# 16LIVES

## JAMES CONNOLLY

## The 16LIVES Series

## LORCAN COLLINS – SERIES EDITOR & AUTHOR OF 16LIVES: JAMES CONNOLLY

Lorcan Collins was born and raised in Dublin. He founded the hugely popular 1916 Walking Tour in 1996. He co-authored *The Easter Rising: A Guide to Dublin in 1916* (O'Brien Press, 2000) with Conor Kostick. Lorcan lectures on Easter 1916 in the United States. He is also a regular contributor to radio, television and historical journals. *16 Lives* is Lorcan's concept and he is co-editor of the series.

## DR RUÁN O'DONNELL – SERIES EDITOR

Dr Ruán O'Donnell is a senior lecturer at the University of Limerick. A graduate of University College Dublin and the Australian National University, O'Donnell has published extensively on Irish Republicanism. Titles include *Robert Emmet and the Rising of 1803*, *The Impact of 1916* (editor) and *Special Category, The IRA in English prisons 1968–1978* and *The O'Brien Pocket History of the Irish Famine*. He is a director of the Irish Manuscript Commission and a frequent contributor to the national and international media on the subject of Irish revolutionary history.

# DEDICATION

For Trish

# ACKNOWLEDGEMENTS

My wife Trish Darcy, to whom this unworthy work is dedicated, for her endurance, commitment, strength, love and unwavering support. My loving children Fionn and Lily May whose first words were James Connolly. My mother Treasa and my father Dermot and their strong sense of Irish culture and heritage. Michael O'Brien for having the vision and bravery to take on this project with such enthusiasm. Mary Webb for her enduring support and guidance. My brilliant series co-editor Dr Ruán O'Donnell. Susan Houlden for her editorial skills. Emma, Ivan, Ide, Kunak, Carol, Helen and everyone at the O'Brien Press. Anne-Marie Ryan for her kindness and everyone at Kilmainham Gaol. Conor Kostick for guidance and suggestions. John Donoghue, James Donoghue, Alan Martin, John Francis, Kenny and all at the International Bar for their constant support. John Gibney. Jim Connolly Heron. John Connolly. Seamus Connolly. Peter Reid. In Troy, New York: MaryEllen Quinn, Samantha Quinn. Jim P Coleman in Albany. Declan Mills. Joe Connell. Everyone at Dublin Tourism. Orla Collins and Mark Childerson, Aoife, Oisín and Ferdia. Diarmuid Collins and Eibhlis Connaughton. Carmel Darcy and Pat Darcy. All the Collins clan, the Farrell family and all the Darcy family. Ciara Gallagher. Rhonda Donagahy, SIPTU. Gary Quinn. Daithí Turner. Prof Andrew Hazucha. Prof Shawn O'Hare, Prof John Wells. Brian Donnelly, Elizabeth McEvoy, Mick Flood and Lorcan Farrell at the National Archives. Keith Murphy at the National Photographic Archives. Gerry Kavanagh, Patrick Sweeney, Michael McHugh, James Harte, Colette O'Daly at the National Library of Ireland. Lisa Dolan, Commandant Victor Laing, Noelle Grothier, Capt Stephen MacEoin, Pte Adrian Short and Hugh Beckett at the Bureau of Military Archives, Cathal Brugha Barracks. Rev Joseph Mallin, Hong Kong. All at Dublin Castle. Honor O Brolchain. All at the GPO. Brian Crowley and everyone at the Pearse Museum. Carol Murphy, SIPTU. Tom Stokes and Frank Allen. Paul Turnell. Shane MacThomáis at Glasnevin Museum. David Kilmartin and the 1916–21 Club. Caoilfhionn Ní Bheachain. Terry O'Donoghue. Caoimhe Nic Dháibhéid. Cliff Housley and the WFR Museum, Sherwood Foresters Archives. Gearóid Breathnach. Coilín O'Dufaigh. Ruarí O'Duinn. Nicky Furlong. Ciaran Wyse at Cork County Library. Dan Burt and Deb Felder. Mick Green, Kevin Lee and Joseph Dowse in Carnew, Wicklow. The *16 Lives* authors – a great collective. Thank you also to all my friends and colleagues for their patience and support and finally thanks to all the Dubliners who pass me by every day with a cheery word or two.

# 16LIVES Timeline

**1845–51.** The Great Hunger in Ireland. One million people die and over the next decades millions more emigrate.

**1858, March 17.** The Irish Republican Brotherhood, or Fenians, are formed with the express intention of overthrowing British rule in Ireland by whatever means necessary.

**1867, February and March.** Fenian Uprising.

**1870, May.** Home Rule movement, founded by Isaac Butt, who had previously campaigned for amnesty for Fenian prisoners

**1879–81.** The Land War. Violent agrarian agitation against English landlords.

**1884, November 1.** The Gaelic Athletic Association founded – immediately infiltrated by the Irish Republican Brotherhood (IRB).

**1893, July 31.** Gaelic League founded by Douglas Hyde and Eoin MacNeill. The *Gaelic Revival*, a period of Irish Nationalism, pride in the language, history, culture and sport.

**1900, September.** *Cumann na nGaedheal* (Irish Council) founded by Arthur Griffith.

**1905–07.** *Cumann na nGaedheal*, the Dungannon Clubs and the National Council are amalgamated to form *Sinn Féin* (We Ourselves).

**1909, August.** Countess Markievicz and Bulmer Hobson organise nationalist youths into *Na Fianna Éireann* (Warriors of Ireland) a kind of boy scout brigade.

**1912, April.** Asquith introduces the Third Home Rule Bill to the British Parliament. Passed by the Commons and rejected by the Lords, the Bill would have to become law due to the Parliament Act. Home Rule expected to be introduced for Ireland by autumn 1914.

**1913, January.** Sir Edward Carson and James Craig set up Ulster Volunteer Force (UVF) with the intention of defending Ulster against Home Rule.

**1913.** Jim Larkin, founder of the Irish Transport and General Workers' Union (ITGWU) calls for a workers' strike for better pay and conditions.

**1913, August 31.** Jim Larkin speaks at a banned rally on Sackville Street; Bloody Sunday.

**1913, November 23.** James Connolly, Jack White and Jim Larkin establish the Irish Citizen Army (ICA) in order to protect strikers.

**1913, November 25.** The Irish Volunteers founded in Dublin to 'secure the rights and liberties common to all the people of Ireland'.

**1914, March 20.** Resignations of British officers force British government not to use British army to enforce Home Rule, an event known as the 'Curragh Mutiny'.

**1914, April 2.** In Dublin, Agnes O'Farrelly, Mary MacSwiney, Countess Markievicz and others establish Cumann na mBan as a women's volunteer force dedicated to establishing Irish freedom and assisting the Irish Volunteers.

**1914, April 24.** A shipment of 35,000 rifles and five million rounds of ammunition is landed at Larne for the UVF.

**1914, July 26.** Irish Volunteers unload a shipment of 900 rifles and 45,000 rounds of ammunition shipped from Germany aboard Erskine Childers' yacht, the *Asgard*. British troops fire on crowd on Bachelors Walk, Dublin. Three citizens are killed.

**1914, August 4.** Britain declares war on Germany. Home Rule for Ireland shelved for the duration of the First World War.

**1914, September 9.** Meeting held at Gaelic League headquarters between IRB and other extreme republicans. Initial decision made to stage an uprising while Britain is at war.

**1914, September.** 170,000 leave the Volunteers and form the National Volunteers or Redmondites. Only 11,000 remain as the Irish Volunteers under Eóin MacNeill.

**1915, May–September.** Military Council of the IRB is formed.

**1915, August 1.** Pearse gives fiery oration at the funeral of Jeremiah O'Donovan Rossa.

**1916, January 19–22.** James Connolly joined the IRB Military Council, thus ensuring that the ICA shall be involved in the Rising. Rising date confirmed for Easter.

**1916, April 20, 4.15pm.** *The Aud* arrives at Tralee Bay, laden with 20,000 German rifles for the Rising. Captain Karl Spindler waits in vain for a signal from shore.

**1916, April 21, 2.15am.** Roger Casement and his two companions go ashore from U-19 and land on Banna Strand. Casement is arrested at McKenna's Fort.

**6.30pm.** *The Aud* is captured by the British navy and forced to sail towards Cork Harbour.

**22 April, 9.30am.** *The Aud* is scuttled by her captain off Daunt's Rock.

**10pm.** Eóin MacNeill as chief-of-staff of the Irish Volunteers issues the countermanding order in Dublin to try to stop the Rising.

**1916, April 23, 9am, Easter Sunday.** The Military Council meets to discuss the situation, considering MacNeill has placed an advertisement in a Sunday newspaper halting all Volunteer operations. The Rising is put on hold for twenty-four hours. Hundreds of copies of *The Proclamation of the Republic* are printed in Liberty Hall.

**1916, April 24, 12 noon, Easter Monday.** The Rising begins in Dublin.

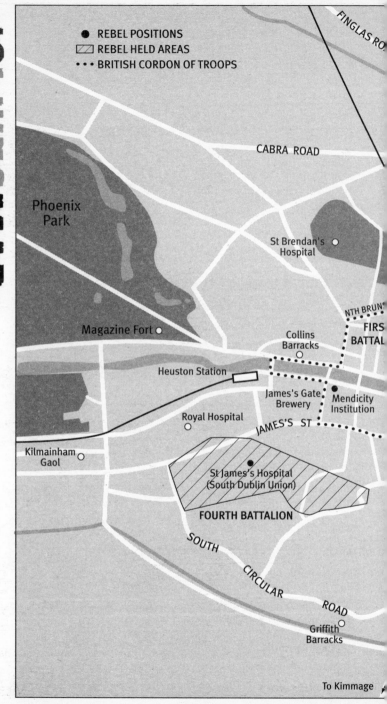

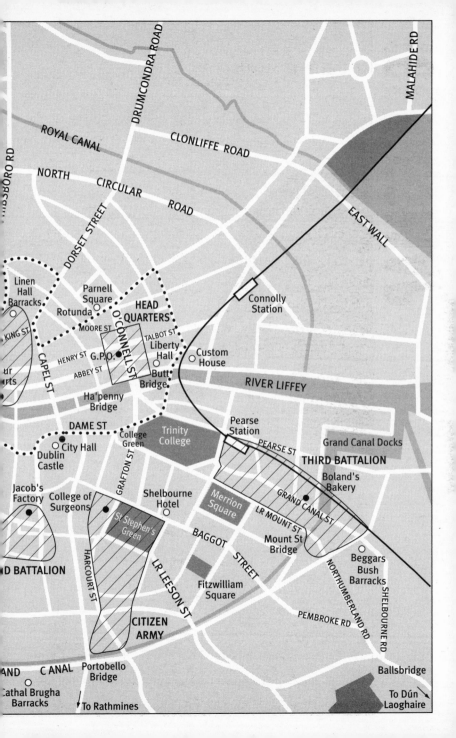

# 16LIVES – Series Introduction

This book is part of a series called *16 LIVES*, conceived with the objective of recording for posterity the lives of the sixteen men who were executed after the 1916 Easter Rising. Who were these people and what drove them to commit themselves to violent revolution?

The rank and file as well as the leadership were all from diverse backgrounds. Some were privileged and some had no material wealth. Some were highly educated writers, poets or teachers and others had little formal schooling. Their common desire, to set Ireland on the road to national freedom, united them under the one banner of the army of the Irish Republic. They occupied key buildings in Dublin and around Ireland for one week before they were forced to surrender. The leaders were singled out for harsh treatment and all sixteen men were executed for their role in the Rising.

Meticulously researched yet written in an accessible fashion, the *16 LIVES* biographies can be read as individual volumes but together they make a highly collectible series.

*Lorcan Collins & Dr Ruán O'Donnell,*
16 Lives *Series Editors*

# CONTENTS

# Introduction

*If you remove the English army to-morrow and hoist the green flag over Dublin Castle, unless you set about the organisation of the Socialist Republic your efforts would be in vain.*[1]

James Connolly (1868–1916) was born in the slums of Edinburgh, where he received only a basic primary education and seemed, like many of his peers, destined to struggle through life, working for low wages in grinding poverty. He joined the British army at a very young age and was posted to Ireland. Being of Irish descent, his sympathy was with the poor and downtrodden of Dublin and the rest of the country. He saw no difference between the lot of the tenant farmer under the yoke of a landlord and that of an Edinburgh factory worker under a capitalist. A strong family man, he dedicated his whole life to attempting to revolutionise the economic system so that his children and future generations would have hope, security and a better life.

His socialist ideas were rejected, often by the very people who he was trying to emancipate. Having founded the Irish Socialist Republican Party in Dublin, it split after a few years and Connolly was forced to emigrate to the United States of America. He was active with a number of socialist organisations, most notably the Industrial Workers of the World (Wobblies) and the Socialist Party of America. However, he returned to Ireland where he spent the last six years of his life fighting against British imperialism and Irish capitalism.

James Connolly linked Irish nationalism with socialism. He saw no reason for merely changing the colour of the flag which flew over Dublin's government buildings; rather he hoped to bring about social change alongside an Irish republic. His articles and books, written in an accessible and straight-forward style, are still read and relevant today. He never wavered on the road to revolution and, as head of the Irish Citizen Army, he joined forces with the Irish Republican Brotherhood and led an insurrection against British rule in Ireland.

Connolly's last moments were spent in a chair in the stone-breakers' yard in Kilmainham Gaol, where, in the early hours of 12 May 1916, a British army firing squad took his life. However, his ideals, his words, his deeds and his dreams live on and, perhaps, one day his wishes for a better world and a better future will be fulfilled.

> But that day will come only when the kings and kaisers, queens and czars, financiers and capitalists who now oppress humanity will be hurled from their place and power, and the emancipated workers of the earth, no longer the blind instruments of rich men's greed, will found a new society, a new civilisation, whose corner stone will be labour, whose inspiring principle will be justice, whose limits humanity alone can bound.[2]

# 1868–1889

# The Early Years

*The cause of labour is the cause of Ireland, the cause of Ireland is the cause of labour. They cannot be dissevered.*[1]

The Great Hunger of the 1840s was a major turning point in the fortunes of Ireland and the Irish. Under direct rule from the British Parliament in Westminster, more than one million people perished from starvation and diseases related to malnutrition, and one million people were forced to emigrate. The social structure of rural Ireland underwent a tremendous upheaval.

During the nineteenth century a very large section of Ireland's citizens existed in some of the poorest and most deprived conditions in Europe. 'The Irish peasant,' wrote James Connolly, 'reduced from the position of a free clansman owning his tribeland and controlling its administration in common with his fellows, was a mere tenant-at-will subject to eviction, dishonour and outrage at the hands of an irresponsible private proprietor. Politically he was non-existent, legally he held no rights, intellectually he sank under the weight of his social abasement, and surrendered to the downward drag of his poverty. He had been conquered, and he suffered all the terrible consequences of defeat at the hands of a ruling class and nation who have always acted upon the old Roman maxim of "Woe to the vanquished."[2]

At that time some argued that British rule in Ireland was benevolent, but little or nothing was done to help the poor and starving. In fact, the great shame is that the British government allowed goods and produce to be **exported** from Ireland during the Great Hunger, hardly a sign of altruism. Emigration, already a common enough problem, speeded up phenomenally. Now known as the Irish Diaspora, the mass exodus saw the population of Ireland cut down to half its original number within a couple of decades. Those who could afford it would pay the fare to Australia, New Zealand, Canada and, of course, America, where those of Irish descent now constitute somewhere in the region of forty million. The logical destinations for the poorest Irish emigrants included England, Wales and Scotland. James Connolly's parents were refugees from the Great Hunger who settled in Scotland.

Over the years, historians have been preoccupied with a desire to prove that James Connolly was born in Ireland. In

1916 the *Weekly Irish Times* published a very detailed *Rebellion Handbook*. One section contained a 'who's who' of the Easter Rising. The entry for James Connolly states that he was 'a Monaghan man'.[3] In 1924, Desmond Ryan, the respected historian and author, wrote of how, in 1880, the Connolly family was forced by poverty to move from their native Monaghan to Scotland. In 1941 the *Irish Press* reported that James Connolly and his family had emigrated from Anlore near Clones, County Monaghan. These and other assertions were simply attempts to ensure the Irish status of Connolly.[4]

To confuse matters further, Connolly put 'County Monaghan' as his birthplace when he filled out the 1901 census. There are at least two possible reasons why he felt it necessary to give this false information. At this time, he was living in Dublin and as an active socialist he often came under fire for not having an Irish accent. Shouts of 'he's not even Irish' were not uncommon during Connolly's lectures, and, as such, he might have felt a need to pretend to have been born on Irish soil. Secondly, it is possible that he felt that the British army was still looking for him to complete his military service, but more about this later.

Whatever the circumstances, it is unfortunate that the concern with Connolly's birthplace should serve as a distraction from his achievements for labour and for Ireland. Nonetheless, for the purposes of definitively proving where the son of two Irish immigrants, John Connolly and Mary

McGinn, was born, an examination can be carried out on his birth certificate. James was born at 107 Cowgate, Edinburgh, Scotland.

Due to the march of time and the Edinburgh slum clearances, the actual house of his birth is long gone, but there is a plaque on a wall which reads:

TO THE MEMORY OF JAMES CONNOLLY

BORN 5th JUNE 1868 AT 107 COWGATE

RENOWNED INTERNATIONAL TRADE UNION
AND WORKING CLASS LEADER

FOUNDER OF IRISH SOCIALIST
REPUBLICAN PARTY

MEMBER OF PROVISIONAL GOVERNMENT
OF IRISH REPUBLIC

EXECUTED 12th MAY 1916 AT KILMAINHAM JAIL
DUBLIN

Beside the new brass plaque are the remnants of the previous memorial, which was vandalised.

Today, the Cowgate area is given over to the world of entertainment, with a plethora of nightclubs and pubs. In James Connolly's youth, these streets were very much part of a divided society and constituted nothing short of a slum, populated for the most part by Catholic Irish immigrants. It was the centre of 'Little Ireland', where thousands of families were living in single-roomed dwellings. Unemployment was high and Connolly's father was deemed lucky to work as a manure carter for the Edinburgh Corporation. This job was at the lower end of the scale and involved shovelling animal excrement into a cart. It was poorly paid night work, but there is little doubt that the removal of dung from the streets was considered a great necessity. Such was the importance of this work that when the manure carters threatened to go on strike, at a meeting held on 13 August 1861, they received their demands at 10am the following day.

John Connolly was promoted shortly after his third and youngest son James was born. It was a good step up the ladder as Connolly's father secured the job of lighting the gas lamps to guide the way for Edinburgh's citizens over her cobbled streets.

Mary Connolly, James's mother, suffered from ill health after the birth of her first child, John. It seems she had chronic bronchitis and suffered for the next thirty years until she passed away.[5]

Young James was formally educated in St Patrick's School, only yards from his birthplace. This was the school that his older brothers John and Thomas also attended. In 1879, at the tender age of eleven, James's formal education came to an end and he began work as a 'printer's devil'. His brother John was employed by the *Edinburgh Evening News* as an apprentice compositor, but James, two years younger than him, was employed at more menial tasks. His job entailed cleaning the ink from the huge print rollers and running errands for more senior staff. Later in life, Connolly would call on the skills that he acquired through his immersion in the printing process when he came to publish his own periodicals.

Newspapers were filled with the stories of the Home Rule movement and land agitation in Ireland. These subjects would have been discussed on the streets, in the public houses, and in the homes of Cowgate. Connolly, like most children, would have picked up snippets of information. Later in life, Connolly would study this period intensively and uncover some Irish idealists who would influence his own thinking, such as James Fintan Lalor (1807–49) and John Mitchel (1815–75).

For the majority of Irish citizens, the most important issue concerned the ownership of land. James Fintan Lalor spread the gospel that the 'entire soil of a country belongs of right to the entire people of that country'.[6] He also held that the return of the land to the people was more important than repeal of the Act of Union.

The figures for the huge change in land ownership due to landlords going bankrupt or simply bailing out of the sinking ship are remarkable. One quarter of the land, five million acres, changed hands in the two decades after the Great Hunger. Of course, it was not the tenant farmers who purchased the land. The new landowners were speculators and hard-nosed businessmen. The Catholic Church, for instance, increased their holdings and invested heavily in land.

In 1879 Michael Davitt founded the National Land League of Mayo, as Connolly later pointedly remarked, 'to denounce the exactions of a certain priest in his capacity as a rackrenting landlord.'[7] The priest, a Canon Bourke, had been forced by the National Land League to reduce the annual rent on his estate by 25 per cent. This was a considerable victory for the tenants, but the demand for a reduction in rent was not the sole underlying principle for the establishment of the League. Tenant farmers were agitating for the famous three 'F's: Fair Rent, Fixity of Tenure, and Freedom of Sale.

Anglo Irish landlords were being targeted under the cover of night: their houses were under the constant threat of attack, and their herds of cattle and sheep proved easy targets. These 'agrarian outrages' were the reinstatement of a tradition from the eighteenth century as an effective but cruel form of protest.

Of a less violent nature, but equally intimidating, was the concept of ostracising landlords or those who collaborated against the Land League. Although not an entirely new idea, it was most effectively and notably used against Captain Charles Cunningham Boycott in 1880. Boycott, an agent for an absentee landlord, not only donated his name to the English language, but required over a thousand soldiers to protect his imported labourers when his tenant farmers refused to harvest the crops from his estate in retaliation for his refusal to reduce rents.

Some years before this, in 1875, the use of the obstructionist policies of Joseph G Biggar (1828–90), a member of the Irish Republican Brotherhood, was introduced in the House of Commons. A fellow Fenian, John O'Connor Power (1846–1919), and a smattering of other Irish MPs soon joined him. Between them they managed to hold up the business of parliament, to the exasperation of all the other members, by talking for hours and hours on various bills that were under discussion. The father of the Home Rule movement, Isaac Butt (1813–79), did not agree with this policy and considered it to be below the conduct expected of gentlemen. But few could argue that Charles Stewart Parnell (1846–91) was not a gentleman, and when this young Protestant landlord threw his lot in with the obstructionists, Isaac Butt's popularity began to decline until his death in 1879.

A year later, in April 1880, after a general election, Parnell became the leader of the Home Rule Party. By this stage Parnell had already joined with Davitt when they founded the Irish National Land League. The democratic Home Rule movement and the Irish National Land League were now intrinsically linked. Both gathered strength from each other at the apparent expense of more revolutionary movements, such as the Irish Republican Brotherhood.

However, it would be unwise to presume that the Fenians

did not have a hand in this alliance. Davitt, as a member of the Brotherhood, had spoken at length with John Devoy (1842–1928) and other Clan na Gael organisers in America concerning his concept of the New Departure, a uniting of everyone from the Irish MPs to the tenant farmers, the IRB, the clergy, the Irish abroad and at home, all working towards the goal of Irish freedom. It would have been folly for the IRB to plan for an open revolution, considering the disastrous attempt of the Young Ireland movement of 1848, and more recently the failed Fenian uprising of 1867. It was clear that the 1880s and 1890s would be a popular time for the Home Rule Party and the Land League, and if the Fenians had at least a part in this success it could only benefit them.

In order to bring some restoration of order, a coercive bill, the Protection of Person and Property Act, was brought into force in 1881. One of the first uses of the bill was to arrest Michael Davitt, which ironically only helped to secure more monetary support from America. Then the Ladies' Land League was formed, a considerable milestone considering that women were traditionally excluded from politics. The Land League also stepped up its activities to the extent that William Gladstone, the Liberal Prime Minister, brought in a Land Act. It was unsatisfactory in its own right, but it was accompanied by a new Coercion Act which added to the indignation of the Irish. Parnell did not want to lose the support of the Liberals and the moderates, so he avoided condemning the Land Act outright within the walls of the British Parliament. Instead, he chose to retain the support of the IRB and the more extreme elements of the Irish Parliamentary Party by launching attacks on parts of the Act in newspapers and through public speeches. In an episode reminiscent of today's political posturing, Parnell called the British Prime Minister a 'masquerading knight errant' who was 'prepared to carry fire and sword' into Irish homesteads. On 13 October 1881, Parnell was arrested and imprisoned in Kilmainham Gaol. He was soon joined by other nationalist MPs such as John Dillon. The editor of Parnell's *United Ireland* newspaper, William O'Brien, was also imprisoned.

For those MPs who found themselves imprisoned in Kilmainham Gaol in the winter of 1881–2, their reputation became allied to the revolutionaries who had gone before. Kilmainham Gaol was a political prison. This was the place where Robert Emmet spent his last night before his execution outside St Catherine's Church on Thomas Street. Emmet's 1803 insurrection was short-lived, but the iconic image of the young Protestant being hanged and beheaded has remained in folk memory to the present day. Emmet's evocative final speech from the dock, in which he implores no man to write his epitaph until his country has taken her place amongst the nations of the world is, two hundred years later, considered among the greatest speeches ever recorded.

Kilmainham also housed political prisoners in 1848 and 1867.

In May1882 the Kilmainham Treaty was signed, despite the fact that it angered the Fenians who believed that Parnell had surrendered. The Treaty was very informal but involved a promise on Parnell's part to suppress the violence of the Land War. Gladstone's compromises included the release of Parnell and the other prisoners, a relaxation of coercion and some minor concessions on the Land Act. The leadership on both sides believed the Land War was effectively finished by the spring of 1882.

During this time of agitation in Ireland, James Connolly's eldest brother left Scotland. John had taken 'the Queen's Shilling', that is, joined the British army, and was stationed in India. At the same time, James's father John was demoted to being a carter, which meant that there was less money for the household. Added to this, a factory inspector had being doing his rounds and paid a visit to James Connolly's place of employment. He soon spotted that James was too young to work at the job he was performing (despite the introduction of a box to give an illusion of height to his small frame); as a result, James was dismissed from the print works. For the next two years Connolly was employed in a bread factory. He once explained to his daughter Nora how crucial it was for him and his family that he have work: 'I'd have preferred to stay at school. There wasn't any alternative ... the few shillings I could get were needed at home. I found work in a bakery. I had to start before six in the morning and stay till late at night. Often I would pray fervently all the way that I would find the place burnt down when I got there. Work is no pleasure for children …'[8]

The census of April 1881 shows that the thirteen-year-old James was listed as a baker's apprentice and that he lived with his brother Thomas and their parents at 2A Kings Stables in Edinburgh. Not long after this, the young baker's health began to suffer badly due to the extreme physical demands made on him – he was, after all, just a boy. Luckily, he found work in a small mosaic factory where he stayed for a year. It would appear that this was much better employment and kinder to the health, but perhaps insufficiently exciting for a young lad of fourteen. Maybe it was the chance of adventure, or perhaps it was for economic reasons, or maybe it was simply to follow in his brother's footsteps, that James Connolly falsified his age and enlisted in the 1st Battalion of the King's Liverpool Regiment.[9] Little information is available on Connolly's time in the British army due to the fact that he was reticent about this period of his life and because he used a false name when he signed up. However, it is possible to follow his movements to a certain degree. Joining the British army resulted in Connolly returning to the land of his father and mother, for, on 30 July 1882, his battalion was shipped to Cork. This was the first time Connolly had set foot on Irish soil. The Ireland that the fourteen-year-old soldier arrived in, that July, was still concerned with the fate of two men who had been assassinated in Dublin a couple of months beforehand.

Just as the Fenians looked on the Kilmainham Treaty as a sell-out, so too did WE Forster, the Chief Secretary of Ireland. Foster was known for his indecisive nature and was nicknamed 'The Pendulum' by those within Dublin Castle circles. For once, he did not swing but made a firm decision; incensed as he was by the British 'surrender', he resigned his position. His callousness was not missed by nationalists, but his replacement was not given much time to prove himself worthy to the Irish. On 6 May 1882, Frederick Cavendish had just arrived in Dublin and was taking a stroll home with his second-in-command, the under-secretary Thomas Burke, towards the Viceregal Lodge in the Phoenix Park. Both men were surprised by a radical new group, the Invincibles, whose members produced knives and stabbed the new chief secretary and under-secretary. The Phoenix Park assassinations caused outrage in Britain. Gladstone (related by marriage to Cavendish) would not honour the terms of the Kilmainham Treaty. Instead of coercion being relaxed, a new Act strengthening these draconian laws was introduced. Furthermore, Parnell, despite offering to resign as an MP, found himself under suspicion to the extent that British detectives followed his every move. These detectives reported to their superiors that he was seen in the company of a married woman, Katherine O'Shea (1845–1921), something that would affect Parnell later. Nonetheless, the Home Rule leader's offer to resign strengthened his reputation amongst the British political figures, and the stand that he took against coercive measures simply served to secure his position with the nationalists.

By December 1882 the Land League was suppressed by the British. The organisation was then replaced by the Irish National League, which came fully under the control of Parnell and the Irish Parliamentary Party. But Parnell was moving away from land reform, soliciting massive donations for the Irish National League and moving more towards the Home Rule issue.

The Ashbourne Act of 1885 enabled more than twenty thousand tenants to borrow the money required to purchase their holdings. This created a temporary period of calm, but the defeat of the Home Rule Bill of 1886 led to a Plan of Campaign where tenants demanded a reduction in rent. Should the landlord refuse, the tenants paid their rent into a fund managed by trustees, who would then use the money for the relief of the evicted. Parnell did not back the tenants on this issue. In 1887, AJ Balfour, as chief secretary, was instrumental in bringing in the Perpetual Crimes Act (or Coercion Act), in an attempt to break the tenants' spirit. In September 1887 three people were shot by the Royal Irish Constabulary at a tenants' meeting in Mitchelstown. The campaign by the

tenants seemed to win the approval of many trade unionists around the globe, but drew the ire of Pope Leo XIII,
who condemned it in an official Papal Rescript. Three more
Conservative Land Acts gave further rights to certain tenants
over the next few years. This policy of 'killing home rule by
kindness' would be British policy in Ireland until 1914, and
the Land Acts also served to diffuse the Land War.

There may not have been a well organised socialist
party, but this does not mean that there were no socialists in Ireland. James Connolly would later write in *Labour
in Irish History* about 'The First Irish Socialist', one William
Thompson (1775–1833) of Clonkeen, Rosscarbery, County
Cork. Thompson was a philosopher and Connolly remarked
how unusual this was as he reckoned that the 'Irish are
not philosophers as a rule, they proceed too rapidly from
thought to action.' 'Thompson's work as an original thinker,'
wrote Connolly, long preceded Karl Marx 'in his insistence
upon the subjection of labour as the cause of all social misery,
modern crime and political dependence ...'[10]

It was not in the barracks that Connolly was introduced to
the writings of William Thompson. That would happen later
in life, when Connolly was engaged in the process of educat-
ing himself. For the moment, in the service of Queen Victoria, he had to content himself with the base nourishment
of barrack-room conversations, which most likely did not
include political debate. From his descriptions of life in the

military, it can be surmised that this intelligent young man had little time for his comrades in the dormitories. Many years later in the *Workers' Republic* newspaper, Connolly described the moral atmosphere of a typical barrack room as being of the 'most revolting character'. The British Army itself he described as a 'veritable moral cesspool corrupting all within its bounds'.

By September 1884, Connolly and the 1st Battalion were stationed in the Curragh Military Camp in County Kildare, not too far from Dublin. Typically, soldiers on leave would have headed for the comfort of Dublin's many public houses and then perhaps taken in the sights of Monto, the notorious red-light district of old. It is unlikely Connolly engaged in such behavior as (most unusually for a young soldier) he was teetotal and seldom used tobacco, but it is clear he visited the city. The following year, in October 1885, his battalion moved to the city, and by June 1886 Connolly was barracked in Beggars Bush.

It was around this time that Connolly first encountered Lillie Reynolds. They met on the street when they were both unsuccessful in hailing a passing tram. This may seem unusual to commuters today, but when the trams were Dublin's main mode of transport; the idea was that potential passengers could hail them at any point on the line. In fact, there was a time when drivers were encouraged to stop beside people and ask them if they needed a tram.

Lillie Reynolds and her twin sister Margaret were born in Carnew, County Wicklow, in 1867. Her father John, a farm labourer, had died at a young age, forcing the family to move to Dublin, to make a living. The twin girls, their two brothers, John and George, and their mother, Margaret, settled in Dublin's Rathmines district. As a young girl, Lillie entered service with a family called Wilson.

The initial attraction between James Connolly and Lillie Reynolds blossomed into romance, and by the end of 1888 they had decided upon marriage. Lillie was Church of Ireland, but inter-faith marriages were not unusual at that time.

In February 1889, James Connolly left Ireland. The reason behind his departure is unclear. His battalion had been ordered to Aldershot in preparation for an overseas posting, possibly to India. Connolly had only a few months left to serve of his seven-year stint; he made the decision to part company, or go AWOL, from the British army.

Around this time, Connolly's father had also fallen ill in Edinburgh and James travelled to the Scottish town of Perth, possibly to be able to visit his father. Lillie was to join him at a later date. It was in Scotland that Connolly became involved in the Socialist League and both their lives were to alter dramatically.

## Chapter Two
. . . . . .

# 1889–1896

# Married with Children

*Governments in capitalist society are but committees of the*
*rich to manage the affairs of the capitalist class.*[1]

In February 1889, not long after arriving in Perth, James
Connolly made his way to the more industrialised town of
Dundee. His elder brother John, who had been stationed in
India with the British army, had served his time and returned
to Scotland, and was now heavily involved in the Scottish labour movement in Dundee. Here the socialists were
conducting a 'freedom of speech' campaign which gained
momentum when local courts banned public meetings. The
Social Democratic Federation (SDF), the radical Marxist
party which had been established in 1881, held huge demonstrations against the ban, and tens of thousands attended.
As one of the organisers of the campaign, John Connolly
introduced his brother to socialism.

When Lillie arrived in Perth, Connolly had already left for Dundee. She remained for a time in Perth. This was the first of many separations that the couple would endure throughout their lives. A year before their marriage, James wrote to 'Lil' from St Mary's Street, Dundee:

For the first time in my life I feel extremely diffident about writing a letter. Usually I feel a sneaking sort of confidence in the possession of what I know to be a pretty firm grasp of the English language for me in my position. But for once I am at a loss. I wish to thank you for your kindness to me, and I am afraid lest by too great protestation of gratitude I might lead you to think that my gratitude is confined to the enclosure which accompanied the letter than the kindly sympathy of the writer. On the other hand I am afraid lest I might by too sparing a use of my thanks lead you to think I am ungrateful to you for your kindness. So in this dilemma I will leave you to judge for yourself my feelings towards you for your generous contributions to the 'Distressed Fund'.

So my love, your unfortunate Jim, is now in Dundee and very near to the 'girl he left behind him' but the want of the immortal cash and the want of the necessary habiliments presses me to remain as far from her as if the Atlantic divided us. But cheer up, perhaps sometime or another, before you leave Perth if you stay in it any time, I may be available to see you again, God send it. I am glad to be able to tell you that I am working at present though and in another man's place, as he is off through illness. So perhaps things are coming round. I could get plenty work in England but you know England might be unhealthy for me, you understand.

Excuse me for the scribbling as the house is full of people. It was only across the street from here a man murdered his wife and they are all discussing whether he is mad or not, pleasant, isn't it. Please write soon. It is always a pleasure to me to hear from you, and especially in my present condition it is like a present voice encouraging me to greater exertion in the future. But I must stop, for I cannot compose my mind to write, owing to the hubbub of voices around me. I will watch for it expectantly, and believe me I will be glad to have the assurance of the sympathy of my own sweetheart.

Yours lovingly, James Connolly[2]

The reference in the letter to 'England might be unhealthy for me' has been taken to refer to the fact that James Connolly was AWOL from the British army.

In the last decade of the nineteenth century, there were many different socialist groups in Scotland. It was not unheard of to be a member of more than one organisation and, in fact, Connolly was associated with them all at one stage. Initially, he joined the Socialist League and later he became a member of the Social Democratic Federation.

The Social Democratic Federation was founded by HM Hyndman in 1881. Although the SDF ethos was based on the ideas of Karl Marx and attracted his daughter, Eleanor, as a member, it was not supported by Friedrich Engels, Marx's long-term collaborator. The party published a popular journal, *Justice*, to which Connolly would later contribute.

Some members of the SDF found aspects of Hyndman's leadership unpalatable. For instance, Hyndman was accused of being dictatorial and that he wielded too great a control over *Justice*. As a result, the Socialist League was founded in 1885 by disgruntled members of the SDF. The League stood for revolutionary socialism and advocated Marxist principles. Early members included Edward Aveling, Ernest Belfort Bax, Edward Carpenter, Walter Crane, Eleanor Marx and William Morris. A journal was also published under the name *Commonweal*. The party was slow to develop but John Bruce Glasier formed a very large and active branch in Glasgow. By the early 1890s a large anarchist section had secured control of the Socialist League, which drove many of the Marxists back towards the SDF and indeed to the Independent Labour Party.

In 1888, James Keir Hardie, Robert Bontine Cunninghame Graham (the first Socialist MP), Henry Hyde Champion, Tom Mann, and other SDF activists formed the Scottish Labour Party. Keir Hardie, a miner, socialist and union activist, was elected to the House of Commons in 1892, where he gained a certain notoriety for his refusal to wear 'acceptable attire' (black frock coat, silk top hat and starched wing collar) in parliament. Instead, he wore a plain tweed suit, a red tie and a deerstalker. He called for the abolition of the House of Lords, votes for women and often attacked the British monarchy in his speeches. The following year Hardie was instrumental in founding the Independent Labour Party. The objective of this party was 'to secure the collective and communal ownership of the means of production, distribution and exchange'; they also called for an eight-hour working day, pensions for the sick, elderly, widowed and orphaned, free education to third level, and universal suffrage. The Edinburgh branch of the ILP was known as the Scottish Labour Party, and would one day have James Connolly as secretary.

There was yet another organisation by the name of the Scottish Socialist Federation, a mixed bag of societies and SDF supporters who worked alongside the ILP to ensure that it did not waiver from its socialist principles. John Leslie became the Edinburgh secretary of the SSF. Connolly was heavily influenced by Leslie's speeches and his 1894 pamphlet, *The Present Position of the Irish Question*. Leslie was a few years older than Connolly but they had a lot in common; they were both Cowgate boys, more Irish than Scottish, and, in fact, had attended the same school. From 1894 the SSF produced the *Labour Chronicle* and Connolly replaced Leslie as secretary. The SSF was calling itself the Edinburgh branch of the SDF by 1895.

A little over a year passed between leaving Dublin and the marriage of James to Lillie. The fact that Lillie was of a different faith did not delay the marriage to any great extent, as permission was sought from the Catholic Bishop of Dunkeld. The lack of finance available to the couple at the time was a problem. Connolly was struggling to feed himself and unable to save the money required to set up home. Although this year was mostly spent apart from each other, the couple continued their courtship by letter. Lillie left Perth and spent a large part of the year working in London. In the meantime, Connolly was employed on a temporary basis as a carter for the Edinburgh Cleansing Department. He wrote a letter, several days before his wedding, expressing his concern, in no uncertain terms, that his bride establish 'legal residence' in Perth in order to marry there. He appears to have been more familiar with the exact nature of the laws concerning marriage than he was with his sweetheart's age. His letter describes preparations for a strike and it is clear that these matters are set to demand his time and attention, despite his pending nuptials:

> Lil, I was very glad to receive your letter as it lifted quite a load off my heart. I was so afraid you had not gone to Perth. Your last letter was so very indignant with me. I am amused to see you are getting some of the anxiety which I have had

this long time. But you need not be afraid. Mrs Angus is wrong. Six weeks was the old law but that has been altered in 1878. If you had done what I told you and gone to the registrar at once, you would have found out for yourself. Seven days is the time now, so please lose no time and go at once, and if all goes well I shall be with you next week and make you mine forever. When giving your name to the registrar I gave it as Lillie.

By the way please write at once as soon as you get this letter and tell me your father and mother's names. Also your father's profession. I want it as soon as ever I can get it also your birthplace. When I gave your age I gave it as 22, was I right. How I am wearying to get beside you, and hear your nonsense once more. It is such a long time since we met, but I trust this time we will meet to part no more. Won't it be pleasant.

By the way if we get married next week I shall be unable to go to Dundee as I promised as my fellow-workmen in the job are preparing for a strike on the end of the month, for a reduction in the hours of labour. As my brother and I are ringleaders in the matter it is necessary we should be on the ground. If we were not we should be looked upon as blacklegs, which the Lord forbid. Mind don't lose a minute's time in writing, and you will greatly gratify your loving Jim. Not James as your last letter was directed.[3]

The wedding ceremony took place on 30 April 1890 in

the Roman Catholic Church, Perth.[4] The groom moved his new bride into his room at 22 West Port, Edinburgh.

The couple found a great friend in John Leslie, secretary of the Edinburgh branch of the SDF, who spoke at many of the 'freedom of speech' meetings in Dundee. Connolly listened and learned much from John Leslie, and not only joined the SDF but became one of their evangelists. Leslie described how Connolly first came to his attention:

> I noticed the silent young man as a very interested and constant attendant at the open-air meetings, accompanied by his uncle whom I knew to be one of the Old Guard of the Fenian movement, and once when a sustained and virulent personal attack was being made upon myself and when I was almost succumbing to it, Connolly sprang upon the stool and to say the least of it, retrieved the situation. I never forgot it. The following week he joined our organisation, and it is needless to say what an acquisition he was. We shortly had five or six more or less capable propagandists and certainly cut a figure in Edinburgh, but with voice and pen Connolly was ever in the forefront. When he started … he had a decided impediment in his speech which greatly detracted from the effect of his utterances, but by sheer force of will he conquered it …'[5]

In May 1891, James's mother Mary finally succumbed to the chronic bronchitis that had marred her health since the birth of her first child. She was fifty-eight years of age and would not live to see James and Lillie's first child. Mona Elizabeth Connolly was born on 11 April while the young parents had rooms in Mary Street at the east end of Cowgate, Edinburgh.

Not being the most salubrious of neighbourhoods, Cowgate had little to recommend it, and in an effort to better their living standards the little family moved to number 6, Lawnmarket, a continuation of High Street. From here they moved into number 6, Lothian Street. This lodging was in a congenial neighbourhood where there was a high population of students and intellectuals, with bookshops and colleges nearby.

As an example of how deep his involvement in the movement was, Connolly's home on Lothian Street was used for meetings of the Scottish Socialist Federation. This also gives an indication of the low numbers of activists; probably so few that they could all sit around the Connollys' kitchen table. Nonetheless, their dedication, and indeed Connolly's resolve, was more than enough to make up for their small size. Throughout the rest of his time in Edinburgh, Connolly's home was often the official headquarters for whatever party he was involved with. Lillie must have been a very patient person to contend with the regular visitors, especially considering that a second baby, Nora Margaret, arrived on 14 November 1893. This was the year that the Edinburgh branch of Keir Hardie's ILP formed, calling themselves the Scottish Labour Party. Connolly also became involved with them while remaining a member of the SSF.

In August 1893, Secretary Connolly announced in *Justice* that the SSF were going to form a branch in the seaport of Leith. His acerbic attack on the citizens of Edinburgh is a fine example of his early writing, a style which he rarely deviated from throughout his career:

The population of Edinburgh is largely composed of snobs, flunkeys, mashers, lawyers, students, middle-class pension-ers and dividend-hunters. Even the working-class portion of the population seemed to have imbibed the snobbish would-be-respectable spirit of their 'betters' and look with aversion upon every movement running counter to con-ventional ideas. But it [the socialist movement] has won, hands down, and is now becoming respectable. More, it is now recognised as an important factor in the public life of the community, a disturbing element which must be taken into account in all the calculations of the political caucuses.

Leith on the other hand is pre-eminently an industrial centre. The overwhelming majority of its population belong to the disinherited class, and having its due proportion of sweaters, slave-drivers, rack-renting slum landlords, shipping-federation agents, and parasites of every description, might therefore have been reasonably expected to develop socialis-tic sentiments much more readily than the modern Athens.

Connolly was twenty-five years old when he gave his first public speech in May 1894. Waiting by the platform, Lillie found she could not bear to witness the event and fled to her new South College Street home as soon as her husband mounted the podium. It was not an easy task for Connolly as he had to speak to a crowd who had been eagerly anticipating the arrival of Keir Hardie. It was raining and Hardie had failed to turn up, which meant that Connolly had to appease a wet, disgruntled and disappointed audience. The crowd listened and Connolly was not lynched. From this moment on, he developed into a skilled orator who 'electrified the audiences on several occasions by passionate interventions, routing hecklers with concentrated and fierce outbursts of eloquence.'[6]

It is worth noting that Connolly felt confident enough to advise Keir Hardie on Irish politics by letter in July 1894:

As an Irishman who has always taken a keen interest in the advanced movements in Ireland … There is a nucleus of a strong Labour movement in Ireland, which only needs judicious handling to flutter the doves in the Home Rule dovecot. Now if you were to visit Dublin and address a good meeting there, putting it in strong and straight, without reference to either the two Irish parties, but rebellious, anti-monarchial and out-spoken on the fleecings of both landlord and capitalist, and the hypocrisy of both political parties for a finale.

Hoping you will excuse me for these hints on what might be done ...[7]

The first time Connolly tested the waters of democracy was when he stood as the SSF's choice for the St Giles ward in Edinburgh in 1894. Five hundred attended the first meeting after he was nominated as a Socialist candidate, and all through late October and early November the pavements in that area were 'chalked white with his name by enthusiastic supporters'.[8] Connolly wrote under the pseudonym 'Rascal' for the *Labour Chronicle*. In an appeal to the Irish voters, he wrote:

Perhaps they will learn how foolish it is to denounce tyranny in Ireland and then to vote for tyrants and instruments of tyranny at their own door. Perhaps they will see that the landlord who grinds his peasants on a Connemara estate and the landlord who rackrents them in a Cowgate slum are brethren in fact and deed.'

He gained 14 per cent of the vote and came in third, despite one of the other candidates describing him as a 'young man of no business ability, advocating ideas repugnant to all right-thinking men'. The rival candidate who said that, Gardiner, attracted a paltry fifty-four votes. One of the reasons why Connolly did not fare too well concerned the reluctance of his potential supporters to register their names as voters. At the time, the debt collectors looked forward with glee to the publication of electoral rolls – a perfect updated list of the addresses of the working-class poor.

The winter of 1894–5 was one of the coldest of the century; the great meandering River Thames froze solid in London. Connolly found himself out of work as the Edinburgh Cleansing Department employed overtime as opposed to casual labour to meet their needs. It was tough all round; soup kitchens sprang up in many areas, and with a couple of small children to feed, Connolly's needs were pressing. With that in mind, he opened up a cobbler's shop at 73 Buccleuch Street. His advertisement in the *Labour Chronicle* wittily claimed that Connolly repaired 'the worn-out understandings of the brethren at standard rates'. Amidst the aroma of hot glue and leather, Connolly sold tickets to fundraisers, waxed lyrical on socialism, and held court. Alas, his cobbling skills left a lot to be desired and customers were thin on the ground. One comrade, Anna Munro, who sympathetically took her family's shoes to him, later remarked that not one single pair could be worn afterwards.

Despite the pressure of running his small business, he still found the time to continue organising and, again, ran as a candidate in the Poor Law Elections of April 1895. The objective behind these elections was to democratise the Poor Law system. Connolly remarked on 'the folly of handing over the care of the poor to those who have made them poor'. The successful candidate, a Catholic priest, polled a little over five hundred votes. Connolly attracted one hundred and sixty-nine, still hovering around the 14 per cent mark. Nonetheless, the SSF still had faith in their secretary and he was re-elected to that position in May.

Regarding the cobbler's shop, Connolly's business acumen was sorely lacking; he wryly commented that he was going to purchase a shaving mirror in order to watch himself slowly starve to death. Try as he did to make a success of the venture, it failed miserably and that summer he had to shut up shop. Instead of mending shoes, he decided that he had served his apprenticeship as a speaker and could legitimately offer his services outside of Edinburgh. The *Labour Leader* ran an advertisement proclaiming the lecturer James Connolly, SSF and ILP, was available for booking through the SDF offices. The few lectures that he gave were just not enough to keep himself and his family, and things were beginning to get desperate. After contesting two elections as a socialist, he was virtually unemployable, and Connolly was forced to consider moving on.

Around this time, the Chilean government was offering free passage, free land and farming tools to young men and their families with the objective of populating this South American country with European settlers. Connolly decided that his family would do better in Chile and so made one of his typically rash decisions to emigrate. He was dissuaded from this speculative adventure by John Leslie and, indeed,

Lillie, who was expecting another child and may have not relished the prospect of a long sea voyage. Leslie subsequently made it his mission to find a job where Connolly's real talents could be utilised, and so with that in mind he made an appeal for employment in *Justice* in December 1895:

> Here is a man among men ... I am not much given to flattery, as those of you who know me are aware, yet I may say that very few men have I met deserving of greater love and respect than James Connolly. I know something of Socialist propaganda and have done a little in that way myself, and I know the movement in Edinburgh to its centre, and I say that no man has done more for the movement than Connolly, if they have done as much. Certainly nobody has dared one half what he has dared in the assertion of his principles. Of his ability I need only say, as one who has had some opportunity of judging, he is the most able propagandist in every sense of the word that Scotland has turned out. And because of it, and for his intrepidity, he is today on the verge of destitution and out of work. And we all know what this means for the unskilled workman, as Connolly is. Now this should not be – most emphatically should not be ...
>
> Connolly's case is scarcely an encouragement for others to go and do likewise. Leaving the Edinburgh Socialists to digest the matter, is there no comrade in Glasgow, Dundee, or anywhere else who could secure a situation for one of the best and most self-sacrificing men in the movement?

Connolly is, I have said, an unskilled labourer, a life-long abstainer, sound in wind and limb (Christ in Heaven! How often I have nearly burst a blood vessel as these questions were asked of myself!). Married, with a young family, and as his necessities are therefore very great, so he may be had cheap.

The Dublin Socialist Club answered this advertisement and offered Connolly a position as club organiser with a weekly wage of one pound per week. In May 1896 the Connolly family sailed for Dublin, the cost of the trip funded by their firm friend John Leslie and a few other comrades from the Edinburgh socialist movement.

## Chapter Three

# 1896–1898

# The Irish Socialist Republican Party

*Irish history has ever been written by the master class – in the interests of the master class.*[1]

On 3 March 1896, a couple of months before the Connolly family moved to Ireland, a third child, Aideen, was born. The family rented a single room in a tenement at 75 Charlemont Street, near the Grand Canal, and close to Rathmines, where Lillie used to live.[2] Connolly was in his element with the prospect of becoming a paid, full-time socialist organiser. His task would be difficult as Irish socialists tended to look towards Britain for guidance. It was up to the new organiser to persuade the Dublin comrades that the emancipation of Ireland and the emancipation of the Irish working class were common causes. Difficult as it would be to convert the socialists in Ireland, the real problem would be convincing the masses; nonetheless, Connolly was confident that he could succeed.

On 29 May 1896, in Ryan's pub at number 50 Thomas Street, eight men disbanded the Dublin Socialist Club at Connolly's behest and founded the Irish Socialist Republican Party. They must have been an interesting-looking cabal, huddled together in the snug, the majority of them drinking lemonade as five of them (including Connolly) were teetotal. Connolly was elected as ISRP organiser and his one-pound wage (a reasonable sum at the time) was to be raised through membership subscriptions or dues of a penny a week and through collections at meetings. The other socialists present at that meeting were Peter Kavanagh, Patrick Cushan, Robert Dorman, John Moore, Alex Kennedy and the two brothers Tom and Murtagh Lyng. The following is the text of the manifesto of the ISRP, drafted a few months after the members formed the party and 'passed by a few lying on the grass in Stephen's Green', after Connolly had read it out to them. Some of these demands were considered radical for their time, but today they are basic rights we take for granted.

### IRISH SOCIALIST REPUBLICAN PARTY

'The great appear great to us only because we are on our knees; LET US RISE.'

OBJECT: Establishment of AN IRISH SOCIALIST

REPUBLIC based upon the public ownership by the Irish people of the land, and instruments of production, distribution and exchange. Agriculture to be administered as a public function, under boards of management elected by the agricultural population and responsible to them and to the nation at large. All other forms of labour necessary to the well-being of the community to be conducted on the same principles.

PROGRAMME: As a means of organising the forces of the Democracy in preparation for any struggle which may precede the realisation of our ideal, of paving the way for its realisation, of restricting the tide of emigration by providing employment at home, and finally of palliating the evils of our present social system, we work by political means to secure the following measures:-

1. Nationalisation of railways and canals.

2. Abolition of private banks and money-lending institutions and establishments of state banks, under popularly elected boards of directors, issuing loans at cost.

3. Establishment at public expense of rural depots for the most improved agricultural machinery, to be lent out to the agricultural population at a rent covering cost and management alone.

4. Graduated income tax on all incomes over £400 per

annum in order to provide funds for pensions to the aged, infirm and widows and orphans.

5. Legislative restriction of hours of labour to 48 per week and establishment of a minimum wage.

6. Free maintenance for all children.

7. Gradual extension of the principle of public ownership and supply to all the necessaries of life.

8. Public control and management of National schools by boards elected by popular ballot for that purpose alone.

9. Free education up to the highest university grades.

10. Universal suffrage.

THE IRISH SOCIALIST REPUBLICAN PARTY HOLDS: That the agricultural and industrial system of a free people, like their political system, ought to be an accurate reflex of the democratic principle by the people for the people, solely in the interests of the people.

That the private ownership, by a class, of the land and instruments of production, distribution and exchange, is opposed to this vital principle of justice, and is the fundamental basis of all oppression, national, political and social.

That the subjection of one nation to another, as of Ireland to the authority of the British Crown, is a barrier to the free political and economic development of the subjected nation, and can only serve the interests of the exploiting classes of both nations.

That, therefore, the national and economic freedom of the Irish people must be sought in the same direction, viz., the establishment of an Irish Socialist Republic, and the consequent conversion of the means of production, distribution and exchange into the common property of society, to be held and controlled by a democratic state in the interests of the entire community.

That the conquest by the Social Democracy of political power in Parliament, and on all public bodies in Ireland, is the readiest and most effective means whereby the revolutionary forces may be organised and disciplined to attain that end.

BRANCHES WANTED EVERYWHERE. ENQUIRIES INVITED. ENTRANCE FEE, 6*d*. MINIMUM WEEKLY SUBSCRIPTION 1*d*.

Offices: 67 MIDDLE ABBEY STREET, DUBLIN.

Wasting no time in launching their new party into the limelight, an open-air meeting 'in favour of an Irish Socialist Republic' was held on 7 June at the Custom House, near the docks on the northside of the Liffey. Further meetings, including a weekly Sunday congregation in the Phoenix Park, continued on into October. A typical meeting would see Tom Lyng as chairman with Connolly and Robert

Dorman as the main speakers, endeavouring to stimulate the political consciousness of Dublin's workers. They were often well received and a type of local celebrity was accorded to them. Their presence did not go unnoticed by the media, but typically it was negative reporting; one journalist wryly commented that the new party had more syllables than members.

As soon as a member paid his sixpence 'entrance fee' he (for the party did not attract any female members at this early juncture) would receive an emerald green membership card, imprinted with the stirring phrase, 'The Great Appear Great Because We Are On Our Knees; Let Us Rise', borrowed from Camille Desmoulins, the French revolutionary.

In a step towards convincing sceptics that socialist principles were held by some of Ireland's revolutionary heroes, Connolly researched the works of James Fintan Lalor and published them in a pamphlet in September 1896. Desmond Ryan, Connolly's first biographer, maintained that the reproduction of Lalor's *Rights of Ireland* and *The Faith of a Felon* 'beyond all doubt did much to rescue Lalor's memory from neglect; as well as insisting upon the great '48 man's social views, then too little heeded.'[3] Lalor wrote: 'Any man who tells you that an act of armed resistance – even if offered by ten men only – even if offered by men armed only with stones – any man who tells you that such an act of resistance is premature, imprudent or dangerous – any and every such man should at once be spurned and spat at. For remark you this and recollect it, that *somewhere*, and *somehow*, and by *somebody*, a *beginning must* be made and that the *first* act of resistance is always, and must be ever, premature, imprudent and dangerous.'

James Fintan Lalor was born in Tonakill, County Laois, and as a young man he joined Daniel O'Connell's Repeal Association. The more radical members of this association, including Lalor, joined the Young Ireland movement. Lalor held that the land of Ireland belonged to all the people of Ireland. In 1845 he founded the Tipperary Tenant League and later wrote pieces for Thomas Davis's *Nation* newspaper. In 1848 Lalor's new journal, the *Irish Felon*, asked, 'Who will draw the first blood for Ireland? Who will win a wreath that shall be green forever?' The French Revolution encouraged the Young Ireland demands for the removal of British rule in Ireland and the return of the land to the people. In a preemptive move by the British, the main leaders of the movement were arrested, including Lalor's comrade John Mitchel (who later escaped from Van Diemen's Land to the United States) and the pacifistic Charles Gavan Duffy (later knighted). Those who took part in the 1848 Rising on 23 July included William Smith O'Brien (transported for life, but later pardoned), Thomas Francis Meagher (also escaped to the US and is remembered as Meagher of the Sword) and Lalor, who was jailed and released due to illness, but engaged in a small rising in 1849 and was jailed again. Lalor died in prison. The legacy of the Young Ireland movement lies less in their revolutionary achievements than in their writings; books by Mitchel and Lalor were amongst Connolly's most treasured items.

In the late summer of 1896, there was a serious strike in the building trade and, by September, Connolly, whose promised pound a week was rarely paid, was obliged to seek extra work. As an unskilled labourer he managed to eke out a few days' work on the Grand Main Drainage Scheme. The Liffey was an open sewer and interceptor sewers were being laid along the quays to bring waste to Ringsend, where it would be pumped out to sea. Weak from the lack of a regular meal, Connolly was not physically able for the work, nor did he even possess decent attire for manual labour. His daughter Nora recalled that the night before he went to work he attempted to repair his footwear as there were two gaping holes in the soles. True to form, his poor cobbling skills resulted in a pair of ruined boots; they literally fell apart. Distraught at the prospect of missing the chance to work, Lillie came to the rescue:

> Look James, those slippers you have on have good strong soles, and the top comes right up to your trousers. If they could be tied on ... you could do with them for a day ... we could buy a second-hand pair tomorrow. We'll be able to do that now that you have got work.' Connolly tied a bit of string around his slippers. 'See, Lillie,' he said. 'You are right. The trousers hide the string. We'll make them do.'[4]

October 1896 saw the publication of Connolly's first major essay, 'Ireland for the Irish'. Published in the ILP journal, the *Labour Leader*, over three weeks, he hypothesised that Home Rule was 'simply a mockery of Irish National aspirations'. But Keir Hardie's *Labour Leader* was not widely read in Ireland, and Connolly needed to reach as broad a section of the Irish populace as possible. The only republican journal in Ireland that would give Connolly some column inches was called *Shan Van Vocht,* a badly anglicised version of '*Sean Bhean Bhocht*' or 'Poor Old Woman' – a symbolic name for Ireland. Alice Milligan, as editor of this Belfast-based paper, was sent a review copy of the Lalor pamphlet which she promoted in her journal. As a result of this, Milligan asked Connolly for a number of articles, the first of which posed the question, 'Can Irish Republicans be Politicians?' He followed up with more essays, one of which was 'Nationalism and Socialism', published in January 1897. In this article, Connolly called for a republic that would be a 'beacon-light to the oppressed of every land', as opposed to the capitalist systems of France and the United States:

> If you remove the English army to-morrow and hoist the green flag over Dublin Castle, unless you set about the organisation of the Socialist Republic your efforts would be in vain.
>
> England would still rule you. She would rule you through her capitalists, through her landlords, through her financiers,

through the whole array of commercial and individualist institutions she has planted in this country and watered with the tears of our mothers and the blood of our martyrs.

England would still rule you to your ruin, even while your lips offered hypocritical homage at the shrine of that Freedom whose cause you had betrayed.[5]

Even if the editor and many of her readers did not necessarily agree with everything Connolly wrote, he was making a name for himself as an insightful political commentator and was already coming to the attention of the Irish Republican Brotherhood.

A selection from the recorded minutes of the ISRP meetings provide an invaluable insight into the party and how they operated:[6]

31 December 1896 – Letter from Socialist Labour Party of America sending greetings to comrades in Ireland and enclosing £1 for 100 cards of membership and quantity of manifestoes [sic] and pamphlets.

7 January 1897 – Letter received from Miss Maud Gonne expressing her entire accord with the republican and socialist ideal of the party, but desiring an interview with the secretary before publicly identifying herself with us. Secretary was instructed to take such steps as were in his power to place Miss Gonne in possession of whatever information she desired … Secretary drew attention to proposed

celebration of the rebellion of '98 and the formation of a committee for the purpose and asked that the ISRP send a delegate to that committee. It was resolved to postpone consideration of the matter until next meeting.

21 January – It was unanimously resolved that the ISRP join in the proposed celebration of the '98 rebellion. Secretary was instructed to write the secretary of Young Ireland League [sic], and apply for permission to send a delegate accordingly.

11 February – Letter from the Committee of the Young Ireland Society relative to the appointment of the '98 celebration Committee. They asked for a list of names... Letter from Secretary Socialist Labour Party of USA expressing sympathy with the objects of the ISRP. It was decided to send 4 names viz. Connolly, Stewart, Power and O'Brien appointed.

18 February – Secretary proposed and it was adopted that we celebrate Commune of Paris on 18th March. Secretary gave motion that next Thursday we discuss the feasibility of starting of a paper.

25 February – Kennedy proposed that a committee be formed to make arrangements for the celebration of the Paris Commune. Seconded by Lyng – Passed. Secretary moved that the discussion as to the feasibility of starting

a paper be postponed till more time be at our disposal – Passed.

3 March – Lyng proposed that the articles written by Connolly for Shan Van Vocht should be used as preface to our new pamphlet.

14 March – Connolly corrected the minutes by saying that it was the Asst. Sect. who was instructed to write to the various persons mentioned in the minutes. Boston Herald forwarded a copy of the paper containing an account of the ISRP. The Secretary proposed a motion against gambling in our Society Rooms. Kennedy proposed that a pamphlet or leaflet be issued by the Society on the forthcoming Queen's Celebration.

25 March – It was resolved to keep refreshments and retail them to members. Secretary moved that assistant secretary be instructed to write to Miss Gonne asking her to speak on our behalf on May Day. It was also resolved to write to the Trades Council asking if they intended to hold a May Day demonstration and informing them of the intention of the ISRP to hold a meeting on that date.

1 April – Correspondence from Sect. Trades Council saying that owing to the small support given in previous years to the Labour Day Celebrations it is improbable that they will hold any meeting this year on Labour Day.

22 April – Lyng formed a branch in Cork and left 60 pamphlets.

29 April – Diamond Jubilee. Consideration of this matter was postponed for a week and the secretary was instructed to draw up a manifesto for the event.

3 May – The proposal that we form ourselves into a branch of the '98 Executive Committee [was] unanimously adopted.

6 May – The secretary read a draft of the proposed manifesto by the Party on the Diamond Jubilee of Queen Victoria. The manifesto was unanimously adopted as it stood and the secretary instructed to get 10,000 printed.

17 June – Letter of resignation from Mr. Dorman. Dorman resignation – Accepted. It was agreed to have 10 poles for black flags and flags, one coffin and one wagonette and D. O'Brien to make letters for coffin. Miss Maud Gonne was reported to be engaged in lettering for black flags. It was resolved to have an anti-jubilee meeting on Monday 21st. Miss Gonne to attend and address meeting.

Connolly's writings from the *Labour Leader* and *Shan Van Vocht* were collected and republished in pamphlet form as *Erin's Hope: The End and the Means* in March 1897. Levenson rightly maintained, 'It was a proud moment for the self-educated, indigent agitator.'[7] The main purpose of publishing the pamphlet was not to massage Connolly's ego but to spread the gospel of republican socialism and to raise some cash for the upkeep of the party. That money would also be required to pay Connolly as his family was growing in number. In early 1897, Ina Mary Connolly, the fourth daughter of James and Lillie, was born.

Connolly spent a large amount of his spare time in the National Library on Kildare Street. He was meticulous when researching facts and figures for his articles and all this study would become the foundation for his greater works, which would be published later. As there was so much interest in 1798, due to the impending centenary, he researched and published half a dozen pamphlets, *Ninety-Eight Readings*, containing sixteen pages of prose, poetry and documents concerning the United Irishmen. The objective behind these was to remind people what Wolfe Tone and the United Irishmen stood for: a separatist republic based on liberty, equality and fraternity – not Home Rule.

As can be seen from the extracted minutes of the ISRP meetings above, an invaluable contact was made in the person of Maud Gonne (1866–1953). One of the leading lights in the feminist and republican movements, she also published a periodical in Paris, *L'Irlande Libre*, to which Connolly would contribute a couple of articles. Maud Gonne, a great beauty and muse for the poet WB Yeats, was independently wealthy, but was more interested in revolutionaries (she later married

John MacBride) and was enthusiastic in organising anti-jubilee demonstrations with Connolly and the ISRP.

Queen Victoria (1819–1901), who succeeded to the throne in 1837, presided over Britain as an imperial nation during the expansion of the British Empire. She also presided over Ireland during the Great Hunger and as a consequence is remembered as 'The Famine Queen'. She had nine children, including the future King Edward VII. Her reign was lengthy and celebrations were to be held to mark her sixtieth year on the throne; thus, 22 June 1897 was earmarked as Diamond Jubilee Day.

Maud Gonne had prepared scores of black flags emblazoned with slogans and facts about the Great Hunger. Connolly had printed up his manifesto, which reminded people that during '… this glorious reign Ireland has seen 1,225,000 of her children die of famine; starved to death whilst the produce of her soil and of their labour was eaten up by a vulture aristocracy – enforcing their rents by the bayonets of a hired assassin army in the pay of the "best of the English Queens" …' Gonne had organised a 'magic lantern' slide show; it projected images and phrases and entranced a small crowd on Parnell Square. A hand-cart, fashioned to resemble a hearse, and carrying a black coffin emblazoned with two words, 'British Empire', was wheeled down Dame Street in the company of Connolly. Following them came a workers' band playing a funeral march. Maud Gonne, accompanied by Yeats, distributed the flags as they solemnly 'buried' the empire. Their route was blocked on O'Connell Bridge by the Dublin Metropolitan Police. During the confrontation that followed, Connolly dumped the coffin into the Liffey, shouting, 'To Hell with the British Empire'. He was promptly arrested and spent the night in jail.

The police made their way up to Parnell Square where they attacked the crowd, mainly women and children fascinated by the 'magic' of the projector. An old woman was beaten so badly she later died of her injuries. As news of the police attacks spread, angry mobs broke every window in the city centre with jubilee decorations or images of Victoria. It seems that not every Dubliner was enthusiastic about the jubilee and the British Empire.

Maud Gonne, having paid the fine to release Connolly, wrote to congratulate him on his efforts:

> Bravo! All my congratulations to you! You were right and I was wrong about this evening. You may have the satisfaction of knowing that you saved Dublin from the humiliation of an English jubilee without a public meeting of protestation. You were the only man who had the courage to organise a public meeting and to carry it through in spite of all discouragement – even from friends.[8]

Two months later, the Duke and Duchess of York visited Dublin. Again the Dublin Metropolitan Police attacked the demonstrations that had been arranged by Connolly and the ISRP. At one such meeting, a couple of banners were unfurled: one a red flag with a pike about to stab a crown with the Latin phrase '*Finis Tyranniae*' (the end of the tyrant, ie the end of monarchy). The other flag was a sunburst on a green background with the phrase 'Truth, Freedom and Justice in Ireland'. The protesters were beaten from Foster Place, off Dame Street, to the ISRP offices on Abbey Street, where they attempted to hold a second meeting but were prevented from doing so by the relentless assault of the DMP. Home Rule newspapers did nothing to report the brutality of the police.

John O'Leary (1830–1907), although he never took the IRB oath, represented Fenian sentiment and 'Romantic Ireland' and therefore made an ideal President of the Centenary Executive, who were charged with organising the celebrations due to be held in 1898. The IRB were involved at a high level and were intent on making some political gain from the renewed interest in republicanism. But the plethora of '98 Clubs came to the attention of the more conservative Home Rule element, who feared that the rise of republicanism would undermine their ambitions and power. They scheduled a meeting of the '98 Clubs in Belfast, away from the Centenary Executive in Dublin. The eventual result, as is usual in Irish life, was a split and the formation of a new Centennial Association, represented by the likes of Joe

Devlin, Joseph Patrick Nannetti, William Martin Murphy and representatives of the Catholic Church. The ISRP's wonderfully named Rank and File '98 Club had tried to get a motion passed that the Centennial Association should only be open to those who approved of the aims and methods of the United Irishmen of 1798. This was blocked, thus proving that the association was a sham. The Rank and File Club refused to associate with such an organisation and held their own weekly assembly immediately after the weekly ISRP meetings. This cemented the link between the ISRP and the younger, radical nationalists who also saw through the platitudinous speeches of the Centennial Association.[9]

When the nationalist newspaper editor Alice Milligan's young brother, Ernest, was on a visit to Dublin, he called upon Connolly on the urging of his sister. He was so impressed by a lecture and a few books he received that he founded a Belfast branch of the ISRP who called themselves the Belfast Socialist Society. Ernest Milligan remembered Connolly as being 'of medium height, thick set in build' and 'endowed with a rich sense of humour'.[10] Descriptions of Connolly left by those who were close to him are more impressive than the few posed portraits of the man. In his book on James Connolly, the author and IRA volunteer Desmond Ryan rather poetically recalled, 'Two full and kindly keen grey eyes burned beneath dark bushy eyebrows; broad forehead crowned by black hair; medium in height; calm and imperturbable outwardly, but beneath invariably a sensitive and tense nervous system.'[11] 'Intimate friends have described Connolly as sensitive to an extreme degree, for all his calm exterior, with a tendency at times to the faults of that trait; a proneness to resent imaginary slights, to groundless suspicions and to fierce personal dislikes.'[12] Tom Bell, a founding member of the Socialist Labour Party, left a fine description of Connolly from when he knew him in 1903:

> A short, stocky man, with heavy auburn moustache, a roguish twinkle in his eye, and pleasant Irish brogue in his speech, Connolly made friends everywhere. His quiet, reticent disposition concealed the store of knowledge he had acquired from extensive reading and wide travel. But, provoked into discussion or debate, he would rout opponents with incisive and merciless logic.
>
> As lecturer, propagandist and organiser, he was unique. A proletarian of proletarians, he had none of that snobbery and pretentiousness that mar so many of our leaders. He was a true son of the working class; devoted and self-sacrificing for the cause of the workers' emancipation from capitalist slavery.[13]

## Chapter Four

# 1898–1900

# The Workers' Republic

*... a people who for centuries have never heard a shot fired in anger upon their shores, yet who encourage their government in its campaign of robbery and murder against an unoffending nation; a people, who, secure in their own homes, permit their rulers to carry devastation and death into the homes of another people, assuredly deserve little respect no matter how loudly they may boast of their liberty-loving spirit.[1]*

The first day of the year 1899 saw the arrival of yet another Connolly girl, Moira Elizabeth, the fifth child of Lillie and James, adding to the burden of feeding the family but also bringing much New Year joy. The constant struggle to make ends meet did not destroy the social structure of the family. A comrade, Robert Lynd, imagined that there 'have been few revolutionary leaders ... in whose life the affections of the home played a greater part. Poverty was there – poverty sometimes so overwhelming that it became a question

whether there was anything else in the house left to pawn –
but it is difficult not to think of that devoted family as being
happy beyond the common lot. There was laughter as well
as anxiety in the air. The family in *Little Women*, indeed, did
not live in an atmosphere richer in human kindness than did
the family of this dangerous agitator.'[2] Lillie had to feed and
clothe the family, as best she could, with the little money that
came into the household. When she passed away in 1938, the
*Irish Press* noted that:

> Lillie Connolly lived a hard life but she was satisfied that
> it should be so because she knew, even when her children
> were hungry and her husband unemployed, when the fire
> was small and everything that could be sold was gone, that
> this was all to be suffered in the cause of changing the mis-
> erable lives of the workers and the poor and making the
> world a better place for all.'[3]

Some interesting insight into Lillie is provided in her
daughter Ina Connolly's recollections:

> I can see myself standing at her side by an open fire wash-
> ing a baby. The joy and love she had for all infants and
> the satisfaction she expressed as she held them close to her
> heart, kissing them and loving them that they should not
> be starved of mother love was her determination. "Bread I
> may not be able to give you one day through the force of
> circumstances that arise out of the capitalist system under

which we live, mother's love no one can deprive me of giving to you" and this she gave most generously.

Ina went on to quote her mother:

"When I left Ireland to be married in Scotland to your father I thought I was the luckiest girl of my acquaintance. I was in some ways, perhaps, not in every sense of the word. We were very happy on very little. To be together and the understandings we had for each other made up for a lot of our shortcomings. Our trials we often tried to look upon as gifts. That was all right as long as they only concerned ourselves, but when the family made its appearance the picture took on another aspect."[4]

It is also apparent that Lillie was a welcoming host.

If mother did not go out much to enjoy herself, I think she lost very little, as we brought everybody we met up to our house and she was always ready to receive them and share with them anything we had, and at times that was very little. They sat down and took whatever was going and mother would say: "eat up, the more you eat the bigger the dividend" as we were members of the Co-operative Society. But we knew better than to eat up, because there would be nothing in the larder to refill the plates.[5]

A bad winter in 1897–8 resulted in the return of the potato blight along the west coast of Ireland. Coupled with this, heavy rains made it impossible to harvest and dry the turf so people were without food *and* fuel. In April 1898 Connolly left Dublin to report on the famine-stricken areas in Kerry. His assignment lasted a couple of weeks; it was on behalf of the *Weekly People*, the American socialist newspaper. At the same time, Maud Gonne went to County Mayo to rouse the people to save themselves. She had given Connolly £25 to cover the expense of printing a manifesto, *The Rights of Life and the Rights of Property*, which they jointly composed; in that Connolly wrote it and Gonne signed it. This pamphlet contained quotes from Catholic popes, cardinals and archbishops to endorse the declaration that the 'very highest authorities on the doctrine of the Church agree that no *human* law can stand between starving people and their right to food including the right to take the food whenever they find it, openly or secretly, with or without the owner's permission.' It also contained a rather revolutionary revelation from a Catholic bishop: 'God created all things that their enjoyment might be common to all, and that the earth might become the common possession of all. Only unjust usurpation has created the right of private property.'

Connolly's movements did not go unnoticed by the police. Dublin Castle dispatched a telegram to the Royal Irish Constabulary district inspector to warn of the impending arrival of the 'Irish Republican Socialist, 35 years, 5ft 4in, black hair, dark brown moustache, black overcoat, black soft hat or grey tweed cap.' The RIC kept a watchful eye on his visits to Sneem, Caherdaniel, Waterville, Valentia Island and Caherciveen.[6] He also took some time to visit Derrynane House, where he inspected Daniel O'Connell's blunderbuss. Connolly had no problem pointing out that Irish heroes can have clay feet: '... it is known now that O'Connell himself, as a member of the lawyers' Yeomanry Corps of Dublin, was turned out on duty to serve against the rebels on the night of Emmet's insurrection ...'[7] His tour of the distressed parts of County Kerry reinforced his socialist doctrine, helped to spread the ISRP message, and also served to build upon his reputation in the US.

The ISRP needed a journal to chronicle their struggle and to promote their cause. A paper could also be expected to bring in some money, but the initial launching cost made such a venture inconceivable. Connolly turned to his connections in Scotland. In the company of his five-year-old daughter Nora, he went to meet Keir Hardie in Glasgow in July 1898 and 'borrowed' £50. It is worth noting that Hardie never got his money back, but it was more of a philanthropic gift to socialism than an investment. Connolly would not forget this gesture and when Keir Hardie passed away in 1915 he paid his respects:

By the death of Comrade James Keir Hardie labour has lost one of its most fearless and incorruptible champions, and the world one of its highest minded and purest souls ... James Keir Hardie was to the labour movement a prophetic anticipation of its own possibilities.[8]

They also paid a visit to Edinburgh, where an aging John Connolly welcomed his son and granddaughter. Nora recalled her grandfather's big red beard and how he loosened her shoe laces to enable her to climb the hills of Edinburgh. He showed her 'a castle high up on a rock, and told her stories about other places'. She decided, 'He was very nice.'[9] Her father also brought her to stay with her aunt Margaret, Lillie's twin sister, and her husband Jack. While Nora enjoyed being spoiled by her aunt, who had no children of her own at the time, her father gave a few lectures in his old town with the help of his comrades from the SDF. He even managed to get a few subscriptions to the soon-to-be-published newspaper, thanks to the advertisement which ran in *Justice*:

IRISHMEN ATTEND! NEW IRISH WEEKLY. ONE PENNY. THE WORKERS' REPUBLIC. A literary champion of Irish Democracy, advocates an Irish Republic, an abolition of landlordism, wage-slavery, the co-operative organisation of industry under Irish representative governing bodies. Every Friday, 1st issue August 12th. Ask your newsagent.

Back in Ireland, the culmination of the 1798 Centenary was to be marked by the laying of the foundation stone of a memorial to the revolutionary leader of the United Irishmen, Theobald Wolfe Tone. The spot chosen for his statue was to be at the northeast corner of St Stephen's Green. The celebrations coincided nicely with the birth of the first issue of the *Workers' Republic*, dated a day later than advertised, 13 August 1898. Containing just eight pages, the type was set by PT Daly, who worked for the small firm contracted to print the paper. On sale for the princely price of one penny, the purpose of the paper was to 'unite the workers and to bury in one common grave the religious hatreds, the provincial jealousies, and the mutual distrusts upon which oppression has so long depended for security'. The editor, Connolly, took a swipe at those who were commemorating Wolfe Tone whilst the injustices he sought to remedy remained in place:

> He was crucified in life, now he is idolised in death, and the men who push forward most arrogantly to burn incense at the altar of his fame are drawn from the very class who, were he alive today, would hasten to repudiate him as a dangerous malcontent.

In the first issue of the *Workers' Republic* Connolly trumpeted:

> We are Socialists because … we recognise in it the only principle by which the working class can … live as men and not as mere profit-making machines … We are Republicans because we are Socialists, and therefore enemies to all privileges; and because we would have the Irish people complete masters of their own destinies, nationally and internationally, fully competent to work out their own salvation.

It was rousing prose:

Nothing can ever be gained by compromise. He who compromises with iniquity, delivers over to the enemy half of
the weapons essential to success. In politics as in geometry,
a right line is the shortest between two given points. Go
straight to the mark of Truth, Freedom and Justice, and all
the stars in their courses will fight on your side, all the
powers of nature, and the irresistible upward march of
human society will bear you onward; but hesitate, halt,
doubt the invincibility of your own enterprise, and the
demons of discord, faction and intrigue will wreck your
cause and blast your hopes.

In the second issue of the *Workers' Republic*, Connolly
remarked on the riots in Belfast that followed the commem-
oration for the Belfast-born Protestant, Wolfe Tone:

The return of the Belfast contingent from Dublin to the
former city was made the occasion of a sectarian outburst
in the streets, in the course of which Protestant and Catholic belaboured each other in the most beautiful manner, in
a truly Christian spirit.

'And proved their doctrine orthodox,

By Apostolic blows and knocks.'[10]

He who could hit the hardest felt himself master of the
soundest theology, and he whose blows did not flatten out
his opponents' skull, was, no doubt, afflicted by conscientious

scruples as to his own orthodoxy. And when Catholic and Protestant workmen absented themselves from work next morning in order to procure the needed sticking-plaster for their craniums, Catholic and Protestant employers stopped their wages accordingly with the most beautiful impartiality.

The *Workers' Republic* enjoyed a little early success in Belfast due to the fact that Ernest Milligan found a wholesaler willing to distribute the paper to newsagents. But its nationalist leaning drew criticism from the Belfast socialists and eventually young Milligan had to abandon his efforts at distribution in the North East. The sales of the ISRP paper were good in Dublin, and the party members were enthusiastic in their efforts to produce and promote the journal. But that initial spurt of energy soon flagged, with the result that the journal's production was suspended at the end of October after eleven issues.

The competing newspapers, especially those of a less radical nature, may have been more attractive to Irish nationalists. This was, after all, the decade of the cultural revival. Eoin MacNeill (1867–1945) had co-founded with Douglas Hyde (1860–1949) the language organisation the Gaelic League in 1893. The revival of the native tongue was interlinked with the desire to preserve Irish culture and promote the language as one of the 'bricks of nationality'. In 1898, the same year that the *Workers' Republic* was launched, the Gaelic League began publication of a widely-read weekly bilingual journal *An Claidheamh Soluis*.[11]

Although temporary, the cessation of the *Workers' Republic* publication would have some bearing on how the ISRP candidate fared in the January 1899 local government elections. The party did not put the more logical choice, Connolly, up for election but instead chose EW Stewart. ISRP advertisements were refused by some mainstream newspapers. Stewart was unsuccessful and the election had drained what little resources there were for the party and its organiser.

Connolly went down to Cork in the middle of February and gave a lecture, 'Labour and the Irish Revolution'. It was well attended and brought in a few contributions, but by early March he was in dire financial straits. Now living in 71 Queen Street, just beside the Liffey on Dublin's northside, he wrote a humble letter to Daniel O'Brien on 11 March 1899:

Dear 'Kumride',

You will be surprised on receiving a letter from yours truly; you will be astounded at the contents thereof. As you are perhaps aware I got a job with the Corporation, navvying, but found myself unable for it. At least I worked Thursday, was not able to go out on Friday, tried again on Saturday (today) but was not allowed to start. So I have now reached the end of my financial tether, and having been on short commons so long, am unable to perform such work when

I get it. My reason for writing to you is to tell you that as the Organiser (?) business is a failure − 7/- per week − and as I don't like to be drawing money from a few comrades − some of whom can ill afford it, perhaps, I am wishful, as a last resort before shaking the dust of Ireland from my feet, to try again my luck at the pedlar's pack. The reason I abandoned that line before was that I never had a sufficient stock to start with, and as a consequence two days good selling left me stranded until I scraped together sufficient for another start.

Therefore I have mustered up all my audacity to ask you if you could find it possible to get me the sum of £2 on loan for that purpose and I will absolutely promise to repay it − at least much sooner than you received the £5 from Miss Gonne. It lowers me in my opinion to ask this, but it would tear my heart strings out to leave Ireland now after all my toil and privation − and unless I succeed in this instance the welfare, nay the mere necessity of feeding my family will leave me no alternative.

I will not be at the meeting tomorrow, and would be obliged if you could give me an answer at my house, or club room, tonight.

Yours fraternally, James Connolly.[12]

It is not known what answer Connolly received to this audacious missive, but it is clear that he was weakened by long bouts of hunger ('short commons') which left him unable to perform hard physical labour. The 'pedlar's pack' was a collection of goods, combs, brushes, small hardware etc. that could be sold from door to door. Connolly seems to have tried that type of work before but it would appear he was unsuited to small capitalist enterprises.

Despite the serious nature of the ISRP's ambitions the members, including Connolly, could also let their hair down and enjoy a good shindig. In March 1899, a celebration of the Paris Commune was held at 87 Marlborough Street in a hall the party used for certain occasions. The minutes of the party meetings recorded that 'a beautiful supply of eatables and refreshments of a less solid nature were provided which suffered a more ruthless dispersion than ever was inflicted upon the Communards ... There were a very large number of songs rendered during the night (and part of the morning) nearly all of which were of the variety Socialist ... The proceedings ended about 2.30 a.m. on Monday morning.'

Connolly decided to resurrect the *Workers' Republic* as a potential source of income. This time they would not incur the expense of paying a printer; instead the party purchased a small hand press and a couple of cases of type. Connolly had picked up a few skills during his days as a printer's devil and now he would put them to some use. One or two of the comrades would help when possible but, for the most part, Connolly wrote the articles, edited the paper, set the type and printed the paper. On 12 May 1899 the *Worker's Republic* hit the stands again. Common financial sense prevailed this time; a new edition would only be released when the previous instalment had sold out. The hand press also proved to be invaluable for producing cheap political pamphlets.

The ISRP continued meeting, on a weekly basis, throughout 1899. The minutes of their meetings indicate how busy they were, organising outdoor meetings, printing leaflets, writing and lecturing. The members voted on a weekly basis as to who would chair the meetings, a very democratic approach. In fact, polls were taken on almost every decision. One particular ballot stands out: 'Vote taken as to whether gas stove should be placed at left side of lecture hall or on the right side.' After all, even revolutionaries have a sense of humour.

Connolly wrote that every 'war now is a capitalist move for new markets, and it is a move capitalism must make or perish.'[13] Not only were new markets required, but raw material wealth, be it gold, diamonds or oil, can often be the underlying reason for international conflict. There is no finer an example of this than the campaign waged by the British against the Boers in South Africa. The ISRP crusaded against the Second Boer War, which Connolly maintained was to enable 'an unscrupulous gang of capitalists to get into their hands the immense riches of the diamond fields … waged by a mighty empire against a nation entirely incapable of replying in any effective manner, by a government of financiers upon a nation of farmers, by a nation of filibusterers upon a nation of workers, by a capitalist ring, who will never see a shot fired during the war, upon a people defending their homes and liberties – such is the war upon which the people of England are criminally or stupidly, and criminally even if stupidly, allowing their government to enter.'[14]

After the defeat of the British at Dundee, South Africa, the minutes of one ISRP meeting described how a 'monster demonstration' had been held in Dublin city centre, which was attacked by the police before it even commenced. The police took possession of a flag inscribed with the phrase 'Down with the Robber Empire'. When some calm returned to the proceedings Tom Lyng proposed 'a resolution congratulating the Boers on their heroic stand and expressing joy at the retreat of the hired assassins of the British Empire from Dundee' and 'Connolly asked for three cheers for the downfall of the British Empire.'

The ISRP were soon joined in their protestations by the editor of the *United Irishman*, Arthur Griffith (1871–1922), a Dublin journalist who had just returned from South Africa. Griffith used his knowledge of the country to denounce the aggression against the Boer Republics. Some people were not content merely to speak out. John MacBride (1865–1916) fought with the Boers in the Irish Brigade and was given the rank of major by the Boer Government.

It must not be forgotten that the Boers' attitude to the

native Africans was brutal. Connolly compared the war to two dogs fighting over a bone which neither of them owned. The point was that Irish nationalists, republicans and socialists did not want to engage in flag-waving jingoism and insisted on their right to express their discontent with the Boer War. They formed themselves into the 'Irish Transvaal Committee' and held a number of open-air public meetings, much to the annoyance of Dublin Castle and the police. At one such meeting, on 18 December 1899, the police banned the event, but the crowds still assembled at Beresford Place, angry that Trinity College was awarding Joseph Chamberlain an honorary degree. Connolly, Maud Gonne, John O'Leary and Pat O'Brien MP were riding in a horse-drawn brake when they were stopped by a cordon of police. Connolly, with some foresight, had chosen to sit beside the driver; he grabbed the reins and drove through the lines of police, who parted and scattered for their lives, to the cheers of the crowds. They managed to get to Beresford Place, and passed their resolution condemning the war; then the four speakers and horse and brake were seized and taken to Store Street DMP Station. The police inspector, somewhat panicked by the arrest of a number of well known radicals, an old Fenian and a member of parliament, told Connolly that they could not stay there. 'We don't want to,' replied Connolly, and the gates to freedom were opened. Their short term of incarceration completed, they led a crowd to Foster Place beside the Old Parliament and re-read their resolution before the police came to scatter them again.

The police seized the opportunity to sabotage Connolly's anti-war stance by attacking the *Worker's Republic*; while all the action was being played out on the streets, a party of DMP officers raided the empty ISRP premises and smashed their small hand press.

# Chapter Five

• • • • • •

## 1900–1902

# Socialism and Nationalism

*Yes, ruling by fooling, is a great British art – with great Irish fools to practise on.*[1]

In the January 1900 municipal elections, an original founding member of the Irish Socialist Republican Party, Murtagh Lyng, stood as the ISRP candidate. 'Vote for Lyng, Labour and Liberty' ran the slogan; but Lyng was trounced, gaining a mere 5 per cent of the votes. He was not alone on the left as Labour, which had done so well in the previous year's election, took a fair battering at the polls. Connolly interpreted it as follows:

> In the North Dock Ward the two extremes of society polled for our capitalist opponent. The propertied class polled to a man, and their understrappers swept up the offscourings of society from out of the brothels and lowest dens of infamy to poll for our capitalist candidate – in their own names

and in the names of others. Between these two classes – equally noxious, and equally parasitical – came the ignorant worker, setting by his vote the political seal on his economic degradation.[2]

Meanwhile, supporters of the old Irish Nationalist Party, divided since the demise of Parnell, had finally patched up their internal differences and by the end of January they were allied under the United Irish League. Led by a conservative middle-class nationalist, John Redmond (1856–1918), the United Irish League was supported by the majority of Irish people and Redmond continued to believe that Home Rule was the answer for Ireland.

The Irish Transvaal Committee and the ISRP were so successful at their anti-recruiting campaign that few, if any, Irishmen were joining the British army. It was decided to send Queen Victoria to Ireland in the hopes that the visit would stimulate some passion and loyalty, resulting in young men signing up to fight for the empire. The organisers were mindful of the fact that the Fenians had once come close to assassinating the queen and they also recalled the violence on the streets of Dublin during her jubilee year. But the potential reward was greater than the risk to the eighty-one-year-old monarch and plans were laid to ensure a loyal welcome. Ships from Belfast, laden with thousands of Harland and Wolff employees and their families, arrived in Dublin to line the proposed route.[3] Guinness, ever the loyal porter-brewing family, gave their employees a day off and an extra shilling to ensure they supported the monarch. Other incentives to encourage people to welcome Queen Victoria included the closure of the schools and the promise of a 'children's treat' courtesy of the Lord Lieutenant.

On 3 April 1900, Victoria arrived in Dun Laoghaire, spent the night aboard her yacht and, after an absence of many decades, set foot on Irish soil the next day to cheers and applause. Thomas Pile, lord mayor of Dublin and self-proclaimed 'nationalist', read a loyal address from Dublin Corporation. In Dublin that night, a torchlight demonstration against the royal visit and the Boer War was attacked by the Dublin Metropolitan Police, who baton-charged the protesters. The police specifically targeted Connolly, Arthur Griffith and another newspaper editor from the *Weekly Independent*.

That Saturday, 7 April, was designated as 'Children's Day'. Loyal youngsters were expected to come to the Phoenix Park, where Victoria would welcome them. Fifteen thousand turned up to enjoy what loyal businesses had charitably contributed:

Jacob & Co. gave one ton of biscuits; Messrs. William & Woods, one ton of jam and 10,000 bags of sweets; Messrs. J. Downes & Co., 1,800 buns; Messrs. Johnston, Mooney & O'Brien 3,000 buns; Messrs. Shuley & Co., 15,000 paper bags; Messrs. M'Cluskey & Co., 750 oranges; Messrs. Cleeve

Brothers, Limerick, 7 cwt. of butter; Messrs. Shaw & Sons, Limerick, 1,250 lbs. of best ham; The Lucan Dairy, 300 gallons of milk; Mr Hamilton Drummond, 2,500 oranges.[4]

Later, on the first day of July, Maud Gonne and a group of nationalist women (mostly from the recently formed *Inghinidhe na hÉireann*) organised the 'Patriotic Children's Treat' in Clonturk Park for minors who did not go to the Phoenix Park to see Victoria.[5] This nationalist treat attracted twenty thousand young people.

Queen Victoria stayed for a month, amidst scenes of civil disturbance and general unrest which Connolly normally revelled in. But sad news from Edinburgh dragged him away from the front line of the battle and back to his old town. On the very day Victoria arrived in Dublin, Connolly's father suffered a brain haemorrhage and seventeen days later he died.

In Dublin, the police seized Arthur Griffith's *United Irishman* as Maud Gonne had written a fairly unflattering article about Victoria entitled 'The Famine Queen'. This attack on freedom of speech spurred Connolly out of mourning and straight back into producing the ISRP's journal, which had not been published for some months. The *Workers' Republic* made a return, at the new lower price of a ha'penny, on 11 May 1900. This time it would be a joint effort; ISRP comrades would work together to produce the paper, with William O'Brien, (who would become general secretary of the

ITGWU) rolling the ink, Murtagh Lyng, (ISRP secretary) pulling the impression, and Murtagh's brother John (later on a good friend to Connolly in New York) 'setting the type from those shapeless hieroglyphics that James substituted for the English alphabet'. Connolly was accused of depriving the printers of Dublin because he used unpaid voluntary labour to produce the paper. His retort was that he could just as well be accused of stealing from the barbers of Dublin as he shaved himself every morning.

In September 1900, Lord Salisbury became British prime minister in the 'Khaki Election,' so called because the British army had worn khaki for the first time during the Second Boer War, then raging in South Africa. The Conservative election manifesto helped to remove the Liberals from power by appealing for support against the Transvaal and Orange Free State:

> The gravest questions must be dealt with. The Imperial Power over the territories of the two South African Republics, which, as events have proved, was unwisely relinquished, must be rebuilt upon durable foundations ... In due time those territories will doubtless enjoy the benignant colonial policy which this country has pursued for half a century, and whose brilliant fruit may be discerned in the affection that so many of our colonies have displayed to the mother country during the recent war.

At the same time, the Home Rulers achieved seventy-seven seats.

By October, the *Workers' Republic* was rolled out for the fourth time since its birth and only for the second time did they make use of newsagents for distribution. In November, Connolly took a look at the use of child labour on the streets of Dublin:

Thus the question of street trading by children is seen to be linked inextricably with the capitalist system. In every country capitalism brings in its train the exploitation and degradation of children; coins into profit their tender limbs, and blots the sunshine out of their young lives. In countries where the factory system has taken root, as in England, the children are caught up into the factory, and there made to supplement by their pitiful earnings the wages of their parents. The millowner reduces the wages of the factory hand and, when remonstrated with, tells his wage-slave to send the children to work and their earnings will make up for the reduction in wages. In Ireland there are few factories, so when the competition for employment drives down labourers' wages, or trade depression throws the labourer out of work, he uses his children also to supplement his earnings, and as he cannot send them to the factory he sends them, too often, to the street. Whose is the fault? The capitalist class, and all who uphold the capitalist class and their accursed social system.[6]

That Christmas was one of the least festive weeks that the Connolly clan would ever have the misfortune to live through. Due to widespread unemployment in Dublin and decreasing sales of the paper, the IRSP could only afford to give Connolly a paltry wage, despite the fact that he had five little children (and his wife was seven months' pregnant).

Nora Connolly recalled that on that Christmas Eve her mother commented to her father that he was very late in coming home. His reply was simply: 'Two shillings was all I got tonight. Two shillings! I was ashamed to come home with them.'[7] The Connolly family simply went without presents and indeed without a decent dinner.

Ina Connolly remembered 11 February 1901, the day when her brother Roderick was born:

> My earliest recollection of my father is his trying to keep the family quiet on the landing as my mother was being delivered of her first son … He was as pleased to have daughters as any farmer would be to have sons. The sex of a child meant very little to him. His concern was: "Is he bodily fit? Are his limbs perfect? Will he be able to take his stand with the rest of the working class, strong and healthy is all that I ask for my family and the average amount of intelligence to be able to work their way through life and leave this world a little better than they found it; not one step backward, but always pushing on, ever forward. To enjoy some of the fruits of this God-given earth and make life somewhat easier for

those who come after is all that he has to inherit." He was making paper hats from discarded newspapers, folding them three-quarter-wise into a poke and tearing some paper up in strips to look like a feather … and we carried sticks on our shoulders. He marched us up and down saying in a soft quiet voice: "for we are the Boers."[8]

*The New Evangel*, a collection of some of Connolly's articles from the *Workers' Republic*, was published in 1901. There was no doubting the appeal of Connolly's prose. It was popular, sold easily and was eminently readable, unlike many of his contemporaries who, despite their educational achievements, lacked the ability to talk or write to the masses. This is one reason why Connolly spent the best part of 1901 flitting back and forth between Ireland and Britain. He addressed the May Day meeting in Glasgow, which suggests that he was beginning to gain some popularity as a speaker. He had, after all, been confident enough to advertise his availability for a lecture tour of Scotland and England.

The printing press belonging to the ISRP was in a pitiful condition and Connolly was keen on acquiring a new machine. WJ Gallagher, a student activist with the Cork branch of the ISRP, discussed it in some correspondence on 23 June 1901: 'O'Lyhane and I feel confident that we shall be able to send you £5 from Cork towards cost, and we think we can do so pretty soon.' A fund for the purpose was set up, but contributions were very slow in materialising. It was exactly one year later that the fund received an £11 loan from the Scottish SDF activist, George Yates, via Connolly, and a second-hand press was purchased. To repay the loan, the ISRP was to print a set quantity of the Scottish Social Democratic Federation (SDF) newpaper, *The Socialist*. It was a perfect marriage: the Irish got their machine, the loan did not have to be repaid with actual money, and the Scottish got a low-cost journal without the hassle of printing it.

In June Connolly again returned to Scotland, this time visiting Falkirk. An observer noted that Connolly 'possesses an attribute comparatively rare among socialist lecturers, that of being at the same time simple and perfectly intelligible to the ordinary man, and also perfectly accurate and rigid in his adherence to scientific verity.'[9] Riding on the success of Falkirk, Connolly proceeded to Aberdeen, Leith and then south to Salford, England, where he gained huge support for the local labour organisations, the South Salford SDF and West Salford ILP, which both shared the cost of the week-long visit. Due to the popularity of the speaker, a further visit was booked for September 1901. Upon his return to Salford, some of the Irish who had worked in the Pendle-ton Pit founded a branch of the ISRP. Connolly was present for their first meeting, where he ensured that the ISRP would not step on the proverbial toes of the SDF and ILP by making membership of the ISRP exclusive to people of Irish birth or ancestry. In truth, this measure would not have affected the majority of those who lived in Pendleton as they were, in the main, Irish.

From Wigan, Connolly wrote to Murtagh Lyng; it's an interesting letter as the writer does not blush at supposing that he was the most important member in Dublin, probably because he actually was:

Dear Comrade.

Enclosed you will find 6/– being payment for 6 doz. papers sold at and around Ashton, the odd coppers I have appropriated to tide me over a temporary emergency.

You will please send on to Ashton 3 doz. assorted pamphlets and an account and they will pay you by return. Also put them down for 2 doz. of each issue of the W.R. [*Workers' Republic*].

I am glad to hear that you are doing so well with meetings and getting so many new members. There were so many evil prophets saying that the movement would go slump if I left Dublin that your progress since I left has been doubly gratifying to me – proving that the ISRP was well able to stand on its own feet, and that its growth depended upon correct principles and not on any man's personality. If all those who can work for Socialism in Ireland would work I might content myself in exile and never be missed, which would be a greater tribute to my work of the past five years than if my presence was indispensable. Please let me know what you are reprinting for the September issue, and what decision you have come to upon the article I sent you.

Tell McLoughlin that his fellow tailor, Mike Clemens, who was in Dublin some years ago and is now in Oldham, came through to hear me on Sunday night in Ashton. He is going to try and establish a branch of ours in Oldham.

Yours fraternally, James Connolly[10]

Connolly went on to Reading, where he spoke to large audiences but had little success in getting new members for the SDF. In Oxford, Connolly's meeting was stoned by students and a large gathering of down-and-outs, who were all very hostile to socialism. The police looked on when the crowd began an attempt to steal the red flag as the socialists began to leave the area. Connolly was maddened; he broke the flag pole in two, flew into the attacking crowd and laid four of them on their backs. Then the police intervened and separated the two factions. Connolly was missing for some hours and, when he returned to his comrades, explained to them that he had been searching the streets for his hat, which he had lost in the fight. More meetings were held in Oxford but it proved too difficult to collect donations, which in turn resulted in Connolly being out of pocket for his expenses.

A branch of the SDF in North London welcomed Connolly, who spoke on the lot of Irish immigrants who traditionally worked the harvest:

They used to be waylaid by farmers wanting to give them a job, they were now waylaid by the farmer's dog, wanting to give them a bite.

The meetings in London were not well attended. On 14 October 1901, Connolly wrote to his comrades in the ISRP:

> The meetings here are awful. McEntee assures me that the smallest meeting we ever had in Foster Place would be considered a demonstration here.[11] Certainly my meetings have been the smallest I have had in England. They said that my meetings were big meetings, but a large proportion of the crowd were Irish and Scotch comrades from other branches in London, who came up to see me personally. So I must still adhere to the opinion I gave Hazell when he asked me my opinion of London.[12] I told him the only hope for it was a 'big fire'![13]

Connolly headed back home to Dublin where, despite his long absence, he was elected to the Dublin Trades Council thanks to the United Labourers' Union. The union also supported him as a Labour candidate in the upcoming corporation elections, when Connolly stood for Wood Quay ward.

Meanwhile, in the south, Con O'Lyhane reported on the state of the Cork branch of the ISRP, which he had founded.[14] Not unusually, they were suffering from a severe lack of finances within the branch as, 'owing to clerical influence', many of the members had 'been frightened away'.

Nevertheless, the letter states that the open-air meetings on Sundays were well attended with 'never less than 200 being present'. O'Lyhane gives us an interesting insight into the personal harassment he suffered and which Connolly would also have faced:

> No serious effort at disturbance has been made yet, but per-
> sonally I have found it convenient to alter my route home
> to avoid the hooting and jeers of some roughs who have
> tried to create scenes as I proceed to dinner from my place
> of business.[15]

In the election held in January 1902, Connolly received 431 votes, whilst the winning candidate received 1,424. Two other ISRP candidates, Edward W Stewart and the tailor William McLoughlin, joined him in defeat. Part of the reason for their failure lay in the general campaign conducted against these socialists from various quarters, including the capitalist press and the Catholic Church. Some priests denounced them from the pulpit, declaring that Connolly was the Antichrist and even threatened excommunication for anyone who voted for them. Today such threats may mean very little, but to working-class Catholics, who lived in abject poverty, their only consolation was often their faith. A couple of months after the elections, the *Workers' Republic* reappeared for one issue. Connolly took time to consider the reason for their failure to win a seat.

In the elections just ended eight hundred votes were cast for Socialism in the only two wards of this city our finances allowed us to contest. These votes were cast for no milk-and-water, ratepaying, ambiguous 'Labour' candidates, but for the candidates of a party which in the very stress and storm of the fight instructed its standard bearers to refuse to sign the pledge of the compromising Labour Electoral body, and to stand or fall by the full spirit and meaning of its revolutionary policy.

These 800 votes were cast for Socialism in spite of a campaign of calumny unequalled in its infamy, in spite of the fact that the solemn terrors of religion were invoked on behalf of the capitalist candidates, in spite of the most shameless violation by our opponents of the spirit of the Corrupt Practices' Act, and despite the boycott of the press. No other party ever had such a dead weight to lift ere they could appear as a recognised force in political life; no other party could have lifted such a weight so gallantly and so well. What is the secret of the wonderful progress of this party? The secret lies not in the personality of leaders, nor in the ability of propagandists; it lies in the fact that all the propaganda and teaching of this party was, from the outset, based upon the Class Struggle – upon a recognition of the fact that the struggle between the Haves and the Have Nots was the controlling factor in politics, and that this fight could only be ended by the working class seizing hold of political power and using this power to transfer the ownership of the means of life, viz. land and machinery of production, from the hands of private individuals to the community, from individual to social or public ownership.

This party had against it all the organised forces of society – of a society founded upon robbery, but it had on its side a latent force stronger than them all, the material interests of the Working Class. The awakened recognition of that material interest has carried us far; it will carry us in triumph to the end.[16]

A sort of fame was thrust upon Connolly when the American Socialist Labor Party republished his pamphlet *Erin's Hope: The End and the Means* in February. This act set in motion a chain of events that would alter the next seven years of Connolly's and his family's future. It had been mooted a few years before, but in April 1902 an official invitation arrived from the SLP in New York confirming that Connolly should come to the US to give a series of lectures. From Glasgow, Connolly confided in a letter to Tom Lyng, the original founder of the ISRP and brother to Murtagh and Jack, that he was not relishing the proposed trip: 'I see the American crowd have finally resolved to go on with the matter of the tour. It makes me nervous.' Even a couple of months later, in a letter to his ISRP comrade, party librarian and sometime treasurer Mark Deering, who was helping to organise the lecture tour, his nerves had not fully settled:

The statement that they have hired Cooper Union, which as you know is the biggest hall in New York, causes a cold chill of nervousness to creep down my spinal column.'[17]

By early August his manner was a little more lighthearted if not darkly humorous when he wrote to Daniel O'Brien:

I am very much afraid that the American trip will be a failure. This conviction has been borne in upon me ever since I saw that engraving in the *Weekly People*. No sensible person would listen to or come to see a person who looked like that picture … The fiend who wrote that preposterous biography, and created a new birthplace and a new year of birth for me, will I hope suffer in this life all the tortures of the damned.[18]

He also sailed to Scotland on 4 April, again to address the May Day rally, this time in Edinburgh for the SDF. It was organised by John Carstairs Matheson, who would faithfully correspond with Connolly over the next decade. In Aberdeen, Connolly spent a week with his comrades and also visited Falkirk. Before returning to Dublin, he went to Salford for a week to see how the ISRP branch had progressed. He was disappointed by its lack of success, but was heartened to see that the SDF and ILP were still co-operating.

Back in Scotland again, this time in his hometown of Edinburgh, Connolly wrote to William O'Brien:

Thank you and McLoughlin for your services to me in the

matter of clothes. I quite understand your difficulty on the night of my leaving Dublin; you will also understand my embarrassment. The whole circumstances of the suit, tho' I may say, made them the dearest I have ever worn, although I paid no cash. That a suit begun in November should not be completed until April and that I had to approach the parties concerned so often and vainly until I felt like a beggar – all this combined to so humiliate me and outrage my self-respect that it at one time nearly, indeed actually, made me resolve never to go back to Dublin again. But having once put my hand to the plough I cannot turn back, and as a matter of fact the movement in Ireland, and Ireland itself, is so twined up in my very existence that I could not abandon it even if I would.[19]

On 16 August 1902, Connolly was, for a week, the guest of the Salford SDF, who threw a *bon voyage* party for him at 43 Trafford Road. He was asked to take the message to America: 'Workers of the World Unite.'

The census of 1901 details the Connolly family living in a single-room tenement at 54 Pimlico in the heart of the Dublin slums.[20] Connolly gave his birthplace as Monaghan; his profession he maintained was that of a 'Printer-Compositor' and he professed an ability to speak Irish.

# Chapter Six

• • • • • •

# 1902–1903

# To America

*None so fitted to break the chains as they who wear them,*
*none so well equipped to decide what is a fetter.* [1]

The American Socialist Labor Party was controlled by
Daniel De Leon (1852–1914), who was eager to have
Connolly, the renowned representative of the Irish working
class, on his side. The journal of the SLP, the *Weekly People*,
under De Leon's editorship, published certain articles from
the *Workers' Republic* in the hopes of ensuring the loyalty of
Irish American socialists. It would be mutually beneficial if a
representative of Irish socialism visited the US on a lecture
tour and Connolly was the logical choice. He was given travelling expenses and a wage, but also hoped to raise subscriptions for the *Workers' Republic* on his journey through the
US. Connolly set sail from Derry on 30 August 1902 and his
visit was considered newsworthy enough to make page two

of *The New York Times* under the heading 'Agitator Connolly Here':

> James Connolly, an Irish Socialist agitator, who founded the Irish Socialist Republican Party in Dublin, Ireland, in 1896, arrived here last week on the Allan Line steamship *Sardinia*. He will start on a tour throughout the United Sates under the auspices of the Socialist Labor Party. His object is to collect information about the trusts so as to make them an object lesson when he returns to Ireland. He will speak at a meeting in Cooper Union Hall to-morrow evening.

De Leon was born on the island of Curaçao, off Venezuela, but he came to the United States in 1874 from Europe, where he had received his education in Germany and the Netherlands. He continued his studies in Columbia Law School where he also lectured for some time but, in 1890, he joined the Socialist Labor Party. Within a couple of years De Leon rose through the ranks of the SLP and became editor of the *Weekly People* and the *Daily People*, positions he retained until his death. He has been described as a 'thin, grey-haired, impetuous, dictatorial pioneer of industrial unionism'.[2] De Leon became the driving force of the SLP, but by being 'his own greatest admirer' tended to irk comrades who railed against the cult of the individual.[3]

Henry Kuhn, the national secretary of the American SLP, worked out an itinerary for Connolly's lecture tour. Initially it was planned for Connolly to go to New Jersey, Connecticut, Rhode Island, Massachusetts, New York, Ohio, Michigan, Kentucky, Indiana, Illinois and Colorado. As word spread about the tour, more bookings for the speaker were made, which resulted in Connolly being on the road for three and a half months.[4]

The resolution welcoming James Connolly to the United States was read out at Cooper Union, New York City, on 15 September 1902:

> Whereas James Connolly is visiting the country as the representative of the Irish Socialist Republican Party, for the purpose of enlisting the interest of the Irish Americans in the Socialist Movement, and
>
> Whereas James Connolly in his mission wishes to destroy the influence of the Irish Home Rulers and the bourgeoisie in Ireland, and their allies who trade on the Irish vote in this country to the economic detriment of the Irish working men in this country, therefore be it resolved:
>
> That we, the members of the Socialist Labor Party, here assembled to receive James Connolly, cordially welcome him to 'our' shores and give his mission our emphatic endorsement.

The hall was packed, despite the harsh weather on the night, and Connolly spoke with such conviction and eloquence that he ensured many enthusiastic receptions and bookings for the next few months. The SLP had promoted the Connolly tour to such an extent that there were many reporters in attendance. He was amused when he was questioned by one journalist as to who his ancestors were and whether or not they had 'estates or castles' in Ireland. Connolly replied that he had no ancestors, and that his people were poor and obscure, like the workers he was addressing in the hall.

The Cooper Union Hall talk was a fine example of the type of lecture Connolly intended to deliver in America. He was smart enough to insist that he was not an Irish Everyman, declaring that he represented 'only the class to which I belong ... I could not represent the entire Irish people on account of the antagonistic interests of these classes, no more than the wolf could represent the lamb or the fisherman the fish.' He then spoke about how the ISRP's tasks were twofold, proclaiming: 'No person can be economically free who is not politically free and no person can be politically free who is not economically free.' Connolly gave an account of living conditions in Dublin and let the Irish Americans know that many of the 'shining lights of the Home Rule executive committee' were in effect slum landlords. Part of his lecture included a fervent appeal to vote for the Socialist Labor Party, for those who supported socialism in America would help to advance the socialist cause in Ireland. The *Daily People* recorded that there was tumultuous applause and a standing ovation, with people throwing their hats in the air.

The next night, 16 September, Connolly spoke to a congregation of four hundred in Getty Square in Yonkers. As a mark of the success of these and subsequent lectures, subscriptions to the *Workers' Republic* began to arrive at SLP headquarters. Remaining in the New Jersey area for a couple of days, he attracted sizeable crowds of three hundred eager listeners in Paterson and Elizabeth.

On 23 September, Connolly wrote from Bridgeport, Connecticut, to Dan O'Brien, secretary of the ISRP, enclosing an international money order for the precise sum of nineteen dollars and ninety-nine cents. There were great dissimilarities between the socialist movements in the US and Ireland. Connolly reported in amazement:

> They never have a red flag. The platform I speak from has generally a desk for the speaker and it is draped with an American flag, Stars and Stripes. And they take a collection before the principal speaker begins to speak. And at a good many meetings they take no collection at all.

In the same letter he also mentions the extreme temperatures:

> It is fearfully hot here for me, but the Americans say it is exceptionally cool. It is obvious to me that hell will be a greater punishment to us than to the Americans. Another injustice to Ireland.[5]

A short trip north brought him to Germania Hall in

Hartford, Connecticut, on 24 September. On this night a man stood up and announced that he was a capitalist as he had managed to save $300 during his working life. He wished to know which party he should vote for. Connolly told him that the socialists would treat him far better than a system that forced him to spend twenty-five long years saving such a miserable sum, much to the amusement of the hall.

As the tour wore on Connolly began to feel the strain of an overburdened lecturer. Each town he arrived in expected a lot of his time and energy, which forced him to complain to Henry Kuhn that he had no free time. Despite Kuhn's efforts, a fierce row ensued in Troy, New York, when Connolly refused to speak at three meetings that had been arranged in succession. He wrote to Dan O'Brien on 16 October:

> Enclosed you will find 16 dollars. This is less than last week due to the fact that I went on strike at Troy and did not speak for three days. This was the first rest I had had for 31 days, and I was determined to have it. But the Troy section had booked me to speak at three meetings, although I had given warning at the Cooper Union meeting in New York [on that date at least] that I would only speak once in Troy. They tried to bluff me into speaking but it did not come off, then they said if I would not speak twice I would not speak at all, but I was not to be coerced, and as a result I did not speak at all.[6]

In fairness to the Troy section, it would be worth looking at the letter they wrote to Connolly on 8 October:

> Comrade Connolly.
>
> You are to speak at Watervliet Friday evening. Watervliet is across the river from Troy, a city of about 1700 people. Saturday as requested by Henry Kuhn you are given a day off. Sunday afternoon at 3 o'clock you speak in City Hall, Troy. Sunday evening you are to speak at Ruissilair, a city six mile south of Troy, on the Hudson. The meetings are all Hall meetings & every arrangement has been made.
>
> Fraternally, Laurence A. Boland, Organizer.

Although he was to be given 'a day off', it is clear that Connolly was miffed at the idea of speaking three times within such a small area, especially as he had already journeyed such a great distance to reach Troy. Frank Passano, the Troy organiser, ended up hurling extreme insults at Connolly, forcing the speaker to complain to the National Executive Committee of the SLP. Later, Henry Kuhn, the SLP secretary, wrote to tell Connolly that Passano had written a letter of retraction and that the Troy section members had 'acted utterly without warrant'. Nonetheless, when Connolly later emigrated to America and lived in Troy, he would constantly clash with Passano.

A fine speech in Boston's Faneuil Hall, known as the 'Cradle of Liberty', resulted in 25 subscriptions to the *Workers' Republic*.

Nora Connolly spoke in the same hall in August 1916 to an estimated crowd of 15,000 – considerably more people than had come to hear her father so many years before.[7] Haverhill, Massachusetts, played host to Connolly on 2 October, and then a couple of days later he was invited to take a small trip south to the town of Lowell.

The list of towns and places visited grew daily: Cleveland, New Bedford, Syracuse, Buffalo, Woburn, Detroit, Chicago, Minneapolis etc. He was constantly on the move as he explained in a letter to the ISRP secretary Daniel O'Brien, from Louisville, Kentucky, on 22 October:

> I suppose you wonder at my short letters, but I have to spend about five hours per day in railway trains, the towns are so far apart, and this does not leave me much time, or inclination, for long letters.[8]

Often overlooked is Connolly's quick wit and speed of retort. Murtagh Lyng wrote in 1902 that Connolly had 'a sledge-hammer repartee'.

There is a story concerning an American heckler who insisted on shouting out inane and irrelevant questions and was succeeding in disturbing the proceedings. 'You seem to know everything,' he shouted up from the crowd. 'Who'll win the Derby?'

'A horse,' replied Connolly, 'but I'm surprised at *an ass* asking!'

The state capital of Minnesota, Saint Paul, on the banks of the great Mississippi River, was populated by German and Irish immigrants who came to hear Connolly speak at Federation Hall in early November. After this talk, he wrote to Daniel O'Brien concerning publication delays in the *Workers' Republic*.

> Here am I, knocking life out of myself, travelling from 200 to 600 miles every day at least, and talking every night, canvassing hard for subscriptions and in order to get them, telling everybody that the paper will appear more regularly in the future than in the past, and you people at home have not the common manliness to try and stand by my word by getting out the paper as promised. You may think it all a joke, but I think that you all ought to be damned well ashamed of yourselves. It is so hard a job for you to get together enough matter to fill a paper once a month – such a terrible strain on your nerves! I am ashamed, heartily ashamed of the whole gang of you.[9]

Sometimes a few words from Connolly concerning his tour would be published in the *Daily People*. In one such issue, he wrote of how he was approached by a man in Salt Lake City who accused De Leon of driving thousands of members from the SLP. Connolly replied that instead of being a 'tyrant', De Leon was 'a somewhat chirpy old gentleman', but was indeed someone who 'scalps a traitor or reveals a corruption, with as little personal feeling as a surgeon in the dissection room'. No doubt De Leon took this as a slanderous description as opposed to the gentle ribbing it was meant to be. De Leon might have been wise to read the report in the *Daily People* concerning the lecture at Century Hall, Minneapolis:

> [Connolly] must be heard to be appreciated. In print, his wit suffers; but spoken in his genuinely Irish proletarian style, it creates both mirth and thought.[10]

Connolly also wrote about his preference for indoor lectures, as they were 'not subject to all the chances of bad weather, brass bands, dog fights and other such circumstances against which Demosthenes himself would contend in vain.'[11]

Meanwhile, in Dublin, the ISRP were receiving regular amounts of dollars and correspondence from the busy lecturer. The Connolly family was also in receipt of a weekly letter, which often contained a newspaper cutting. Nora Connolly noted that 'some of the papers called him the Socialist Silver Tongue. She would say it over to herself while waiting for the postman. It had a lovely sound.'[12]

A welcome break of five days was spent with some cousins in San Francisco, where he spoke on 18 November at the Pioneer Hall. Over the next three nights he found himself in San Jose, Bakersfield and Los Angeles. On 24 November he was in Phoenix, Arizona, and then three days later in Colorado. A report of a meeting in Pueblo, Colorado, on 29 November declared that 'two hundred workingmen listened to Comrade Connolly'. The lecturer spoke of how the greatest power the master classes use against the workers is political power or in other words, as Connolly explained, the government. He went on to say that 'it makes no difference whether the robber is Irish, American or German … a robber he will remain so long as the workingmen give to him the political power by their votes.'[13]

At the beginning of December, Connolly spoke at Columbia Hall in Denver to over 500 people. Many others had to be turned away due to lack of space in the venue. A curious show called 'Captain Jinks of the Horse Marines' was at the Opera House in Grand Junction on the same night as Connolly lectured in the Court House; nonetheless, the socialist speaker still attracted a fair crowd. Following this, he went to St Louis, Missouri, where his date was cancelled as SLP members reckoned 'the venture would not warrant undertaking'. The next two nights he crossed the state line to Illinois to speak in Jacksonville (where they could not hire a hall for the occasion) and Springfield. Taking no rest, he was due to go to Marion, Indiana, on 10 December, but rather ridiculously the local SLP could only schedule talks on weekends so nothing could be arranged for Connolly. Luckily, the Indianapolis branch of the SLP picked up this slot and

organised a lecture for him. Things were not going too well
in the last weeks of the tour. A scheduled talk in Detroit on
the eleventh had to be cancelled as Connolly had no way
of reaching the city on time. The Canadians were a little
more coordinated and hosted a couple of meetings across the
border. As on many occasions when he had to meet strangers
in new places, the national secretary of the Canadian SLP
wrote to tell him to 'come to London (Ontario) … you will
be met by comrades wearing the red button.'

Despite the troubles he had encountered earlier on with
the Troy SLP, Connolly spoke there on 19 December. More
importantly, he could now take a small vacation with his
cousins, Thomas and Margaret Humes of 447 Tenth Street,
Troy, New York.[14] The intensity and duration of the tour
suggests Connolly was indefatigable. In fact, he even wrote
to Dan O'Brien to see if he could arrange a meeting in Cork
for him on his return journey.

A farewell meeting was held for Connolly in the Manhat-
tan Lyceum on 26 December 1902, and was addressed by De
Leon.[15] Having introduced Connolly to an excited audience,
the chairman implored Connolly to give his impressions of
America and the movement. Connolly rose to speak and
was met with 'tremendous cheers'. He began by expressing
his appreciation of America and that there were many great
aspects to it. But he pulled no punches in asserting that there
were many things that required improvement. Besides what

he called a general disregard for law, particularly amongst the capitalists, he pointed out that individualism was practised systematically. He went on to say that even the trade unions were infected by lawlessness and then remarked that the country as a whole was backward in its understanding of class struggle. On the positive side, he 'reaffirmed his belief in the policy of the Socialist Labor Party' and stated that it was 'the only one likely to carry the working class to emancipation'.[16]

When it came for De Leon's turn to speak, the leader of the American Socialist Labour Party firmly rejected the accusation of American socialist backwardness and indeed insisted that it was the socialists of the Old World who needed to 'knock into their heads' that America would be the strategic battleground when it came to the fight between Capitalism and Socialism. De Leon received 'round upon round of applause'.[17]

Finally, early the next afternoon, on 27 December, Connolly boarded the Cunard steamer *Etruria*. When he eventually got home to Pimlico it was early in the New Year and there was great excitement amongst the Connolly children as their father had brought presents for them all. Years later, Nora could still recall that there were books about China and America, some moccasins, a ball and a doll.

Not all of the Dublin comrades were as enthusiastic as his clan upon Connolly's return. An unreasonable situation had occurred during his absence which saw the establishment of a licensed bar at ISRP headquarters. Connolly, regardless of his teetotal nature, could not condone the misappropriation of funds (which he had collected in America) towards making up for a shortfall in the bar takings. He also voiced his annoyance that the *Workers' Republic* was produced in such a lackadaisical fashion whilst he was away. He berated his comrades for the number of complaints he had received from new subscribers to the ISRP journal. Some complainants did not receive the newspaper at all and the luckier ones often received it when it was more than a month out of date. This clearly distressed Connolly, having worked so hard over the previous few months to secure the financial security of the paper and the party.

This was the tense atmosphere in which the ISRP contested the local elections with Connolly as their candidate for the Wood Quay ward. An unlikely supporter, Arthur Griffith, in the *United Irishman,* voiced his opinion that Connolly deserved the vote of every nationalist in the ward. Griffith wrote that the 'able and honest men who are going forward as candidates can be counted on the fingers of one hand. Foremost amongst them is Mr. James Connolly … He is opposed by the shoneens, the tenement house rack-renters of the poor, the publicans, and we regret to say, the priests. We are not Socialists, but we would be intensely gratified to see a man of Mr. Connolly's character returned to the Dublin Corporation, to let the light in on the corruption that sits enthroned on Cork Hill …'[18]

Perhaps due to his long absence and lack of preparation, Connolly only polled a disappointing two hundred and forty three votes, a little more than half the number he received in the last election. Other factors may include some underhand tactics used by the other candidates:

> … let us remember how the paid canvassers of the capitalist candidate – hired slanderers – gave a different account of Mr. Connolly to every section of the electors. How they said to the Catholics that he was an Orangeman, to the Protestants that he was a Fenian, to the Jews that he was an anti-Semite, to others that he was a Jew, to the labourers that he was a journalist on the make, and to the tradesmen and professional classes that he was an ignorant labourer; that he was born in Belfast, Derry, England, Scotland and Italy, according to the person the canvasser was talking to.[19]

In February 1903 Connolly resigned from the ISRP in protest over non-payment of monies owed. He wrote to the ISRP secretary, EW Stewart:

> The members will not, I know, believe me to be animated by any considerations for the 'rights of property', but as a man who has some knowledge of the world and of its Socialist movements I know that there must be a certain code of honour observed towards those who have business dealings with us, or else our very existence will become

impossible. I despair of any party controlled by men who will not recognise the market value, even, of a modicum of honour and honesty in its business relations.

I wonder would the mover and supporters of the motion that we pay no rent, practise in his own household, towards their own landlords, the same rules they seek to apply to the Party premises. By no means; they would be too careful of their individual reputation. But the integrity of the Party's name and reputation were and are as dear to me as those of my household, and therefore my refusal to countenance in the one case what I would not dream of in the other.'[20]

Not only was the rent due; the paper manufacturer was also owed money. This could have resulted in a withdrawal of supplies, which in turn could have seen the termination of the *Workers' Republic*. Considering that Connolly had managed to secure large amounts of subscriptions to ensure the life of the paper, he was understandably vexed. His name would also be worthless in America if the newspapers did not arrive.

He returned to the party within two weeks when the members agreed to pay the rent. However, the row cause a split and a few key figures resigned from the ISRP, including the secretary, EW Stewart, who Connolly saw as being no great loss. But Jack Mulray, Tom Lyng and William O'Brien also left the party. Connolly wrote to O'Brien, offering to resign himself if the younger man would come back to the organisation. This period was an all-time low for the ISRP.

With little happening in Dublin, Connolly began to suspect that he had made a mistake in returning from the US. He accepted an engagement as a lecturer in Scotland for the Social Democratic Federation. He wrote a letter to John Carstairs Matheson as follows:

> I am wearying for my Scotch tour to commence. It is the centrepiece of my plans for the whole year as I intend to go to America in the Autumn and bring my family out after me … in any case I consider that the party here has no longer that exclusive demand on my life which led me in the past to sacrifice my children's welfare for years in order to build it up. I only wish that I had known it in America before I came home, as when there I received tempting offers to stay, and it is not likely that having rejected them once I will receive them again.[21]

Connolly asked his comrade not to broadcast this news as he continued to hope that he could still make a decent living in either Scotland or Ireland.

From Edinburgh he edited two issues of the *Workers' Republic*, but the ISRP as a political party was in turmoil. In fact, as an organisation, it was practically nonexistent at this time and eventually the *Workers' Republic* suspended publication. Connolly, perhaps recognising the need to advance his skills, utilised some of his free time in Scotland to train in a college as a linotype operator. The linotype machine essentially forged lines of typed words from hot lead, thus speeding up the printing operation hugely. Before its invention, each individual letter had to be placed on a printing plate by a compositor.

During his time in Scotland the SDF suffered a split, which resulted in Connolly going over to the newly formed Socialist Labour Party. For the next few months, on a salary of thirty shillings a week, Connolly was busy journeying around the country of his birth, organising for the new party, which at this stage was ideologically indiscernible from De Leon's American SLP. He was also elected as national organiser for the Scottish SLP.

It was agreed that the party's paper, *The Socialist*, could be sent to those Americans who has subscribed to the absent *Workers' Republic*. Meanwhile, back in Dublin, the ISRP had begun to reorganise, thanks to John Lyng and William O'Brien (who had returned to the party), ensuring that the finances were available to post the Scottish periodical to the US.

Connolly worked determinedly as the national organiser and also set about holding classes for budding speakers. He used some very interesting teaching methods. 'Students' would gather around a table reading from newspapers while one of their comrades sat in a chair on top of the table. Questions on current issues would be fired from the floor, with Connolly acting as an anti-socialist heckler, to prepare potential speakers for the rigours and dangers of debating at street corners and in halls.

Tom Bell, co-founder of the SLP, remembered that he learned a lot from Connolly in 1903.

I carried the platform and took the chair for him at meetings. He took great pains to coach us and to assist us in becoming public speakers. He would arrange to put one of us up for ten minutes before he took the meeting. Afterwards he would give us friendly criticism and words of encouragement to go on and do better. Connolly's speeches were a model of simplicity, conciseness, and burning class invective; always backed up by quotations and statistics of fact. Being Irish, he excelled in repartee, his ready wit silencing all opposition, though he went to no end of pains to clear up doubts in the minds of workers honestly seeking the truth.

One example of his repartee – We were holding a meeting at the Wellington Monument, Falkirk, one Sunday night. At question time, a man in the audience tried to be clever and in a facetious tone of voice asked: 'Mr. Speaker – if you had been born with a silver spoon in your mouth, what would you have done?'

Without any hesitation Connolly replied: 'I would have cried like the devil till they took it out of my mouth and put me on the breast.'

Another Saturday night, at Rutherglen Cross, a few drunks gathered round, and for a time there was a lot of interruption, prompting one individual to ask: 'Is this a public meeting?' 'Yes,' said Connolly, 'what do you think it is – a public house?' The laughter put the crowd in good humour, and the meeting went on.[22]

One of Connolly's pressing concerns was that Lillie and the children were still in Dublin. Moving the whole family to Scotland was out of the question, especially as a few financially disastrous meetings, in July 1903, resulted in Connolly being left without basic living expenses. Finally a decision was made, after five arduous months, much to the sadness of his Scottish comrades, who were 'filled with emotion when he sailed from the Broomielaw one September night, in the Irish boat, to go to Dublin, in preparation for emigration to New York.'[23]

It is worth noting that none of his comrades in Dublin came to wish him luck on his second voyage to America. In the view of Connolly, he was being exiled. Certainly he displayed a slight persecution complex when he wrote to O'Brien before his departure:

These things have changed the whole course of my life, but my conscience is clear, as my judgment was correct; let those who are responsible for those acts be assured that no amount of belated praise can gild the pill, or sweeten the bitterness of my exile. My career has been unique in many things. In this last it is so also. Men have been driven out of Ireland by the British Government, and by the landlords, but am I the first driven forth by the 'Socialists'?[24]

Although he left his family in Dublin, the plan was that they would join him as soon as he could earn their passage. Mona, his eldest daughter, was due to make the trip with him, but Margaret Humes, who had forwarded Connolly the boat fare, could not afford to lend him the price of two tickets. Margaret Humes was definitely Connolly's cousin. Some authors have called her Helen Humes and maintained that she may have been Lillie's cousin. She wrote 'Dear Cousin Lillie' in a letter, dated 29 June 1903, but in the same envelope she included a letter to 'Dear Cousin James'. In this letter to James she thanks him for visiting her parents in Scotland and talks candidly about her estranged brother John Carlin.[25] Added to this, the Carlins lived in Edinburgh, which is additional proof that they were more likely the real cousins. Curiously, she did have a daughter Helen and it is possible that this is where the initial mistake came from. Margaret also had a son Joseph, but these children were not born when Connolly lived in the US. Margaret's husband Thomas was a labourer, a grocer and, from 1906, a school janitor, so it is understandable why they could only afford to pay for one person to come from Ireland.

Upon his arrival in New York City, Connolly had hoped

to get a position with *The People*, but his relations with Daniel De Leon, the leader of the American Socialist Labor Party, had cooled and De Leon did not have it in mind to employ Connolly as a writer or as a printer. Connolly was not in possession of an American Federation of Labor (AFL) union card, so it would not have been possible for a socialist newspaper to employ a non-union linotype operator. On the other hand, how difficult would it have been for the SLP to procure a union card for him? Basically, anyone who disagreed with De Leon was shunted to the side and, as the ISRP were no longer that strong in Ireland, Connolly was not as useful as before. Connolly soon travelled north to Troy, where he was again welcomed in the Humes' household. Even disregarding the former difficulties with the SLP in this town, Troy would have been too small for Connolly to become a paid organiser. With the obvious need to finance his family in Dublin, Connolly gained employment as a collector of dues for the Metropolitan Life Insurance Company and agitated during his spare time.

By Christmas of 1903 it appears that Connolly was, like his politics, in the red. John Carstairs Matheson was called upon to send twenty shillings from Scotland to Lillie in Dublin. Matheson softened the embarrassment by writing: 'If I was in a hole you would be the very first man I would appeal to.'[26]

One of the more bizarre episodes of Connolly's time in America occurred a little over six months after his arrival.

Many historians and experts on Marx, Connolly and De Leon have written deep probing analyses of a very public spat between De Leon and Connolly.[27] It is not intended here to repeat such detailed work, rather to briefly explain the argument between both individuals. On 9 April 1904, De Leon published a friendly but provocative letter by Connolly on 'Wages, Marriage and the Church' in the *Weekly People*. The letter examined 'whether or not workers should struggle for higher wages in the advance toward Socialism'.[28] Connolly's point was that some SLP speakers believed that strikes for better wages were futile, as prices would only rise. The other minor points that Connolly made were that some SLP members were against monogamy and marriage and that anti-religious agitation was driving believers from the SLP.

De Leon, as editor, placed his own personal reply right beside Connolly's. He used Marx to try to undermine Connolly's statements but was inconsistent if not circuitous in his attempt. As with all good controversies, this one lasted for months, and many letters (mostly in support of De Leon) were published in *The People*. The SLP leader was an intolerant man and 'it was said that everybody who stood on his own two legs had trouble with De Leon.'[29] The fact is that, despite the few letters published in support of Connolly's stance, the editor of the paper did not give Connolly any more column inches to reiterate or explain further his position.

Unbelievably, the Troy branch of the SLP put Connolly 'on trial', but rather than expelling him came over to his side and requested that De Leon print a brilliant statement by Connolly proving how correct he was in the first place. Of course, this never appeared in *The People*, but De Leon continued to try and undermine Connolly at the SLP convention that July. Due to work commitments, Connolly could not attend, but later he wrote to a comrade explaining how De Leon had behaved at the convention, saying, 'Dan played a very smart trick ... he read my correspondence, paragraph by paragraph, adding his own criticism in between so that the delegates could not discern where I ended and my quotations began ... tearing me to pieces ... The result is that throughout the SLP, I am looked upon as an incipient traitor ...'[30] With few friends in the movement, it was fortuitous that his family would soon be joining him in America after a year of separation.

## Chapter Seven

· · · · · · ·

# 1904–1905

# A Tragedy

*We realised that their children are about all the workers of*
*Dublin have left to comfort them, that amidst the squalor and*
*wretchedness of their surroundings the love of their little ones*
*shines like a star of redemption, and that to part with their*
*dear ones would be like wrenching their hearts asunder.*[1]

In June 1904 Connolly wrote to his faithful correspondent
John Carstairs Matheson, editor of *The Socialist* and founding member of the Socialist Labour Party in Scotland:

> At present you must excuse this short letter as I have just
> received word from Dublin that my wife is dangerously ill,
> and may not recover, and my children have all had to be
> taken away in the homes of neighbours and friends. I am
> too upset to think of anything else now.[2]

As the Atlantic separated them, he was in no position to

do anything but hope. Happily, he received word a month later, as he explained to Matheson:

> Along with your letter comes one from Mrs. Connolly announcing that she was out of bed for the first time in nearly two months, and expects to join me in the middle of August. Her boat leaves Liverpool on the 5th of that month.[3]

On 14 August 1904, the Connolly family, consisting of Lillie and her children Nora, Aideen, Ina, Moira and Roderick, arrived on board the SS *Cedric* at New York. Their father had been waiting for them with some anxiety; they were late. Every time a ship arrived from Ireland he went to Ellis Island to collect them. There was some confusion when they finally arrived as Connolly was expecting Lillie and *six* children. He was devastated to discover that Mona, his eldest daughter, had died in horrific circumstances in Dublin the previous week.

Ina Connolly was an eye witness to the events and recalled that her 'mother had to go through that awful ordeal of explaining to the officials that we were his family and were one short. Just imagine the meeting, to hear of the loss of your firstborn under such circumstances amongst strangers in a foreign land. This was a sad meeting when an official had to bring Father over to hear the sad story and identify his wife and family.'[4]

Ina's recollections of this terrible event are written in a very matter-of-fact style.[5] She was only seven years old but recalled the tragedy with clarity:

> One of Father's very dear friends came to spend the last day with my mother and to help prepare us for sailing that night. As there seemed so many of us crowded in the one room falling over one another, each and all of us were afraid to put a nose outside the door in case we would be left behind. The thought of going out to play for an hour or so would not do. This thing – a trip across the Atlantic – was something new to us. We had not heard of this joyride before and none of us would make ourselves scarce and give a little more room for breathing space, until things got to such a pitch that this kindly friend offered to send my eldest sister and me to her house which was on the other side of the city and see if we would tidy up her place for an hour or two. My eldest sister did not like the idea of deserting Mother on her last day in Dublin and said so, but as she was ever obedient, she got me ready and we went forth on this errand of duty much against our wishes. We had to travel in the tram and she talked about it being our last trip across the city. "This time tomorrow we will be on the high seas on our way out to Father. Will he think I've grown big? I wonder will he know me?" These were all her dreams. She had herself worn out thinking about him, longing to see him. To be near him for evermore was her last wish on earth.
>
> We found the street of my Aunt Alice's house – as we

**Right:** James Connolly and his wife, Lillie Reynolds, and their young children in Edinburgh, 1894. Mona, their first child, is sitting on the stool and Nora is in Lillie's arms.

**Left:** Connolly in Belfast in 1913.

**Left:** Born in Wicklow and raised in the Church of Ireland faith, Lillie Connolly suffered great hardship to enable her husband pursue his political career but bore it all with great dignity.

**Below:** Lillie Connolly and her youngest child Fiona in 1916, after James Connolly's execution.

**Inset:** Connolly in Liverpool in 1913. Note the red hand badge of the ITGWU which eventually became the badge of the ICA.

**Left:** Countess Markievicz was a great comrade to Connolly and a friend to the Connolly family. During the 1916 Rising she was second-in-command in St Stephen's Green, where she fought as a lieutenant with the ICA.

**Right:** Nora Connolly dressed in Archie Heron's Volunteer uniform. She sent this photograph to James Connolly and signed it 'Peter', a little joke between herself and her father. Archie Heron later married Nora's sister Ina.

**Below:** Irish Women Workers' Union on the steps of Liberty Hall. Delia Larkin, Big Jim's sister, was the Secretary of the IWWU which was an integral part of the 1913 Lockout.

Three of James Connolly's children, Fiona, Roderick and Nora.

**Left:** The newspaper banner for the *Workers' Republic*, founded by Connolly in 1898.

**Right:** An advertisement in the *Labour Chronicle* for Connolly's cobbler shop. To support Connolly, Anna Munro, a comrade, brought her family's shoes to him for repair and later remarked that not one single pair could be worn afterwards.

**Left:** The organ of the Social Democratic Federation, *Justice*, a newspaper to which Connolly often contributed.

**Below:** 'The Starry Plough', flag of the ICA. The flag was designed by a Galway art teacher Billy Megahy and woven by the Dun Emer Guild. During the Easter Rising The Starry Plough flew from the roof of The Imperial Hotel opposite the GPO.

James Connolly's daughter, Ina Connolly, in Celtic dress with future husband Archie Heron.

**Above:** National Executive of the Irish Trade Union Congress and Labour Party, 1914. Standing, left to right: James Connolly, William O'Brien, Michael J Egan, Thomas Cassidy, WE Hill and Richard O'Carroll. Seated, left to right: Thomas MacPartlin, David Campbell, PT Daly, Jim Larkin and Michael J O'Lehane.

**Below:** The Irish Citizen Army on parade beside Croydon House, Dublin, in 1915. The park surrounding the house was used by the ICA for training purposes.

**Right:** Standing, left to right: 'Big' Jim Larkin, James Connolly and 'Big' Bill Haywood of the Industrial Workers of the World. Seated: Mary 'Ma' Bamber, organiser for the Warehouse Workers' Union. This photograph was taken in Liverpool, in 1913, not long after Haywood had reviewed the ICA in Croydon Park, Dublin, in November.

**Left:** James Connolly, in 1910, before he returned to Ireland.

called her. She had no children and was always interested in our family. My sister was disgusted to find there was no housework to do. Everything was in apple-pie order. She was very vexed. She felt she had been misled into believing that she was sent to be of some assistance instead of being put out of the way. This deception she very much resented as she had been always treated as an adult, and when reasoned with she always accepted the better judgment of her elders and would abide by their decision. She cried for a while and then thought better of it and, looking on the bright side of things, started to anticipate the joys that lay before her that night. "There is nothing to be done. How will we fill in our time for a couple of hours?"

The poor child was all worked up with excitement of going aboard a boat tonight and could not sit still. It was really cruel to have sent her on this fool's errand, she that was so sensitive. Little did her elders dream of the torments and trials she was passing through. She was no ordinary child and therefore needed the time and understanding not necessary for the average girl of her years. She went from one room to another. It was only a small house – a parlour and kitchen and two bedrooms and small garden back and front. When she discovered that the washing had not been done, "this," she thought, "is the work for me to do."

The fire was in the kitchen range and, as any other little *mháthairín* would do, she got going on the washing, and, putting me up beside her to help by the way – more likely to be better able to keep her eyes on me and keep me out of harm's way – she let me dabble in the tub of water.

Things were going very nicely; all was happy and well. She was one of those lovely people who, whatever she did she had to do well. The washing of clothes had its recompense. She had to boil what she thought called for that thoroughness before she would put them on the line. The largest saucepan procurable was filled with white articles and hot water on the floor. She then removed the ring cover on the top of the range and stooped down to lift up her saucepan which she held with her apron. This apron unfortunately became caught in under the saucepan and when she went to lift up the saucepan to release the apron she realised it had become ignited.

I screamed when I saw her all in flames as the flimsiness of her attire was more responsible for the quickness of the conflagration than the fire would have been in the ordinary way. She bid me keep away from her and ran into the back garden where there was a water tap and bending down to reach the fall of water thereby putting the upper portion of her body in more danger and there exposed her breast and neck to the naked flames.

The cries and screams of me drew the attention of a man in a nearby garden. He could see the flames. He jumped the garden walls and came to our assistance, putting out the fire the best he could and then taking my poor unfortunate sister to hospital ...

Meanwhile my mother was feeling uncomfortable at our not returning ... Aunt Alice decided she would go and fetch us ... Curiously enough, she simultaneously arrived at her door as her husband did to be encountered by a few neighbours who had me in their keeping, and when they got an account of the accident, learned of the child in hospital, their first thoughts flew to Mother.

What a catastrophe! She, sitting with her brood waiting to go aboard ship that night! How would they tell her? Who would break the news? Taking me in their arms, they both made their way towards returning to Mother immediately – to bring her to the hospital there to see her first-born child lying unconscious, all wrapped in bandages, with her dreams she never lived to see come true, in a sleep she would never come out of. She had passed out of all her suffering and left Mother with more cares and heartbreaks than she would ever have wished, had she but known.

The records of Glasnevin Cemetery confirm that Mona Connolly, aged thirteen, died of burns in Drumcondra Hospital on Thursday, 4 August 1904. She was buried three days later. The address of her mother, Lillian, is given as 54 Pimlico, Dublin. The bitter poverty that haunted the Connolly family at that time is revealed by the fact that Mona was buried in an unmarked pauper's grave.[6] It is also evident that Lillie and the other children were unable to make it to Mona's funeral; having had to postpone their initial sailing, they had to accept the next available ship, which left from Cork on the day Mona was buried. One can only imagine Lillie's grief on the voyage. A poignant and intriguing aspect of this sad story is that the ship's manifest, a list of passengers presented upon arrival in port, still contained Mona's details.[7]

Connolly kept in touch with John 'Jack' Mulray, whom he had chanced to encounter on a New York street when he had been waiting for Lillie and the children's arrival. Mulray, a tailor, was one of those members who had resigned from the ISRP in early 1903. Jack and James had left their acrimonious argument in Dublin and became firm friends again. The loss of Mona also served to warm Connolly to his old comrades. He wrote to Mulray about this not long after his family arrived:

> Mrs. Connolly informs me that the Socialists in Dublin showed great sympathy for her in her last great trouble. I am thankful to them for that proof of kindliness, and also as a token that old time relations were not entirely blotted out.[8]

The first few months in the new Connolly home at 96 Ingalls Avenue, Troy, were busy and gradually they settled into American life.[9] The family now had money as their father was still in full-time employment with the Metropolitan Life Insurance Company. In addition, Troy was one of the centres of the textile industry, so Lillie and the older children picked up work sewing and starching shirt collars. Even the younger members of the family were able to bring in a few cents:

We children were employed carrying baskets of collars from factories to the homes of the workers. On our way to school we would deliver a large basket of finished articles to the factories and call for their refills on our way home in the evening. In this way the whole populace was striving to increase the output. This work we enjoyed as everybody was doing it. It became part of our school life; we knew no other. All was well. We were very happy and things were looking bright. Mother and Father were entering into the spirit of their new environment and even going out at night, sledge riding with the other neighbours. This was a big change for Mother. What would the people who knew her in Dublin think if they saw her out in such attire as was necessary for those winter nights.

The people here all took part in winter sports. It helped to keep them warm and it was their form of social evenings. We had a wonderful Christmas here. It was just one long dream. Things happened here that we had never dreamed of. Just imagine a big Christmas tree of our own in our parlour lit up with candles and presents for every member of the family and all who came to see it, which also meant that we got presents from trees that we went to see. We never thought that life could be so pleasant and happy. Now we had all forgotten the sad poor days of the past. Here there was plenty and lashings *go leor*. But how long was it to last? Could it really come to an end, this laughing, singing, joy-rides and food for all?[10]

The winter of 1904–5 was a long, bitterly cold one. Along-side the cold came an economic depression that resulted in many textile workers losing their jobs. The first thing they stopped paying for were insurance dues and, as a direct consequence, Connolly lost his job with Metropolitan Life. In December, in a bit of a panic, he wrote to Mulray:

I lost my job … I have not yet found an exploiter … I will go down to New York on Sunday and have a run around the Insurance Offices … The immediate purpose of this letter is to ask you if you could get me a bed anywhere …[11]

Mulray kindly shared his lodgings with Connolly and therein began a long relationship. Both men tried to secure work whenever they could, but it seems that when one of them found employment the other got his cards. Connolly spent some months in Greenwich Village. John Lyng was also in New York, so Connolly was usually to be found in his company or with Mulray; either wandering the streets trying to find work or searching for the cheapest meals, usually something under ten cents.[12] Connolly enjoyed inventing names for the cheap diners they ate in. There was 'The

Waldorf', so named because it was the complete opposite to the famous hotel. There was 'The Coffee Without Onions', where Connolly had once found stray vegetables in the bottom of his cup. Upon his next visit he asked for 'coffee without onions' and broke down laughing when the waiter shouted the order through the hatch.

Connolly was active throughout these years and still an SLP supporter, despite his troubles with De Leon. He claimed that SLP members were being treated as 'automatons', whose duty was to repeat in varying accents the words of their director general. Nonetheless, he was still asked to give lectures whenever the chance arose. Between February and March he talked in New York City on 'Everyday Illustrations of Socialist Teaching', 'Labour Laws and Trade Unionism' and 'The Unfulfilled Mission of Trade Unionism'.

Although he was often hungry, the family in Troy were at least eating, as Ina recalled rather rosily:

> This was a wonderful place to live. We had many outings of gathering nuts … Some of these were sold to the stores … and we had enough nuts to last us the year … I remember the tomato crop my mother had … they were preserved, skinned and bottled … we had apricots, quince, apples and pears … you had a supply of these lovely fruits and savouries the whole winter through and there was never a shortage of these luxuries.[13]

Connolly moved back to Troy to be with his family and by June 1905 he somehow managed to pass himself off as being financially sound enough to accept the post of district manager for the Pacific Mutual Life Insurance Company of California (Life Accident and Health), Eastern Department:

> I have the right to employ agents and have a big enough margin of profit left to pay them more than they would get from most companies, but as the company is new to this district agents are hard to get. ... At present I am taking side-leaps with the hunger, although to get this job I had to represent myself as worth $3,000, and get a bond for $2,000 from the National Surety Company. I was playing the American capitalists at their own bunco game, and succeeded, so far.[14]

However, the business turned out not to be viable, especially as it was a new company trying to establish its presence during a three-month-long shirtmakers' strike; one way or another, by July he was getting bitter about Troy:

> And in addition to this when a man or a family is hard up in New York everybody need not know about it as they do here. Here in Troy you cannot get less than 2 lbs. of sugar at a time, and there is no half-way house between a half ton of coal and a bucketful. And it is the same all round. Nothing under a 20 cent meal can be got in the town. Of course there are advantages also. But for a man in the fix I am in, I

think the big city has the advantages, as well as being nearer
the centre of socialist activity.[15]

By September 1905 he was lodging in Newark, having
secured work posing as an engineer or machinist for Singer,
the sewing machine manufacturers. A socialist foreman had
managed to get him the job, but after six weeks, upon the
foreman's suggestion, he transferred to the Singer sewing-
machine factory in Elizabeth. Now that their father had
secured some work, the Connolly family moved from Troy
to 543 Fifteenth Avenue, Newark.

Ina recalled that the houses the Irish were renting 'in this
part of the States were detached wooden ones with verandas
and with three storeys, each floor with two self-contained
flats, large under-ground cellars ... very useful for children
to play in when the weather was wet. It was a country district and a newly built up area was in progress ... It had a lot
of conveniences, a big public park, a swimming pool, a large
school nearby, shops, church and library.'[16]

Connolly commuted between Elizabeth and Newark on special trains laid on for the thousands who worked in the Singer
factory. The job was not mentally challenging by any stretch
of the imagination and, doubtless, Connolly would rather have
been organising, as he wrote to Mulray: 'I have started work in
Singer's Factory – it is a pretty bum job, so far.'[17]

Matheson suggested to Connolly, who had complained
about the US, that they could buy the ISRP's press and

have a go at making a living through a socialist journal in Scotland. In the last few days of 1905 Connolly reflected on his situation to Matheson:

> At present I am earning an average of $15.00 per week – the average wage for most mechanics here … I have emerged out of the depths, else I would have not written to you, and am only troubled by my health which is indeed giving me great trouble of late. As you gathered from my letter I do not like the country, indeed my chief motive in coming here was to provide a better field for my girls than was open for them at home. But the girl for whose immediate benefit the change was made was stricken down by death on the eve of our departure, and the blow darkened my life and changed all our hopes and prospects. My wife, who was as enthusiastic about coming here as I was careless, is now mad to get out of the country. But to shift a family across the Atlantic is no picnic … But let me know how your proposal was taken by the EC. All I can say at present is that I am not averse to it.[18]

Although nothing ever came of this suggestion, comments such as these from Scottish and Irish correspondents served to plant a seed in Connolly's head that one day he would be able to return.

Like all the Irish emigrants, it was important for the Connollys to remind themselves of their roots. Ina remembered how Connolly would take them downtown 'to see the St. Patrick's Day parade and to see the huge numbers of Irish nationalists out marching, carrying banners representing different interests of the homeland and we sporting our bunch of shamrock on our coats together with the green ribbon on our hair.'[19]

Connolly also wanted to keep up with news from Scotland. In April 1906 he made a plea to Matheson:

Send me the paper now and then; it will keep me posted on things. I am in absolute ignorance of what is really going on in the Labour movement. The only information I got lately was when a little Scotchman in the shop told me that "the Hearts were in the final of the Scottish Cup; they knockt hell oot o' tha Hibs." Wherat I felt very much depressed.[20]

Connolly was a fan of the Edinburgh football club, Hibernian.

In the same letter, he also mentioned that he had been contributing two columns per week to *The Sunday People*, and that he was absent from home for fourteen hours a day. How he found time to write and to work such hours is difficult to imagine, but he found time for studying on the train, at breaktime, and even during the short hours that he was at home. Nora recalled:

Daddy was always reading or writing when he was at home. All the little ones could play or fight around him, but he would keep on reading or writing … often when Mama spoke to him he would not hear her till she put her hand on his shoulder, then he would look up very slowly as if his head was very far away.[21]

Nora's sister also recalled a patient father:

[Our] home was always open to any person or to as many children as we cared to bring in. Indeed I can see pictures of my father sitting at the table writing and a crowd of children playing round on the floor, not alone his own family but others as well, and we were never told not to make noise or to stop talking or singing as father was writing. We could go up to him and show him our dolls and carts or balls and he would stop to listen to what we had to say and then continue as if we were not there.[22]

## Chapter Eight

# 1906–1908

# The Wobblies

*The moment the worker no longer believes in the all-conquering*
*strength of the employer is the moment when the way opens*
*out to the emancipation of our class. The master class realise*
*this, and hence all their agencies bend their energies towards*
*drugging, stupefying and poisoning the minds of the workers –*
*sowing distrust and fear amongst them.*[1]

In the summer of 1905, in Chicago, Illinois, a couple of hundred socialists, anarchists and labour enthusiasts gathered
together with the express intention of forming a grassroots
socialist union. The revolutionary organisation they created was
given the international and ambitious title Industrial Workers
of the World (IWW). Early founding members and organisers
included such luminaries as William 'Big Bill' Haywood of the
militant Western Federation of Miners (WFM); Eugene Debs,
organiser of the American Railway Union; Cork-born Mary

Harris 'Mother' Jones, who fought vigorously against the use of child labour; Bill Trautmann, of the United Brewery Workers' Union; Charles Moyer, the president of the WFM, and the radical priest Tom Hagerty, who preached that the ballot box was simply a capitalist concession and that direct action was the only way to free the working class. They were tired of the lack of action within Marxist parties; Hagerty described them amusingly as 'slowcialists'. Using their motto, 'An injury to one is an injury to all', the IWW railed against the corruption and craft unionism and of the American Federation of Labour (AFL), preferring instead a system of industrial unionism. Unlike the craft unions, the IWW, or 'Wobblies' as they were affectionately known later, accepted all workers into their ranks regardless of gender, religion or ethnicity. Haywood said upon the foundation of the IWW:

> We are going down in the gutter to get at the mass of the workers and bring them up to a decent plane of living.[2]

Their badge contained the phrase 'One Big Union', an ideal that the ITGWU also adopted in Ireland and included on their member's badge as OBU.

Frank Stennenberg, the anti-unionist former governor of Idaho, was killed in a bomb attack in February 1906. Charles Moyer and 'Big Bill' Haywood, as officials from the Western Federation of Mineworkers (closely associated with the IWW), and George Pettibone, a union supporter, were accused of the crime. They were held in jail for over a year, pending trial, while no evidence against them was produced. James Connolly was on the Newark Haywood–Moyer Defence Committee. His task included organising protests and raising finance for the defence of these two socialists. Eventually, one Albert Horsley, alias Harry Orchard, was found guilty of the murder. But it also transpired that Orchard had been encouraged by the famous Pinkerton detective McParland to say that Haywood and Moyer had ordered him to execute Stennenberg. Haywood was found not guilty and charges against Moyer were dropped. The trial exposed the depths that capitalists in America were willing to sink to in order to undermine radical unions. The trial also exposed Connolly to a wider audience; from the early developmental stages of the IWW he had shown himself to be an active and enthusiastic supporter. With the able assistance of Patrick Quinlan, 'the two men made the IWW known in Newark.'[3]

Connolly wrote to Matheson in April 1906, enclosing fifty cents for Hugo's *Simplified German Teacher*, the budding student explained that in the department of Singer's where he worked, the majority of employees were Germans and German was the principal language spoken. Some of Connolly's biographers claimed that he learned and spoke other languages with confidence: German, Italian, French, Irish, Yiddish and Esperanto. His daughter Nora maintained that he 'had a little bit of this language and a little bit of that. I think my father knew a bit of French, but not enough to be able to write anything, or read anything completely. I think he knew some German, but I am not sure. But he was perfect in Italian. He used to organise among the Italians in New York. A short while ago when I went over to New York I spoke to someone who had been finding out a lot about the Italians in New York. He had been amazed at the number of people who told him, according to their age, that their father or grandfather had known James Connolly.'[4]

With only a smattering of Irish, he was never a member of the Gaelic League. Initially he commented that it was useless to teach starving men the Irish language, but his time in the US changed his opinion on the matter and later he called the destruction of the Irish language an act of imperialism.

Patrick Pearse believed that a country without a language was a country without a soul and, likewise, Connolly also saw that the defence of the language was as important as the defence of the soil.[5] With that in mind, he undertook to study Irish, but he never became fluent, although he did claim in the 1911 Census that he spoke both English and Irish. Whatever his proficiency level was in European languages, his attempts to learn them at all, in order to communicate with other workers, is an admirable quality. In fact, he felt confident enough to translate a German song into English and he translated and published many Italian socialist articles.

Elizabeth Gurley Flynn (1890–1964), a labour activist and

IWW organiser, later wrote her memoirs of that time and recalled one particular occasion in 1907 when she shared a platform with Connolly at a meeting organised by the Italian Socialist Federation. Elizabeth was most surprised to hear Connolly speak to the audience in their native tongue. An extremely pleased group of Italian workers 'viva'd loudly' throughout his lecture.[6]

In late 1906, after almost a full year's employment, Connolly left the Singer Factory. The fourteen-hour day spent travelling and working had left him too little time to pursue his activities for the IWW and write articles for the SLP journal, the *Weekly People*. It is also possible that the very cause he worked for resulted in him losing his job. The SLP organised a picket for union recognition at the gates of the factory, thus placing Connolly in a very difficult position, one that all trade unionists inevitably face: feed the family or pass the picket. Connolly would never pass a picket, let alone one organised by his party. His daughter Nora maintained that the reason for leaving was that pressure had been exerted on Connolly's foreman, Magnette, who had got him the job in Singer's initially. According to her, Magnette was getting a hard time as it had been discovered that Connolly was a socialist agitator. She wrote that her father left the firm rather than get the foreman into further trouble.[7]

By December 1906 the Connollys were living at 152 Hawthorn Avenue, Newark. Connolly wrote to Matheson about his appointment to a senior position within the National Executive Committee (NEC) of the SLP: 'By the way I have been nominated as a delegate for the NEC from New Jersey, the unanimous choice of the state. Hurroo.'[8]

Nora Connolly wrote of how her father's books were a treasure to him. These included classic works by John Mitchel, Karl Marx, Michael Davitt and James Fintan Lalor. Propser-Olivier Lissagaray's *History of the Paris Commune* also graced his shelves. Now that he was no longer working such long hours operating a lathe, he began in earnest, in 1907, to write his *tour de force*, a book destined to become a classic itself, *Labour in Irish History*. In essence, the seed for this book had been planted nearly a decade before, during the Queen Victoria Jubilee demonstrations, when he researched facts and figures on the Great Hunger. Essentially he built upon his articles from the *Workers' Republic* and produced a simple, straightforward history book. His proficiency in reading, studying and journalism, coupled with the confidence gained from the publication of his pamphlets, paved the way for his attempt to quantify in one small volume the relationship between the Irish working class and the Irish nationalist movement. It was no easy task, but he was a determined writer; although he finished it relatively quickly, it was not published until 1910.

There were many 'Race Federations' in America who were aligned to the SLP, for example the Hungarian Federation and the Swedish Federation. Elizabeth Gurley Flynn wrote:

> [Connolly] felt keenly that not enough understanding and
> sympathy was shown by American Socialists for the cause
> of Ireland's national liberation, that the Irish workers here
> were too readily abandoned by the Socialists as "reactionar-
> ies" and that there was not sufficient effort made to bring
> the message of socialism to the Irish-American workers.
> In 1907 George B. McClellan, Mayor of New York City,
> made a speech in which he said: "There are Russian Social-
> ists and Jewish Socialists and German Socialists! But, thank
> God! There are no Irish Socialists!" This was a challenge to
> Connolly.[9]

In March 1907 a *ceilí* was held to launch a permanent association of Irish socialists in the New York area. This organisation, the Irish Socialist Federation (ISF), would become
very active in Irish circles and was quite appealing to Irish
immigrants. The purpose of the group was to develop the
spirit of revolutionary class-consciousness amongst the Irish
working class in America, to spread knowledge of the socialist movement in Ireland and to educate its members upon the
historical development of the class struggle in Ireland. As well
as Connolly, the illustrious list of organisers included two old
comrades from the ISRP in Dublin, Jack Mulray, and one
of the Lyng brothers, John, who was now living in New
York. A Limerick man who emigrated to the US, joined

the SLP in New York, and befriended Connolly, Patrick Quinlan, also helped to found the ISF alongside the 'young prodigy' Elizabeth Gurley Flynn.

The ISF was to be organised 'against every party recognising British rule in Ireland in any form or manner' and wished to seek 'the Workers' Republic: the administration of all the land and all the instruments of Labour …' The federation held a good many meetings in New York that summer and by the following year had branched out to Chicago. Like all respectable socialist organisations, the ISF had a flag. It was green (of course), and surrounded by harps and shamrocks was the Irish phrase *Fág an Bealach* or 'Clear the Way'. Initially, their appearance on street corners met with derision and sometimes abuse. In order to deter more aggressive hecklers, a comrade from Germany, an expert blacksmith, constructed an iron platform with removable legs that served as defensive cudgels.

Meanwhile, Connolly had already been in touch with a new party back home in Dublin. They called themselves the Irish Socialist Party and were formed in March 1904 through the fusion of the ISRP and the Socialist Labour Party. The ISP not only agreed to affiliate to their New York comrades in the Irish Socialist Federation but also agreed to reprint the *New Evangel* by Connolly, first published back in 1901. Doubtless Connolly was happy to reacquaint himself with the comrades at home as it appears from the vast amount of correspondence between Dublin and New York that his heart was always in the Irish capital.

The seventh and final child to join the Connolly family came in 1907. Another girl, Fiona, was the only one to have been born in the US. As a mark of the friendship that had developed between Mulray and the Connollys, Jack was asked to be godfather to Fiona. Despite being surrounded by children, neighbours and comrades, Connolly seemed to have suffered bouts of loneliness bordering on depression. Even after the excitement of Lillie's pregnancy and becoming part of the Irish Socialist Federation, he still complained to Matheson in April: 'I feel rather lonely and friendless now, and hope you will not delay long in writing, as outside of the Irish and Scotch whom I meet, there are few comrades who have anything for me but coldness or hostility.'[10]

This hostility came to a head when the old spat with De Leon reared up again, this time as a two-headed monster. The first dispute centred on whether or not a sub-committee of the party could insert material into *The People* without the permission of the National Executive Committee (NEC). The editor, De Leon, did not want to lose control of the paper and Connolly wanted to undermine De Leon's dictatorial role. Although it seems to be a trifling matter, it snowballed into a controversy that even infected the IWW. Connolly ended up resigning his position as New Jersey delegate to the NEC in protest, but he still retained his membership of the SLP., or, rather, he tried to resign from the NEC, but they refused to accept his resignation, preferring to draft a condemnatory resolution and a resolution removing him from all governing bodies within the SLP.

Secondly, in February 1907, the 'Wages Controversy' was raised again in *The People*; this time De Leon used a form of double-speak and simultaneously agreed and disagreed that an increase in wages would not cause a rise in the price of goods. Later on in the year Connolly wrote an article in the IWW journal and reminded readers of the stance he took in 1904. He reiterated that prices of goods rose first and that wages climbed slowly behind them. This time Connolly had full access to the *Industrial Union Bulletin*, unlike previously when *The People* editor controlled the content. In round two of the 'Wages Controversy' Connolly's position was accepted by the IWW and De Leon's policy was considered 'antiquated and exploded'.

The IWW offered Connolly a position as head organiser of the District Council of New York City in July 1907. At the end of the summer Connolly wrote to Matheson to explain the events of the previous few months:

> My friend Dan made a grand effort to destroy me at general party meetings here in New York, after the July NEC meeting, but he was routed, horse, foot, and artillery. As a result he made enemies of nearly all the American, German, Swedish, Irish and British members of the party in New

York, and has nobody left he can trust outside of the Jewish elements. The Jews, you know, are still looking for a saviour. The rest of us have had our saviour already, and as he made a mess of it we intend to mistrust saviours in the future ... At present I am an organiser for the IWW in New York, and am paid by the building trades and machinists. They asked me to take the job when the fight between Dan and I was at its height and when I believed I was utterly discredited in the party. Instead I found to my surprise that they had come to the conclusion that I had the real grasp of the revolutionary situation, and they were willing to attest their belief by their purses. So after some persuasion I accepted and I have now been about three months in their pay.[11]

The New York stock market suffered a crash in October 1907. The immediate fall-out was felt by the workers, especially those who were unskilled labourers, immigrants or African-American. Wages were slashed, and any workers who went on strike were dismissed and replaced by the multitudinous hungry, willing to scab to feed themselves and their families. Race riots and horrific lynchings were carried out in certain areas of the country. Obviously subscriptions to the IWW fell drastically and Connolly, amongst others in the Wobblies, was barely surviving. In fact, William Trautmann, as general secretary-treasurer, would shortly announce that he could not guarantee the salary of any organiser since more than one-third of the IWW members were unemployed.[12] Towards the end of October 1907 Connolly wrote to Matheson:

> Personally I am always living on the margin of subsistence.
> Of course better fed and housed than in the old country,
> but regretting the day I ever saw America. I expect to have
> to move into New York soon, and then I will not be so well
> housed. Rooms there are only boxes and rents are fearful.
> I will not be able to get a house under $18 per month,
> and to get that I must live away about 12 miles from the
> centre of the city. Health is pretty good, since I left the fac-
> tory, wages sometimes uncertain. Am sending you a copy of
> my new song book … Remember me to old friends. My
> mouth waters when you mention a lecturing tour of the
> Old Country.[13]

The new song book that Connolly was referring to was
called *Songs of Freedom by Irish Authors* subtitled *The 'Take and
Hold' Book* in honour of the SLP phrase 'Take and Hold'. In
the introduction, Connolly clearly stated the aim of publishing the book:

> No revolutionary movement is complete without its poeti-
> cal expression. If such a movement has caught hold of the
> imagination of the masses, they will seek a vent in song for
> the aspirations, the fears and hopes, the loves and hatreds
> engendered by the struggle. Until the movement is marked
> by the joyous, defiant, singing of revolutionary songs, it
> lacks one of the distinctive marks of a popular revolutionary

movement – it is a dogma of a few, and not the faith of the multitude.

The small book included nine of Connolly's songs, three by his old Scottish comrade John Leslie, *The Red Flag* by Jim Connell and of course *The Marseillaise*. In *Be Moderate*, which he wrote in 1904, he attacks hesitant union leaders:

*The 'Labour Fakir' full of guile,*
*Base doctrine ever preaches,*
*And, whilst he bleeds the rank and file,*
*Tame moderation teaches.*
*Yet, in his despite, we'll see the day*
*When, with sword in its girth,*
*Labour shall march in war array,*
*To seize its own, THE EARTH.*

Lillie once remarked to her husband that it seemed to be their fate never to spend more than five years in any one place; she was getting tired of building up a home knowing that it would be broken up again. Their relatively enjoyable suburban life in Newark ended abruptly in November 1907; they now found themselves in a six-storey brownstone near Elton Avenue in the Bronx, 684 East 155 Street, New York. Happily there were plenty of Irish and Scottish neighbours in this area alongside plenty of other nationalities; Ina recalled that they made friends quickly in this area. They were not too far away from Elizabeth Gurley Flynn and her family.

Trouble was brewing for Connolly, for at a general SLP

meeting on 7 December 1907, the proceedings were taken up with a debate on the 'criminal actions' of James Connolly. All manner of accusations were heaped upon him: they dragged up his refusal to speak three times in Troy in 1902; they accused him of wanting to be the editor of *The People* and that was his reason for undermining De Leon; that he founded the Irish Socialist Federation in order to divide the working class and that he purposely disrupted the ISRP in Dublin. De Leon was twisting the knife by twisting history. A few days after the meeting, Connolly wrote to Matheson:

> Yet now five years after the event these lying slanders are hurled at my head and I am refused the opportunity to refute them. Great is Democracy. Well, I suppose I weary you with all these things. But you are the only person to whom I open the inner sanctuaries of my heart in this matter; to all others I simply strive to school my countenance to hide the effects of these stabs. I do not want the vermin to know how much they hurt me.[14]

Coincidently, a special meeting of the General Executive Board of the IWW was held in New York three weeks after the SLP meeting. The reason for meeting in New York as opposed to Chicago was that Connolly had been working on bringing a large block of longshoremen into the Wobblies and such a move needed to be discussed at executive level. The applicants, about ten thousand men, were Irish and Italian workers; naturally they were, in the main, of the Catholic persuasion. De Leon claimed in a closed executive board session that Connolly was an agent of the Jesuit order who was employed to break up the labour movement; that there was a secret agreement between the ten thousand workers, Connolly, and the Jesuits to demoralise the IWW. Even if Connolly was a devout, practising Catholic, it would have stretched the imagination to see him as a Jesuit agent. On the subject of religion, Connolly wrote frankly to Matheson on his faith:

> For myself tho' I have usually posed as a Catholic I have not gone to my duty for 15 years, and have not the slightest tincture of faith left. I only assumed the Catholic pose in order to query the raw freethinker whose ridiculous dogmatism did and does annoy me as much as the dogmatism of the Orthodox. In fact I respect the good Catholic more than the average freethinker.[15]

What the accusations by De Leon did accomplish was to undermine the SLP leader. As the charges were so ridiculous, no one took them seriously and his standing in the IWW was not greatly affected. Connolly could look back on 1907 as being a good year for him: organiser for the IWW, the publication of his song book, another child, a new book in the pipeline, the foundation of his race federation and a little win against De Leon to ice the cake.

Connolly asked the Dublin comrades in the Irish Socialist Party for contributions to the new journal of the ISF, *The Harp*. 'It is our desire to make the paper thoroughly interesting to the Irish Working Class here and as an antidote to the Home Rule and Sinn Féin drivel.'[16] The very first issue of *The Harp* was published in January 1908. Rather than the ISF or Connolly accepting financial responsibility for it, the journal was owned and published by JEC Donnelly, a professional printer and sympathiser. In a throw-back to his *Workers' Republic* days, Connolly was editor, chief journalist, correspondent and features writer. His 'Harp Strings' was a regular feature with news from Ireland, plucking at the ties that bound the two nations. In the very first issue Connolly explained: 'We propose to show all the workers of our fighting race that Socialism will make them better fighters for freedom, without being less Irish.' Although it was an Irish journal, it also championed the rights of all workers; Connolly railed against the 'vilification and discrimination', the 'abuse and ignominy', which was once the lot of the Irish but was 'now poured so freely upon the Italian, the Pole, the Hungarian, the Slav and the Jew.'

*The Harp* was also peppered with plenty of that dry sense of humour that Connolly possessed:

Our great American institution today is the bread line. Every night in New York, thousands of men and women stand in line in the public streets, waiting for their turn to receive a few crusts of bread to keep body and soul together. The same in every other city and town from East to West. The bread line is a great American institution. But I do not think I would shoulder a rifle in defence of it.[17]

As a journal, *The Harp* had some success in that it was printed regularly for a couple of years. The quality of the content is reflected in the fact that some articles were reprinted by other newspapers, for example John Devoy's *Gaelic American*. Although its circulation was never much higher than the two thousand mark, Connolly, as in most of his socialist enterprises, was adamant that it could be made a success. He often stood out in all weather, trying to make a few sales. 'It was a pathetic sight to see him,' said Elizabeth Gurley Flynn, 'standing, poorly clad, at the door of Cooper Union or some other East Side hall, selling his little paper. None of the prosperous, professional Irish, who shouted their admiration for him after his death, lent him a helping hand at that time.'[18]

In April 1908 Connolly wrote to Matheson in Scotland, vainly trying to suppress his excitement at the prospect of returning home:

Last week I received a letter from Dublin from a young comrade who ... says that a number of comrades have asked him to write to me and to inquire whether I would be willing to return to Dublin if some provision could be made for my upkeep ... Now in a letter you sent to me

157

you also suggest that it would be good if I could get home. Well, you people are all contributing to make me home sick. I wrote to my Dublin comrade, saying that I had all the will and all the desire in the world to get home out of this cursed country, but I can't. The District Council owes me over 80 dollars back salary. I am now off the pay roll, and the misery and hunger now in New York are dreadful. I am simply frightened at the immediate outlook for the family and myself. How then get home?'[19]

Connolly was not exaggerating the extent of the poverty. Newspapers reported that destitute people lined up to eat the food left by picnickers that summer on Coney Island.[20]

Connolly finally severed all links with the American Socialist Labour Party in April 1908. No doubt it was a relief to De Leon's friends and Connolly's, but one wonders why he stayed in the SLP for so long. Perhaps he did not want to allow De Leon the pleasure of seeing him off. Or perhaps he suddenly saw that there was another socialist party that he could swing over to. Leaving the SLP essentially paved the way for him to concentrate more on *The Harp*, the IWW, and opened the door to membership of the Socialist Party of America. Doubtless, Connolly hoped that Matheson would never tell anyone that the new member had once described the leaders of the Socialist Party as corrupt and incapable.

After six months or so, *The Harp* was selling reasonably well but needed a boost. In a repeat of his first trip to the

United States, it was decided that Connolly should embark on another tour of the country. *The Harp*'s publisher, Donnelly, was happy to see Connolly spread the word of the organ to Oregon, Pennsylvania, Illinois, Massachusetts, New England, Vermouth, Maine and New Hampshire. The year 1908 was a presidential election campaign year and Eugene Debs was running as the Socialist Party candidate. Connolly included a call to vote for Debs at his lectures. There was a fairly simple way that IWW locals and Socialist Party branches could secure a lecture from Connolly. One hundred advance copies of *The Harp* entitled the purchaser to one lecture. A full week of lectures would be granted to those who purchased five hundred copies. It proved to be a very successful lecture tour and went a long way to ensuring Connolly became a full-time organiser for the Socialist Party of America.

Ina Connolly recollected:

> We saw little of father, for he was travelling full time, helping to organise trade unions and lecturing about the country. Once in a while his work brought him to the city, and we had grand weekends. He often took us to large public meetings and it was a treat to hear him speak.
>
> Upon occasions, during these brief reunions, father took us on outings of the Socialist Party. Father was popular, not only for his organising activities, but also because he was founder and editor of the Irish Socialist paper, *The Harp*.

The catering at these affairs was done by the Party members. There were sandwiches, sweet cakes, ice cream, soda pop and – for the men – beer out of the barrel.

Father didn't drink. He was not partial to it, and if he were, he used to say, he would not have been able to afford it. Nevertheless, in organising the men, he often had to make contact with them in saloons. He used to complain to mother: "What with the quantities of ginger beer I've drunk, my stomach is in worse condition than any toper's."

There were grand speeches at the outings, and the band played with gusto. We danced and sang to our heart's content. Mother did not share our enthusiasm, however; travelling with a young family in a New York summer was a trial. I can understand her remark when we returned from one such picnic: "I'd rather do two days' washing than ever again face such a day's pleasure."[21]

On 27 September 1908 Connolly took no small pleasure in informing his comrade Matheson what had happened at the Fourth Convention of the IWW in Chicago the previous week. An attempt was made to bar De Leon from attending the convention as he was not a wage worker. Connolly witnessed the fall of the SLP leader: 'De Leon himself was thrown out by 40 votes to 21. He was thrown out on the technical point that although he was engaged in the printing trade as editor of a paper he refused to join the printers IWW local, but stayed in a local of store and office workers.'[22]

Connolly managed to attend this convention despite the fact that there was very little cash around. The IWW could not even afford a stenographer to record the proceedings. Connolly's funds were just as low, but he succeeded in attending the convention during his lecture tour with the assistance of a comrade who lent him five dollars.

It was while he was in Chicago that he formed a branch of the Irish Socialist Federation. He also met the publisher Charles H Kerr, who ran 'a Socialist publishing house owned co-operatively by over 2,000 Socialist locals and individuals'. Kerr liked Connolly's articles which had been published in the *International Socialist Review*, a journal which Kerr printed. They discussed at length the possibility of publishing these and other articles in book format.

Another year ended on a positive note as a letter arrived in early December 1908 from the national headquarters of the Socialist Party: 'This is to notify you that you have been placed in nomination as a candidate for member of the National Executive Committee.'[23] Connolly, however, had to decline the invitation as he intended touring New York State for the Socialist Party in early 1909 and he was busy with *The Harp* and writing *Labour in Irish History*.

# Chapter Nine

• • • • • •

# 1909–1910

# Socialism Made Easy

*... the Irish propertied classes became more English than the English, and so have continued to our day.*[1]

**V**ery few people are aware that James Connolly wrote ballads and poetry. More surprisingly, he also wrote a play entitled *Under Which Flag*. This short work, set in 1867, the year of the Fenian Uprising, is hardly one of the great masterpieces of Irish theatre, but it does provide a useful insight into the beliefs of the 'aspiring dramatist'.

The protagonist, young John O'Donnell, is looking for ways to better himself and thoughts of emigration are in his head. He remarks that Ireland is no place for a man and goes on to say: 'I'm for America, as soon as ever I can. Ireland is only fit for slaves. America is the place where a man is a man, a free man. Here in Ireland we are always slaving for other people: landlords, and the Royal family, and all the rest of the tribe that lives upon the poor.'

His mother Ellen pours cold water upon his dreams and spells out the harsh reality of the emigrant's lot, remarking: 'America, you poor boy. Far off hills are always green. Always slaving for other people, is it? And do you think you will get out of that by going to America? Faith, then, you won't. The poor of the world are always slaving for other people, always going hungry that others may be fed, naked that others may be clothed, badly housed that others may live in palaces. 'Tis the way of the world in America as well as in Ireland.'[2]

Connolly spent years struggling in America and was qualified to highlight this warning to young Irishmen and Irishwomen that the grass was no greener across the Atlantic. It seems ironic then, that in his seventh and final year in the US, just as he was really beginning to establish himself financially, he should decide to leave the country. There is no doubting how money was a necessity for him with a large family to feed, but he never let the lack of it or the excess of it change his decisions.

The first decent few dollars to find their way into the Connolly family arrived on foot of that fortuitous meeting in Chicago with the socialist publisher Charles Kerr. The result was *Socialism Made Easy*, a collection of essays and articles written by Connolly from *The Harp*, the *Industrial Union Bulletin* and the *International Socialist Review*. On 15 March 1909 Kerr sent a letter to him enclosing a cheque for $45:

The first copies of your book are just being bound and

trimmed, and we are sending you a hundred, for which please credit us $5.00.

We understand that you are soon to start out on the road again, and trust you will let us keep you supplied with your book ...[3]

If *Socialism Made Easy* was the first book of Connolly's to make some money for him, it follows that it was also the most widely read, at least in 1909. The book sold thousands in the USA, Canada, Ireland, Britain and even as far away as Australia, where it was republished numerous times under the title *Axe To The Root*.[4] He had really made a name for himself now amongst the socialists of America. Part of the book's appeal lay, like most of Connolly's writings, in the simple style and positive light that it is written in – it does what it says on the cover, it makes socialism easy.

Meanwhile *The Harp* was still being churned out with Connolly writing articles, sometimes from hundreds of miles away. Bernard McMahon of Chicago recalled reading the journal for the first time:

Looking it over casually, I saw that it was a Socialist paper with a special appeal to the Irish race and that its editor was James Connolly, of whom I had heard. I read every line of it and concluded ... that it was worthy of Bronterre O'Brien, Fintan Lalor or John Mitchel, three of Ireland's greatest writers on economic subjects ...[5]

McMahon, who was the original founder of the Chicago chapter of the Irish Socialist Federation, urged the Socialist Party to build upon Connolly's successful New York tour and engage him as a lecturer on a tour of the whole country.

With that in mind, the National Office of the Socialist Party of America sent a circular to all Locals. 'Comrade Connolly has already toured Massachusetts, Maine, New Hampshire, Pennsylvania and Illinois during the recent campaign, and the National Office has received from all those states the most glowing reports of his abilities, and especially of his tactfulness in dealing with such delicate questions as religion ... He is, however, equally entertaining and convincing on the broad question of Socialism in general. His terms for your state will be $5.00 flat per lecture.'[6]

Connolly's tour lasted eleven months in total. It was a long time to be separated from the family, but the rewards were great. He got three dollars a day, seven days a week, had his expenses reimbursed, and was entitled to the proceeds from the sale of literature. The tour brought him to Washington, Ohio, Indiana, Missouri, Iowa, Colorado, Texas, Arizona, Montana and California, to name but a few of the states that hosted talks.

All through the year of the tour, he engaged in lengthy correspondence about the potential of his return to Ireland. An unusually short communication in the form of a telegram sent from Philadelphia to William O'Brien in May

1909 simply states: 'Fifty shillings. Connolly.' It is an answer as to what salary Connolly would need if he was appointed editor of the proposed Dublin Trades and Labour Council newspaper. The potential of getting such a job back home really piqued his desire to return to Ireland and he bares his soul in a letter from Washington DC to O'Brien:

> I may confess to you that I regard my emigration to America as the great mistake of my life, and, as Jack Mulray can tell you, I have never ceased to regret it … My family are growing, and their needs are pressing. I am at present on a tour, and possibly six months from now I might have some money to spare, but just now I am only painfully recovering from the long financial depression of the winter. If by any possibility you get that job for me, the task of raising the money for the passage would fall entirely upon the comrades in Ireland. Also … owing to the terrible accident which blighted our last separation, my wife would never consent to make the trip without me accompanying her. So that if I go to Ireland I have to bring my family along with me. To do that would require about 200 dollars, £40, and I do not see how in heaven that money is to be raised.

On a lighter note, Connolly suggested that O'Brien could 'break into the Bank of Ireland when the cashier is not looking'.[7]

He was determined not to split up the family again. Months later, in December 1909, he had not changed his mind on the matter when he wrote from Tucson, Arizona: 'When I go back to Ireland my family will accompany me or I do not go.'[8] Connolly need not have bothered getting too excited about the editor's position as it was given to PT Daly, the same comrade who used to help with the *Workers' Republic* back in the day.

He wrote to Lillie from Cleveland, Ohio, on 7 June 1909: 'I enclose $12 to pull you through for this week. I got Mollie's post card this morning, and although it was late I was glad to see that some one remembered me.'[9] It had been Connolly's forty-first birthday, on 5 June, and he was obviously feeling a little sorry for himself and perhaps a little lonely. At the same time, he had money to spare, was being well received in lecture halls and had been made one of six national organisers for the Socialist Party. But it still did little to quench that desire to return home.

In July 1909, Connolly was in Brazil, Indiana. He penned a missive to O'Brien concerning his fears that a return to Dublin would be a return to poverty: 'of course I could not go into the Dublin slums again to live; one experience of that is enough in a lifetime. My children are now growing up, and it is a part of my creed that when I have climbed any part of the ladder towards social comfort I must never descend it again.'[10] He continued in the same vein when he wrote again, on 12 September, this time from Springfield, Illinois:

It makes me shudder even yet when I think of the hard grind of those poverty-stricken years, of the hunger and the wretchedness we endured to build up a party in Ireland … National organisers are generally laid off in December … But I am to be kept on through the winter, and to be brought right through to the Pacific coast for a trip, through Washington, Montana etc. and back through San Francisco and California. Thus the money which I would have to use to supplement the earnings of the winter months (if necessary) until April, I can save and apply to the purchase of tickets for Ireland. This is where I am going to get the money … although it is the best job I ever had in my life, I am willing to resign it if I can get a living at a tradesman's wages in Ireland.[11]

In November 1909 a rather disgruntled Connolly wrote to O'Brien:

Some six weeks or more ago (rather more) I sent you per Chas. Kerr & Co. Chicago, one hundred copies of *Socialism Made Easy* as a present from your humble servant to the Socialist Party of Ireland. At the same time I sent to the Party, by Donnelly in New York, one hundred copies of *Songs of Freedom*. These 200 books I paid for and sent to the Party, carriage paid, in order to help it to get a start. But up to the present no one has condescended to acknowledge the receipt of these books.[12]

If Connolly was trying to endear himself to the former comrades in Dublin, he had a strange way of going about it.

On the tour Connolly covered thousands of miles, mostly by train, which afforded him time to put the finishing touches to *Labour in Irish History*. The first draft for *Labour in Irish History* was ready in September 1909, but he was concerned that American publishers were 'ridiculously conservative', with the exception of Kerr, but that publisher would only reach a socialist audience and Connolly wanted this book to 'reach the Irish public in Ireland, and also in Great Britain.'[13] In March 1910 Connolly casually alluded that a large section of the book went missing:

> I sent the copy of the "Labour in Irish History" book to be typewritten, and three of the last chapters have got lost in the mail. I am afraid I will have to write it all over again …[14]

Connolly decided that he might be able to print *The Harp* in Ireland; it would be cheaper, might get more subscriptions there and would have more appeal to Irish Americans if it literally came from the home country. Connolly decided that he could edit the paper for a few months from New York as long as he could find someone to organise things for him in Dublin. Typical of a man who gives his all to a project, he expected that O'Brien should drop whatever he was doing and fulfil a list of demands that Connolly made upon him:

> So I will be frank with you. My whole plan is this. I had

to take over *The Harp*. But having taken it over I wanted to utilise it to prepare the way for my return. For that purpose I want it to be sold in Ireland and Great Britain. In Ireland, that I may once more be "remembered in Erin", and in Great Britain because I believed it may be necessary for me to do some lecturing in England before my footing was secure in Ireland ... If I got a circulation in Ireland and England first, I could easily get dates for lectures afterwards, and the purpose you propose for my trip would be accomplished at a small expense.[15]

There were many proposals and counter-proposals but eventually, in January 1910, the printing of *The Harp* was transferred to Dublin where WP Ryan of *The Nation* took on the job, purely as a business venture.

Jim Larkin, about whom Connolly had been reading since he arrived in Belfast in 1907, had become a very successful union leader in Ireland, having founded the Irish Transport Workers' Union in 1909. Larkin was taken by the first Dublin issue of *The Harp* and decided to offer his managerial services, much to Connolly's delight. This in turn impressed the Dublin comrades, who were now a little more enthused with the prospect of Connolly's tour as he was now 'approved' by Larkin.

In April 1910 O'Brien convened a meeting of the Socialist Party of Ireland (SPI) and other socialists, where they approved a motion to set up a guarantee fund for the Connolly tour.

They proposed to raise £20 and O'Brien also mentioned that they had discussed what his relationship to the Socialist Party of Ireland would be. In a rather presumptuous fashion Connolly suggested that he place his services 'as the disposal of the SPI as, say, National Organiser', whilst he was in the country.

As Connolly felt that it was not going to be possible to emigrate back to Ireland, he settled for the next best thing: a tour of the old country. This way he could legitimately leave the family in New York, on the understanding that he would return. It is difficult to believe that he ever intended to return to the United States, but maybe he even convinced himself at this stage that it would be a 'mere experimental trip or trip of exploration …' Back home in New York, in May 1910, he wrote to O'Brien:

Well the fact is that I am torn between desire and fear … But in order to put the matter to a final issue my wife and myself held a Committee of Ways and Means, with the understanding that its decision should be final. So we have decided to inform you that I will be in Dublin in the last week in July. This is definite.[16]

In New Castle, Pennsylvania, a bitter steelworkers' strike had been going on for nearly a year. Two local newspapers had been supporting the strikers against the giant US Steel Trust: the IWW paper *Solidarity* and the weekly socialist *New*

*Castle Free Press*. Connolly had visited the strikers a number of times on his *Harp* tour and his Socialist Party tour. On one such occasion the *Free Press* announced Connolly's visit under the headline 'Very Special'. He had written about the strikes in *The Harp* and the *Free Press*, and editor Charles McKeever republished some of these articles. The situation before the strike was appalling. Men worked for seven days a week, on twelve hour shifts, for a dollar a day. Connolly reported in *The Harp*:

> Family life is destroyed, not in any imaginary way, but by the appalling number of preventable accidents, and a typhoid fever rate that has already been commented upon throughout the civilised world as a disgrace to the American People.[17]

The companies refused to recognise the strike and used thugs and the police to try and demoralise the workers. Running battles between state troopers were recorded, with many deaths on both sides. McKeever was arrested as part of a clampdown and, at the request of the Socialist Party, Connolly took over as temporary managing editor of the *Free Press* for six weeks. Public opinion in the United States eventually forced the Steel Trust to tone down its tactics against the workers and the leaders, allowing Connolly to return home to New York and thence home to Ireland.

There was a 'Farewell Dinner to James Connolly' organised

by the Irish Socialist Federation in Cavanagh's Restaurant on Thursday, 14 July 1910. Connolly was described as the national organiser of the Socialist Party of Ireland. 'A feast of mirth' and a night of real Irish songs and stories was promised if one bought a one-dollar ticket. Ticket holders were encouraged not to 'miss this occasion to tell Connolly what you think of him!' This was Connolly's second 'farewell' to the US and, two days later, he departed from his wife, family and New York City, never to return again.

# Chapter Ten

● ● ● ● ● ●

# 1910–1913

# Back Home to Ireland

*... as the working class has no subject class beneath it,*
*therefore to the working class of necessity belongs the honour*
*of being the class destined to put an end to class rule, since,*
*in emancipating itself, it cannot help emancipating all other*
*classes.*[1]

**J**ames Connolly was forty-two years of age when he upped sticks and came home from America. He left New York and his family on 16 July 1910 on board the *Furnissia*, and arrived in Derry after ten days' sailing. He immediately sent a telegram to the Socialist Party of Ireland activist and former ISRP comrade, the man who had effectively organised his trip to Ireland, William O'Brien: 'Just landed. Arrive Dublin on Tuesday, Connolly.' Upon the return of his old comrade, O'Brien noticed that 'it was at once apparent that he had greatly developed as a speaker, writer and man of affairs.' His appearance, too, had improved, and when O'Brien's mother commented upon this, Connolly replied: 'While I was away I got something to eat.'[2]

During his absence, the workers of Belfast and Dublin also got something to eat, due, in the main, to Jim Larkin, who had achieved notoriety and popularity during the Belfast Strikes of 1907. The leadership within the National Union of Dock Labourers disliked Larkin's militant tendencies and, in December 1908, he was suspended without pay. His reaction to his 'sacking' was to establish the Irish Transport Workers' Union on 4 January 1909. Larkin was the general secretary, Thomas Foran was the general president, and William O'Brien added the word 'General' to the union's name. The 'Transport Union', as they were also known, operated from a 'sparsely furnished office rented at 10, Beresford Place' for a few years.[3] From March 1912 the ITGWU moved into the former Northumberland Hotel on the corner of Beresford Place and Eden Quay. Their new headquarters was renamed Liberty Hall.

In the summer of 1910 Larkin was incarcerated on a trumped-up 'misuse of funds' case. The first thing that Connolly did when he got to Dublin was to visit the union leader in Mountjoy Jail, as Larkin had requested a meeting. The two had never met face to face; they knew enough about each other to establish an instant, respectful relationship, but this never became a friendship. Doubtless, Connolly informed Larkin that he would agitate for his release.

The next night, a welcome reception was held for Connolly, but immediately after that he set about organising his tour, giving talks in many of his old haunts and finishing off the text of *Labour, Nationality and Religion* by day. The main reason for compiling *Labour, Nationality and Religion* was to counter the anti-socialist preaching of a certain Fr Kane. As there had been a sudden swing to socialism through Larkin, this Jesuit priest devoted a series of Lenten lectures designed to attack the practicality of socialism as a system. Fr Kane's arguments showed a lack of understanding of the subject, believing that socialism meant state ownership of children, free love and obligatory atheism. Throughout the book, Connolly managed to avoid an attack on the Catholic Church as an institution, for that would have played into Kane's hands. Rather, he quoted from Catholic sources, which unintentionally endorse socialist doctrine, such as St Chrysostom's statement that 'The rich man is a thief' or the comment from Gregory the Great that 'The earth of which they are born is common to all, and therefore the fruit the earth brings forth belongs without distinction to all.' Connolly's pamphlet destroyed any arguments that the priest had made and proved to be a very popular book. Small wonder when his prose contained such delightful nuggets as 'in every European country the title deeds to aristocratic property have been written in the blood of the poor, and that the tree of capitalism has been watered with the tears of the toilers in every age and clime and country.'[4]

He spoke every night as 'the famous Irish-American orator' and was impressed by the numbers and outlook of the people who had been infused with confidence through Larkin. He spent a week up in Belfast where he helped to establish a branch of the Socialist Party of Ireland. He was, after all, the national organiser. In Cork, Connolly drew a crowd of six hundred one week and two thousand the following week. At that meeting in Daunt Square the SPI sold two hundred copies of *Labour, Nationality and Religion*. A Cork branch of the SPI was founded with a membership of twenty-four comrades. Connolly was on a roll.

On the other hand, *The Harp* would sound no more. Its silence was not due to Larkin's imprisonment or the fact that most of the subscriptions had run out. Rather, the blame might be laid at Larkin's unbridled but graceless style of journalism. Six months later, Connolly still appeared angry when he wrote to John Carstairs Matheson of the Social Democratic Federation (SDF) in Edinburgh:

> The Harp has been suspended since June. There were four libel actions instituted against it over its last issue, and as the whole thing had been mismanaged since its transfer to Dublin I did not feel able to lose any more money upon it. I return you your sub.[5]

A new manifesto was adopted by the Socialist Party of

Ireland in September 1910. Drafted by Connolly and Francis Sheehy Skeffington, it aimed to organise the workers of Ireland, irrespective of race or creed, into one great party of Labour. It encouraged the Irish working class to organise itself industrially and politically, with a view to gaining control of the entire resources of the country. By the use of the ballot box, it was hoped to secure the election of socialists to public bodies, and thus to gradually transfer the political power of the State to those who would extend the principle of public ownership. Their agreed aim was to make the people of Ireland the sole owners of Ireland.

In late September, O'Brien thought he had good news for Connolly. After an informal national conference of the SPI, they proposed an offer of a six-month national organiser contract. Connolly had gone to Glasgow and was due to embark on a lecture tour of Britain to help supplement the costs of his stay, but he was despondent:

I am making my plans up with the understanding that I am going back to America ... Your offer was for 36s. per week for six months. In order to accept it I would require to bring my family home from America.

[The wages] works out at about £41.16s.0d.; to bring my family home would take about £45 to say nothing of the sacrifice of my furniture on our side and the stocking of a new home on the other. Thus I would be working six months for nothing, so to speak, and at the end of that period might be left idle altogether, for I can see that my activities in Belfast might not help me in Great Britain. I may be wrong in this latter fear, but you can understand that I cannot run too much risk on this affair.[6]

A loose proposal was announced to set up a fund to raise enough money to retain Connolly, who said a man with his 'responsibilities could not maintain life on less than £2 per week.' Connolly clearly wanted to have a definite idea of how much money would be available. He had heard of 'guaranteed' wages before during his years as organiser for the ISRP. O'Brien informed Connolly that the most they could probably raise would be about £65 for the organiser.

Then, on 1 October 1910, came Larkin's release from Mountjoy Jail. O'Brien had a word with Larkin and seems to have suggested that the ITGWU could find a position for Connolly. But Connolly was understandably perplexed by the apparent confusion surrounding the Organiser Fund and he did not wish to impose himself upon the union. Witness his reply to O'Brien:

Your letter informing me that your Committee refuse to make an effort to ascertain definitely what money is available for an Irish organiser came duly to hand. It came to hand the morning after I had parted with Jim Larkin who told me that he had been asked to come to Glasgow from Liverpool to confer with me about the above post, and that he, after consultation with you people, was sure that there was no difficulty in the way; also that he had already deposited some money in the bank for that purpose. That he was making arrangement with some friends of his own for the purposes of creating the fund and assisting it, and all the time he was with me he was speaking of the Fund as an actuality, and of my remaining in Ireland as a foregone conclusion … But what was the meaning of the Larkin visit to me if the Committee have no intention of going on with it? … So at the bottom of the negotiation we will write the words FINIS – all off. Me for America.[7]

However, Larkin's involvement, although typically impulsive, meant that the SPI felt more confident and suddenly they were convinced that they *could* afford Connolly. A direct appeal to the public and to the SPI members was drafted (by Connolly) with a target of £100. This 'Appeal for Organisation Fund' was, it seems, enough for Connolly finally to decide to stay.

Ina Connolly recollected that Lillie was not overly keen on returning to Ireland:

She had practically settled down in the States and was looking forward to a few years to come when some of her children would be able to leave school and find suitable employment, thereby helping her to lighten the burden of supporting the rest of the family.[8]

However, she was left with little choice when 'the fatal letter' arrived on 13 November 1910:

> I want you to come back to Ireland. Now after you have drawn your breath let me tell you the particulars. My engagement is for two pounds a week and most of the money is already in hand. Also, I am sure that I have a more promising future in Ireland than in America, not so often and so long away from home as I would be if we stayed in the U.S. You are not coming back to the misery you left. Do not be afraid of that ...[9]

*Labour in Irish History* was published in November 1910. Desmond Ryan called it 'that strangely burning and sincere book, which may well serve as Connolly's testament.' Published by Maunsell, and 'written in haste ... in a crowded life, by a man who had to struggle hard to win his daily bread', the book is a 'work of genius'.[10] Essentially it is a collection of articles that challenges the accepted version of Irish history and examines it instead from a working-class perspective. Like his other books, the research is meticulous, the writing is appealing, the message is clear, and Connolly believed that it could 'justly be looked upon as part of the literature of the Gaelic revival'. Here was a masterpiece written by someone who was not 'of the master class'; but in fact it was Irish history written by an incorruptible inheritor of the fight for freedom in Ireland.

Meanwhile, in New York, the Connolly family were packing up, selling their few bits of furniture and saying farewell to neighbours and friends. Ina recalled:

> Some had come a long distance to see us off and many were crying as well as mother. Wasn't she coming with us and going to see father and her brothers, so why the tears? I later heard her say that she was leaving the land where she had spent the best five or six years of her life.[11]

While the Connollys were sailing home, their father reacquainted himself with Maud Gonne. They had kept in touch only once or twice, but old friends became new again and they launched into a campaign to extend into Ireland the Provision of School Meals Act (1906). Despite Ireland being ruled from Westminster, the feeding of hungry Irish children was not covered by this Act. The nationalists were reluctant to support this call, and the Catholic Church were against it as the hierarchy tended towards the notion that it was the responsibility of the family, not the State, to feed children. Nonetheless, the SPI continued for many months to campaign with the assistance of *Inghinidhe na hÉireann* (Daughters of Ireland) and the Irish Women's Franchise League.

When Connolly met his family in Derry, he brought them on a tour of the famous walls. Lillie told him that everyone on board the ship thought they must be very wealthy to be returning back to Ireland; they called them 'the millionaire's family'! 'You mean the madman's family,' retorted Connolly. After a night in a hotel, they all travelled to Dublin. Connolly had to reintroduce the children to the town as they had been young when they left for America. He pointed out Nelson's Pillar. 'It is a landmark,' said Connolly. 'If in doubt of your direction, ask for the Pillar and start off from her. Then you will be making some use of a terrible eyesore.'[12] The Connolly family moved into a house at 70 Rosetta Terrace, South Lotts Road, Ringsend. The Dublin comrades organised an evening's entertainment in the Antient Concert Rooms, headquarters of the SPI, to welcome them back to Dublin and introduce them to party members and their friends.

During Connolly's lecture tour in the autumn of 1910, he met the editor of a Scottish journal *Forward*. Thomas Johnston produced this weekly journal of socialist thought and Connolly, always happy to voice his ideas, was a regular contributor between 1911 and 1914.

Connolly often stayed in Danny and Emily McDevitt's house at 5 Rosemary Street when he was organising for the SPI in Belfast. Danny was heavily involved in the movement and his wife was destined to be a founding member of the Belfast Cumann na mBan. On 14 February 1911 he wrote to William O'Brien from the McDevitts' home, to keep him informed of the progress of the movement in the city. He may appear to be embroidering the significance of a few new members, but it should be borne in mind that socialists were thin on the ground:

> Since I reorganised the branch we are doing nicely, getting lots of new members. I issued six cards on Sunday, and got three more applications. And more coming.[13]

A very strange incident happened to Connolly when he was down in Cobh in March 1911, giving a lecture on the school feeding campaign. Although Cork City was generally welcoming, Cobh, also known as Queenstown, was a little less enthused by socialists. A certain Councillor Healy, a laundry owner who paid his girls an unbelievably low wage of just under three shillings per week, led the heckling. He asked Connolly if he had written 'a book that said the Jesuits killed Popes'. Another woman shouted, 'What about free love?' It's unclear whether she was asking for it or denouncing it, but with that comment the crowd rushed the platform and Connolly had to be escorted by the police to the train station. A further attempt to speak there the following week was similarly disrupted; this time Connolly and the SPI members were lucky to make it out unscathed as the crowd had armed themselves with chair legs and cudgels to show them that their 'atheist' ideas were not welcome in Cobh, a town which Connolly later described rather poetically as 'that nest of parasites feeding on parasites'.

At a public meeting held at Sinn Féin's headquarters on

24 March 1911, Connolly was, despite his non-attendance, 'unanimously elected to act on the Committee which was formed to consider the forthcoming visit of the English King to Dublin.'[14] George V (1865–1936) visited Dublin from 8–12 July 1911. He received a cordial welcome in St Patrick's College, Maynooth, where great men of the cloth entertained the new King of Great Britain and Ireland. Connolly issued a manifesto which SPI members distributed around as a handbill:

> ... a people mentally poisoned by the adulation of royalty can never attain to that spirit of self-reliant democracy necessary for the attainment of social freedom. The mind accustomed to political kings can easily be reconciled to social kings – capitalist kings of the workshop, the mill, the railway, the ships and the docks ... Monarchy is a survival of the tyranny imposed by the hand of greed and treachery upon the human race in the darkest and most ignorant days of our history.

Ina recalled that the family eventually found their footing in Dublin, despite Connolly's regular absence as SPI organiser. Nora could not find any work in Dublin, but she found a position as a seamstress in Belfast. Her father often spent a week or two in that city and he began to see, especially as his SPI income was shrinking by the week, that it seemed very wasteful to keep two homes going. He also decided to join the Belfast branch of the ITGWU. A decision was made to bring Lillie and the rest of the children up from Dublin.[15] Number 1 Glenalina Terrace, Falls Road, the very heart of nationalist Belfast, became the new Connolly home. Despite Connolly's promise to Lillie that they were not returning to poverty in Ireland, in mid-June he was compelled to write to Richard Hoskin, who was responsible for the SPI's organising funds which in turn paid Connolly:

> The whole affair had me nearly crazy. Between the railway fare of my family to Belfast, the transportation of my furniture and incidental expenses in taking the house it cost me about £4 to move to Belfast and on the same week I had to raise the instalment on my loan – making a total of £9 – exclusive of that interest, all to be paid inside of two weeks. Hence, my past and present anxiety about money … Mrs Connolly is under the impression that when the Dublin comrades got us out of Dublin they left us to starve, as she has already been 3 days in Belfast, a strange town, without a penny to buy food, and I away in Scotland. Such an impression on her makes my work in the movement rather difficult.[16]

It is difficult to comprehend why Connolly himself was not in Belfast. He left at the beginning of June and was away for three weeks, instead of helping the family to settle into their new home and ensuring that they had food. It depressed him that his promised £2 per week had dried up. Little wonder that he remarked later in Edinburgh to John Leslie, his old comrade who had encouraged him to go to Ireland in 1896, that he had made two grave errors in life: one in going to America and the other in returning. Connolly was considering moving to England, but Leslie gave him some sound advice, with remarkable foresight, that he should stick to Ireland where he 'would find a niche in the temple of fame'.

On 3 July 1911, Jim Larkin sent Connolly a money order for £4 as wages and expenses. Connolly had been appointed secretary and Ulster district organiser of the Irish Transport Workers' Union. Maybe Connolly gambled on Larkin giving him a job and that was his real reason for moving to Belfast. It is true that O'Brien had Larkin's ear, but the money to employ someone in that position was never there before. Larkin's union was back on track with over five thousand members. He had become a dominant force in the Dublin Trades Council and the Irish Trades Union Congress. The timing of the job could not have been better; Connolly had spent nearly a year back home and there was a serious need for strong leadership in Belfast. Really, there was no better man for the job than Connolly, especially as a strike had broken out in the city. Without hesitation, Connolly opened up offices at 122 Corporation Street and immediately set about organising.

Conditions in the Belfast docks were appalling; it had

been some years since Larkin had left the city for Dublin and the workers lacked leadership. The employers were intent on 'speeding-up' the offloading of cargo. Pathetic bonuses were offered for a doubling of the work load, and intimidation through threats of dismissal and physical violence were used to demoralise the dockers into acceptance of their conditions.

For days and weeks, Connolly lectured along the docks on solidarity with those seamen who were on strike. Slowly but surely a few labourers took notice. Finally word came about that the Ulster SS Company paid their own workers less than the same company was paying workers in Bristol. Connolly managed to persuade six hundred workers out on strike, which achieved an increase in pay and, as a bonus, some improved conditions.

After a further series of a dozen lightning strikes, Connolly achieved general pay increases all round and an abolition of the 'speeding-up' system. This was made possible through a localising of decision-making rather than awaiting a decision on strike action from Dublin. The success of the strike brought the ITGWU and Connolly to great prominence in Belfast. The 'Non-Sectarian Labour Band', composed of Protestant and Catholic workers and founded by Connolly, became a familiar sight on the streets of Belfast and was to prove an effective fund-raising and eyebrow-raising tool.

Larkin had founded a union newspaper in July called the

*Irish Worker.* It was an immediate success due to Larkin's habit of naming and shaming bad bosses. Within months, its weekly circulation was twenty thousand, in comparison to Griffith's heavily subsidised *Sinn Féin*, which only sold a couple of thousand. As a newspaper, it also achieved more popularity than the *Workers' Republic* or *The Harp.*

Not long after the strike was settled, the United Irish League of Great Britain helped to organise a trip to Wales for Connolly. The Independent Labour Party of Pontypridd booked him for a whole week of lectures in late August 1911. He was back on form, doing what he liked best, organising workers at home and travelling around giving talks.

The Belfast mills were described by Connolly as 'slaughter-houses for the women and penitentiaries for the children'. Staffed almost entirely by female workers, they operated under desperate conditions and stubbornly rejected their regular unions' call for calm in the face of a threatened lockout.[17] Instead, 3,000 women packed into a hall to proclaim their allegiance to a new textile branch of the ITGWU. The girls lasted on strike for as long as the funds were there to keep them from starving, but the bosses stood firm, and eventually Connolly had to advise them to return to work. However, he continued to call for the workers to stick together when any individual was being harassed:

> If a girl is checked for singing, let the whole room start singing at once; if you are checked for laughing, let the whole room laugh at once; and if any one is dismissed, all

put on your shawls and come out in a body.

Cathal O'Shannon wrote that Connolly:

... was not exactly a great orator, although he could rise to oratory too. But he had a method, a style, a manner that exactly fitted and adorned the splendid material he used in his speeches. He was never slipshod, never flamboyant, but always earnest, simple and informative ... From Connolly you got a cogent, coherent and reasoned statement of a case, presented in the clearest manner, illustrated by the most telling allusions, with the argument marshalled in the coldest and calmest fashion, yet warmed with the burning fire of sincerity and sympathy.[18]

Ina recalled their own nationalist activities in Belfast:

Shortly after we arrived I got to hear about Fianna Éireann who used to meet and drill in St. Mary's Hall. I went down there one evening by myself and joined as a member ... It was at St. Mary's Hall that the Gaelic League also met and gave the Irish classes. My father used to take us to ceilidhthe there. We learned drilling, Irish dancing, Irish history, Irish language and first aid. At the weekend we used to march and parade up to Sean's Park at Whiterock Road. All the labour supporters, as well as nationalists, used to march there on Sundays ... My father, though in full sympathy, had not joined the National Movement. It was through the Fianna that he met those noble young souls, Liam Mellows, Sean Heuston and Con Colbert, who later sacrificed their lives for Ireland. Liam Mellows, in particular, became firmly attached to my father and family. Here, too, I met Eamon Martin who, in troubled times, out of sincere admiration for my father, became a firm friend of the family.[19]

In December, Connolly reflected that his life in Belfast had separated him from the Dublin scene in the SPI:

I have almost lost track of Dublin. No one from there ever drops me a line, or in any way communicates with me. I wrote to the secretary acquainting him of the dispatch of 1,000 pamphlets to Dublin, wrote again asking if they had been received and also giving instructions re my dues to the branch, but to neither communication have I yet received an answer. Whether the branch is yet alive I could not know except by the medium of the Irish Worker. Please break this terrible, this awful silence.

As to the Belfast end of the struggle, my absorption in the Union's work makes it difficult for me to get much done ...[20]

The union was taking precedence over Connolly's work as party organiser. But it was the union work that paid the bills.

The printer and city councillor Patrick Thomas Daly resigned from the Sinn Féin party and came over to the socialists and the ITGWU. Daly was sent to Wexford to help with the strikes there, but had found himself on the wrong side of the law, having been arrested for 'inciting to riot'. The town had witnessed a long battle when the foundries' owners refused to recognise Larkin's union by locking out members. Michael O'Leary, one of the striking workers, was brutally beaten to death by the police. Both sides were entrenched when Connolly arrived in January of 1912. He managed to convince the employers to accept an Irish Foundry Workers' Union and secured a complete reinstatement of all workers who had been dismissed for striking. That the IFWU was affiliated to the ITGWU did not seem to bother the employers. It was a triumph for Connolly, a drawn battle according to the foundry owners, and the men of Wexford were content to resume work with union recognition and heads held high. Daly's imprisonment was illegal, according to Connolly, and the matter was even raised in Westminster; he was released in March, thus allowing Connolly to return to Belfast quite elated.

Around this time, a curious offer came to the Connolly family, one that could have easily altered the course of Irish history. Ina Connolly recalled how her 'grandfather's brother, Peter, who was a Fenian, had been obliged to flee to Scotland before that, having changed his name because there was a price on his head. He had procured work in the Corporation and it was probably through him that my grandfather obtained employment. Peter never married. I remember him

coming in 1912 to Belfast, where we were living at the time
to take my father with him down to Monaghan to take over
the family farm, the lease of which had run out. My father
refused to go as he was engaged in a strike in Larne. He
said what could he do with a farm with a houseful of girls.
He had no money to pay the rent and rates of a farm. My
mother was heartbroken that he would not show an interest
in the farm. She was a country girl herself from Wicklow.'[21]

In May 1912 Connolly called for independent Labour
representation on all public boards at the Irish Trades Union
Congress in Clonmel. Much support and enthusiasm for
Connolly came from other delegates, including Jim Larkin
and William O'Brien. Congress decided to form an Irish
Labour Party independent of all other parties. Previous
to this Connolly had sought a motion within the Belfast
branch of the ITGWU calling for such a party to be founded
– something William Walker of the Belfast ILP railed against.
The general tendency within Irish socialism was to support
the British Labour Party. Connolly and Walker held a long
and public debate on socialism and national independence.
Connolly quoted Marx on the need for English workers to
fight for Irish freedom. Walker did not even support Home
Rule and their debate turned very sour when personal insults
were made against Connolly. Walker later left the movement
and went to work for the British Government.

By September 1912 Larkin's lack of interest in the Labour

Party was a cause of disappointment for Connolly. He confided in O'Brien:

> I begin to fear that our friend Jim has arrived at the highest elevation, and that he will pull us all down with him in his fall.
>
> He does not seem to want a democratic Labour movement; he seems to want a Larkinite movement only.
>
> I am sick of all this playing to one man, but am prepared to advise it for the sake of the movement. In fact the general inactivity since the Congress has made me sick and sorry I ever returned.[22]

Larkin was no De Leon, but for those who knew Connolly intimately, there was probable cause to fret about a repetition of that great battle.

Winifred Carney came to work for Connolly and the union as a secretary in September 1912. Connolly would pay her wages out of the salary he received as secretary of the Approved Society, ie the insurance section of the union. It is clear that Connolly was under great pressure from a letter to O'Brien where he complained that he was 'up to the neck in trade union and Insurance and other allied work'. Carney and Connolly became great comrades – they developed a close relationship that would last until she joined him in the General Post Office (GPO) in 1916. One aspect of Connolly's character was that he enjoyed constant contact through correspondence. The number of letters he sent to Matheson and O'Brien is proof of that. Once his relationship with 'Miss Carney' had been cemented they corresponded very regularly. At one stage, in late 1915, it became a daily occurrence.

Of course the great issue, especially in the northeast of Ireland, was the third Home Rule Bill. Introduced by the Liberal Prime Minister, Herbert Henry Asquith, in April 1912, and despite the usual opposition from the House of Lords, it would have to become law by 1914 by virtue of the Parliament Act. On 28 September, thousands of Unionists signed Ulster's Solemn League and Covenant, promising to 'use all means which may be found necessary to defeat the present conspiracy to set up a Home Rule Parliament in Ireland.' Edward Carson and his sidekick, James Craig, stalwarts of Orange intransigence, had massed the majority of unionists, generally Protestants, into a frenzy of anti–Home Rule agitation and passionate loyalty to King George V.

Around this period, Connolly gave a series of lectures on what he termed 'The Re-Conquest of Ireland'. In 1915 these lectures were published in pamphlet form.

Sometimes, at one of these lectures, the odd uncompromising Orangeman would attempt to disrupt proceedings. An old comrade recalled one such occasion when Connolly 'was speaking at Library Street on a Sunday evening and was expatiating on Irish history when one of this type interrupted him, and drawing a copy of the Solemn League and Covenant from his pocket brandished it in the air and remarked there would be no Home Rule for Ireland and that he and his thousands of co-signatories would see to it. Connolly, with a sardonic smile, advised him to take the document home and frame it, adding "your children will laugh at it".[23]

At the beginning of 1913, Connolly fought for a seat in the municipal elections. The Dock ward, in which he stood was a mixed area (Connolly exaggerated it as an 'Orange Ward' in a letter to O'Brien), but many of those entitled to vote would not have agreed with his advocacy of socialism, independence and equality.[24] In an appeal for support, he explained his motivation to the voters:

> I desire to be returned in order to advocate, among other things, that the Act for the feeding of children at school at present in force in Great Britain, be applied to Ireland. We have a right to demand equal treatment for Irish and British workers, and as the British workers have secured that their children must be fed before being educated (because it is impossible to educate hungry children), we also claim that when the poverty, or neglect, of the parents is such that the children are suffering, that the Local Authorities should be empowered to make provision for the supply of at least one good meal per day to each child. To those who object that this would 'pauperise' the children, I answer that the children of the working class have as much right to be

maintained thus as have the children of royalty. If it does not pauperise the one it cannot pauperise the other.

The Corporation of Dublin and many other Public Boards in Ireland have declared for this measure; it is time Belfast City Council was interesting itself more about such matters and less about the perpetuation of the religious discords that make Belfast a byword among civilised nations.

Believing that the present system of society is based upon the robbery of the working class, and that capitalist property cannot exist without the plundering of labour, I desire to see capitalism abolished, and a democratic system of common or public ownership erected in its stead. This democratic system, which is called socialism, will, I believe, come as a result of the continuous increase of power of the working class. Only by this means can we secure the abolition of destitution, and all the misery, crime, and immorality which flow from that unnecessary evil. All the reform legislation of the present day is moving in that direction even now, but working-class action on above lines will secure that direct, voluntary, conscious, and orderly cooperation by all for the good of all, will more quickly replace the blundering and often reluctant legislation of capitalist governments.

Connolly did manage to attract about nine hundred votes but the Unionist candidate polled one and a half thousand, perhaps to do with the following line in Connolly's election manifesto:

As a lifelong advocate of national independence for Ireland, I am in favour of Home Rule, and believe that Ireland should be ruled, governed, and owned by the people of Ireland.[25]

In the same month, January, a meeting of the Ulster Unionist Council consolidated the various local anti-Home Rule militias into the Ulster Volunteer Force. There had been numerous small groups of militant unionists but now they became a formidable political entity, especially as they were receiving popular support from British Conservatives and were being trained by ex-British army officers. The UVF imported a significant consignment of weapons at Larne in April 1914, but the threat of civil war over Home Rule dissipated when the vast majority of the UVF joined the 36th Ulster Division with the outbreak of what would eventually be known as World War I.

Belfast in June 1913 was in turmoil. Connolly was in the thick of it; writing to O'Brien, he said: 'I am in the midst of strife and tribulation here, a strike on in the brickworks, 300 men out; a strike in Larne, the same number out; and a rival union established on the docks to fight us – the Belfast Transport Workers' Union. This is an Orange move, fostered by the employers, and directed by a Councillor Finnigan, an Orange leader. I see ahead the fight of our life.'[26] With the anti-Home Rule fever heaped upon an already suspicious population, socialism became a difficult creed to preach.

Connolly noted the change in the atmosphere in an article in the socialist newspaper *Forward*, the organ of the Independent Labour Party: 'Socialist meetings in Belfast can only be held in the business centre of the town where the passing crowd is of mixed or uncertain nature.'[27]

In mid-July Connolly wrote a letter to Larkin castigating him:

> On the occasion of your last visit here you asked me for a statement of our expenditure which was furnished you on July 1st. Since that time I have on more than one occasion asked for a settlement that we might start this quarter clear. Everything here is in arrears, our clerks' salaries atrociously so. But no notice is taken of my appeal.[28]

Connolly was understandably perplexed with Larkin. He decided the best course of action would be to absent himself on holiday, effectively issuing an ultimatum. By the end of July 1913 Connolly was complaining bitterly about Larkin. He wrote to O'Brien:

> To make matters worse I confess to you in confidence that I don't think I can stand Larkin as a boss much longer. He is simply unbearable. He is forever snarling at me and drawing comparisons between what he accomplished in Belfast in 1907, and what I have done, conveniently ignoring the fact that he was then the secretary of an English organisation, and that as soon as he started an Irish one his union fell to

pieces, and he had to leave the members to their fate. He is consumed with jealousy and hatred of anyone who will not cringe to him and beslaver him all over.

He tried to bully me out of the monies due to our branch for administration benefit of the Insurance Act and it was this that brought me to Dublin last week. He did not succeed, and had to pay £37 which was due my staff as wages. I told him that if he was Larkin twenty times over he could not bully me, that I was charging for not one cent he had not contracted to pay for, and that I was not going to hire clerks, and leave them without their wages to suit him.

I would formerly have trusted to his generosity in financial matters, now I would not trust him at all.

Larkin seems to think he can use Socialists as he pleases and then, when his end is served, throw them out if they will not bow down to his majesty. He will never get me to bow to him.[29]

Less than one month after writing this letter, Connolly would be forced to cast aside his problems with Larkin and join him the epic struggle that was the 1913–14 Lockout.

## Chapter Eleven

# 1913–1914

# The Great Lockout and the Irish Citizen Army

*Remember that the whole history of Ireland is a record of betrayals by politicians and statesmen, and remembering this, spurn their lying promises and stand up for a United Ireland – an Ireland broad based upon the union of Labour and Nationality.*[1]

William Martin Murphy (1844–1919) was the epitome of the wealthy Irish capitalist employer who relied on Church, Empire and cheap labour to oil his balance sheet. As Murphy was the Dublin Employers' Federation leader and the proprietor of the *Irish Independent*, his was the loudest voice against any move to improve workers' rights, conditions and pay.[2] The writer GK Chesterton famously maintained that the largest shareholder of the Dublin United

Tramways Company was 'like some morbid prince of the fifteenth century, full of cold anger, but not without perverted piety'.[3] Murphy has also been described as a 'venerable old man, with pointed beard, pallid face, pinched features, piercing eyes, and stoop' who 'owned half of Dublin and much elsewhere'.[4] James Larkin, on the other hand, was the working-class agitator, born to Irish parents in Liverpool, and a tough union man; he was 'trumpet tongued' and defiant of any power who might chance to stand in his way. Murphy wanted to implement a purge of 'Larkinism' within his business empire and that meant that he would have to battle the Irish Transport and General Workers' Union.

On 15 August 1913, sixty workers at the *Irish Independent* were sacked for refusing to renounce their union membership. That night the city's newspaper boys refused to sell Murphy's *Independent* and the 'sympathetic strike' ideal began to spread. For instance, two days later a large number of tramworkers refused to carry the *Independent*, resulting in *their* instant dismissal. At precisely 9.40am on 26 August 1913, the first day of the Dublin Horse Show, two hundred tram conductors and drivers, many sporting the Red Hand badge of the Irish Transport and General Workers' Union, abandoned their vehicles and began an official general strike. Larkin announced in the newspapers that the ITGWU would hold a huge meeting on O'Connell Street on the following Sunday. The chief divisional magistrate in the Dublin

Metropolitan District, EG Swifte, immediately issued a proclamation, dated 29 August, and using the typical language of
the judiciary proscribed Larkin's meeting:

> Whereas it has been represented to me … that a number
> of persons will meet or assemble at SACKVILLE STREET
> OR ITS NEIGHBOURHOOD in the said County of the
> City of Dublin … and that the object of such Meeting
> or Assemblage is seditious, and that the said Meeting or
> Assemblage would cause terror and alarm to, and dissension
> between, His Majesty's subjects, and would be an unlawful
> assembly … I do hereby prohibit such Meeting or Assem-
> blage.

On Friday, Connolly arrived hastily from Belfast and that
evening himself and Larkin spoke to a crowd outside Liberty
Hall. Connolly held Swifte's banning order aloft and asked
those present if they knew where 'Sackville Street' was:

> Perhaps it is in Jerusalem or Timbuctoo, but there is no such
> street in Dublin. There is an O'Connell Street, and there
> we will come on Sunday, in a very peaceful way, to see if
> the government has sold themselves body and soul to the
> capitalists.[5]

Never one to be outdone, Larkin set fire to the document
in front of his supporters, much to the chagrin of the police
and a few detectives who were furiously scribbling notes

on the speakers' comments. It would appear that when the meeting ended, about twenty members of the Dublin Metropolitan Police attacked the peaceable spectators. The attack on the crowd, 'of which a good proportion were women and children', was unwarranted and set the 'standard' of policing in the city for the coming weekend.[6]

The following afternoon, Saturday, 30 August, Connolly was taken from Liberty Hall by the DMP and charged with incitement to cause a breach of the peace on the previous night. Connolly refused to be bound over and informed the court that he did not recognise the English government in Ireland. This treasonous talk resulted in a sentence of three months.

Meanwhile, a group of strikers gathered at Ringsend's Shelbourne Football Club. Shelbourne were about to play against Bohemians, a famous Dublin club who Larkin said had 'scabs' amongst their players. As the Bohemian fans entered the stadium they jeered the strikers, who were then joined by numerous sympathetic locals. Small scuffles broke out and before long a few trams in the area, driven by 'blacklegs', were attacked. When the DMP intervened, a full-scale riot ensued. There was much cheering when 'Inspector Chase of the mounted police was unhorsed by an ex-cavalry man who seized him by the stirrup and hoisted him up so that he lost his balance and fell. A big striker grabbed his sword and wielded it with great effect, clearing a space round him.'[7] The trouble stretched from Ringsend Bridge all the way up Great Brunswick Street and lasted over the course of the afternoon.[8] Battered and bruised, the crowds gathered at Liberty Hall, in the hope of gaining some leadership or direction, but Larkin was in Rathmines hiding out in Countess Markievicz's home, Surrey House, and Connolly was in a cell.

PT Daly tried in vain to get the agitated crowd to go home or at least leave Beresford Row. A DMP inspector attempted to arrest a man who was about to throw a stone. Missiles began to rain down on the police and when reinforcements arrived they charged full force into the strikers. Many of the police had drink taken and in a repeat of the previous night began to batter the unprotected heads of men, women and children.[9] The police attacks were relentless and scores of citizens were injured. Sean O'Casey attributed his conversion to Irish Republicanism to the police batons of constables 33B and 188B that Saturday night.[10]

On Eden Quay, James Nolan, a member of the Transport Union, was so badly beaten that he died of his injuries the following day. James Byrne, a labourer, was brutally clubbed by a gang of policemen on the opposite side of the Liffey, Burgh Quay. Byrne died a few days later; Dublin had unfortunately gained its first two Labour martyrs.

Eventually the bulk of the crowds were dispersed towards Montgomery Street.[11] But this was a tough working-class district, where many residents relished the chance to return some of the compliments that the police had paid them over the years. Perhaps for the first time in this area of Dublin, the citizens won a small victory over the crown forces. The DMP effectively retreated under a hail of bottles, sticks, stones and lumps of coal from Corporation Buildings on Corporation Street.[12]

On Sunday, after all the trouble on the streets, all eyes were on Larkin. Would he risk capture and further street disturbances to honour his pledge to speak on O'Connell Street? Fully cognisant of the DMP's eagerness to arrest him, Larkin was in the Abbey Theatre, assuming a new but temporary persona. Sporting Count Casimir Markievicz's frock coat, silk top hat and a rather ad-hoc beard fashioned by Helena Molony, the union leader began to resemble one of Dublin's employers.[13] Larkin had earlier booked a first-floor suite under a false name and now disguised and ably assisted by his 'niece' Nellie Gifford, he waltzed past the DMP into the Imperial Hotel, opposite the GPO, taking no small pleasure in the irony that William Martin Murphy owned the establishment.[14]

As soon as a bellowing figure appeared in the window of the Imperial the DMP wasted no time in arresting him. Cries of 'It's Larkin' drew the strikers and the ordinary citizens towards the door of the hotel. Larkin was manhandled out onto the street and Countess Markievicz ran to shake his hand. She received a policeman's fist into her face for her trouble. She was not the only person under attack, for the police came from every corner and wielded their batons with deadly accuracy, having spent the previous couple of days in practice. There was pandemonium on O'Connell Street and although the attack lasted for only ten minutes the three hundred policemen involved ensured many hundreds of people were badly injured. Amongst others, Countess Markievicz's recollections provide a clear picture of the events on Dublin's main thoroughfare:

> I saw a woman trying to get out of the way. She was struck from behind on the head by a policeman with his baton. As she fell her hat slipped over her face and I saw her hair was grey … I saw a barefooted boy with papers hunted and hit about the shoulders as he ran away. I shall never forget the look on his face as he turned when he was struck …
> I noticed that the policeman who struck me, smelt very strongly of stout, and that they all seemed very excited. They appeared to be arranged in a hollow square and to be gradually driving the people into the street, and then closing in on them and batoning them.[15]

The DMP spent the remainder of the day indiscriminately attacking citizens. For instance, they charged into Amiens Street Station and assaulted passengers who were innocently awaiting their train.[16] A large body of police headed for Corporation Buildings to seek revenge for the previous night's humiliating defeat, breaking windows, bursting into people's flats, smashing every stick of furniture and beating everyone who did not manage to escape. One unfortunate resident, John McDonagh, who was paralysed, was so severely beaten in his bed that he subsequently died in hospital. The day was quickly named Bloody Sunday by those who were on the receiving end of the batons.[17]

Tom Clarke, tobacconist and IRB activist, wrote a letter of protest to the papers. He declared that he had personally witnessed much brutality during his life yet nothing he knew of could 'match the downright inhuman savagery that was witnessed recently in the streets and some of the homes of our city when the police were let loose to run amok and indiscriminately bludgeon every man, woman and child they came across, in many cases kicking them on the ground after felling them with the baton.'[18]

Little wonder the police treated the citizens with such a lack of respect when one considers that the *Irish Catholic* referred to the workers as 'all the foul reserves of the slums, human beings whom life in the most darksome depths of a great city has deprived of most of the characteristics of civilisation.' It may come as no surprise to learn that William Martin Murphy also owned the *Irish Catholic*.

When the dust settled and Dubliners began to assess the weekend of violence, Murphy held a meeting of the Employers' Federation and, as Connolly put it, '... strung together in bonds of gold and self-interest … laid their plans with the wisdom of the serpent, and the unscrupulousness of the father of evil.'[19] Part of Murphy's plan was that employers should insist that all employees sign the following declaration:

> I hereby undertake to carry out all instructions given me by or on behalf of my employers, and further I agree to immediately resign my membership of the Irish Transport and General Workers' Union (if a member) and I further undertake that I will not join or in any way support this union.

The four hundred main employers, some of whom were normally reasonable characters, were shaken by the terror of the civil disobedience over the weekend and rushed to implement Murphy's idea. Those employees who refused to sign the undertaking were locked out.

Meanwhile, James Connolly was in Mountjoy Jail while all the action was going on outside. On 7 September, taking inspiration from the Women's Suffrage Movement, he refused to take food, thus becoming one of Ireland's first political hunger strikers. It also transpired that Magistrate Swifte, who had sentenced Connolly and proclaimed Larkin's meeting, was hardly what one might call impartial as he held a large number of shares in the Dublin United Tramways Company. A week into the hunger strike, a deputation led by the pacifist Francis Sheehy Skeffington went to the Lord Lieutenant, Aberdeen, to appeal for clemency in Connolly's case. Later that day, a messenger arrived at Eamon Martin's home where Lillie and the Connolly children were lodging. The message contained a direct order for the release of the hunger striker. They brought the letter to Mountjoy Jail, and an extremely weak Connolly was taken to Surrey House, where he recuperated under the care of Constance Markievicz. A few days later, he made his way home; his daughter recalled the excitement:

> We were expecting father to arrive in Belfast on Thursday. What a wonderful reception he got! The dockers all turned out to a man and all the mill girls in their shawls. The Fianna boys and girls were there in strength. The railway gates were closed, nobody was allowed inside. I managed to squeeze my way through as someone was getting his ticket punched. The train came in. There was a roar of greeting and a shout of song. Someone started singing: 'For he's a jolly good fellow.' The whole place rang with the chorus. The band played and through the struggling throng we managed to get father to the entrance of the station and he was put on a sidecar with myself beside him and Mother on the other side. The crowd swelling bigger than ever cheered and stood and called for 'Speech! Speech!' We drove through the city towards the famous steps of the Custom House. The crowd, grown to a great size, would not move, but kept on demanding a speech, not realising what the poor man was going through.

He seemed fatigued after the journey. It was only a few days since his release and the crowd was so overjoyed at his victory that they had forgotten the circumstances in which he achieved it. As they continued calling for a speech he turned to me and said: 'I think the best thing for you to do, Ina, is to stand up on the seat and thank them for the glorious welcome they have given me. It's far more than I ever expected or deserved. Tell them I am too weak tonight to thank them, but I will do so in a day or two. Advise them to go home quietly and not give the authorities any excuse to show their bad manners here tonight.' I was a very proud girl delivering that short speech by my father's side to a very responsive and enthusiastic audience.

As they dispersed, we drove home quietly, at least we thought it would be quietly; but, to our surprise, on the Falls Road we were met by bonfires outside our own home which was at the top of the Falls Road. In the space outside the City Cemetery the biggest bonfire of all was flaming.[20]

The women of Dublin also refused to bow down to the demands of the Employers' Federation. They were not being directly targeted by Murphy but defiantly rejected the proposal to get them to sign the pledge against the ITGWU. Connolly urged men who might shirk the fight to think of the women.

Did they care to evade the issue, they might have remained

at work, for the first part of the agreement asks them to merely repudiate the Irish Transport and General Workers' Union, and as women they are members of the Irish Women Workers' Union, not of the Irish Transport and General Workers' Union. But the second part pledges them to refuse to 'help' the Irish Transport and General Workers' Union – and in every shop, factory and sweating hell-hole in Dublin, as the agreement is presented, they march out with pinched faces, threadbare clothes, and miserable footgear, but with high hopes, undaunted spirit, and glorious resolve shining out of their eyes. Happy the men who will secure such wives; thrice blessed the nation which has such girls as the future mothers of the race! Ah, comrades, it is good to have lived in Dublin in these days![21]

On 7 October 1913, George (AE) Russell (1867−1935), the writer, artist and promoter of the co−operative movement, wrote an open letter to the employers in the *Irish Times*. It was a dire warning to the 'aristocracy of industry' that they would suffer the fate of the landed aristocracy who were 'already becoming a memory'. The letter provides some insight into how the intellectual literati viewed the Lockout.

You have allowed the poor to be herded together, so that one thinks of certain places in Dublin as of a pestilence. There are twenty thousand rooms, in each of which live entire families, and sometimes more, where no functions of the body can be concealed and delicacy and modesty are creatures that are stifled ere they are born. The obvious duty of you in regard to these things you might have left undone, and it would be imputed to ignorance or forgetfulness; but your collective and conscious action as a class in the present labour dispute, has revealed you to the world in so malign an aspect that the mirror must be held up to you, so that you may see yourselves as every humane person sees you.

... You determined deliberately in cold anger, to starve out one-third of the population of this city, to break the manhood of the men by the sight of the suffering of their wives and the hunger of their children ... You reminded Labour you could always have your three meals a day while it went hungry.

You may succeed in your policy and ensure your own damnation by your victory. The men whose manhood you have broken will loathe you, and will always be brooding and scheming to strike a fresh blow. The children will be taught to curse you. The infant being moulded in the womb will have breathed into its starved body the vitality of hate. It is not they – it is you who are blind Samsons pulling down the pillars of the social order. You are sounding the death-knell of autocracy in industry. There was autocracy in political life, and it was superseded by democracy. So surely will democratic power wrest from you the control of industry. The fate of you, the aristocracy of industry, will be as the fate of the aristocracy of land, if you do not show that you have some humanity still among you. Humanity abhors, above all things, a vacuum in itself, and your class will be cut off from humanity as the surgeon cuts the cancer and the alien growth from the body. Be warned ere it is too late.

Yours, A.E.

'Scabs', or 'Free Labourers' as the employers called them, a small number who were from Dublin with others from rural Ireland, and many from England, were not long in appearing on the scene. Connolly was quick to denounce them in the pages of the *Irish Worker*:

During the progress of the present dispute we have seen imported into Dublin some of the lowest elements from the very dregs of the Criminal population of Great Britain and Ireland. This scum of the underworld have come here excited by appeals to the vilest instincts of their natures; these appeals being framed and made by the gentlemen employers of Dublin.[22]

Not only did they receive the protection of the DMP but some of them openly carried weapons, including revolvers. In December 1913, a sixteen year-old girl, Alice Brady, was shot by a scab labourer whom she was jeering. She died two weeks later, her funeral being a massive show of support for the locked-out workers. Alice had been a member of the

Irish Women Workers' Union.[23] Larkin gave the funeral oration and Connolly followed with a brief statement:

> Every scab and every employer of scab labour in Dublin is morally responsible for the death of the young girl we have just buried.[24]

Even today, in Dublin, one of the worst insults that can be hurled is to call someone a 'scab'. The word was in the vernacular but really gained popularity during the Lockout and its meaning has expanded over the years to describe mean people, skinflints, borrowers, or indeed it can also be used as a verb to describe a form of sneaky pilfering. One striker in 1913, up on a charge of 'using language of an intimidatory nature', was defended by his solicitor who explained to the judge that the word 'scab' is 'being used by the children on the street just now; if a boy takes another's top he is called a scab!'[25]

An idea to alleviate the suffering of the children was devised by three women: Lucille Rand, whose father, Henry Gage, was a former governor of California and American ambassador to Portugal; Grace Neal, organiser of the Domestic Workers' Union in England; and Dora Montefiore, feminist, socialist and suffrage activist. Dora first proposed the idea of fostering the Dublin children to English families during a public meeting about the Lockout in Memorial Hall in London, at which Larkin had spoken about the hunger in

Dublin.[26] It was resolved to send some of the children of the strikers away to be fed and clothed in sympathetic houses in England and Scotland for the duration of the strike. It may appear anachronistic now, but the archbishop of Dublin, William Walsh, denounced the practice as it was a danger to the children's faith. Walsh was clearly of the opinion that it was better to go hungry than be fed by Protestants. The same man was at the receiving end of James Joyce's acerbic wit in his wonderful poem 'Gas From A Burner' written in 1912:

> *For everyone knows the Pope can't belch*
> *Without the consent of Billy Walsh.*[27]

Inevitably, riots ensued on the docks, led by priests and members of the Hibernians, oftentimes resulting in the departing children (whose souls the priests were attempting to save) being injured in the trouble. Connolly, as a father to a large family himself, saw the dilemma faced by the workers regarding the 'evacuation' of their offspring.

Nobody wants to send the children away – the Irish Transport and General Workers' Union least of all desires such a sacrifice. But neither do we wish the children to starve. We love the children of Ireland, we are sacrificing our own ease and comfort in order that the future of these children may be sweeter and happier than the lot of their fathers and mothers. We know that progress cannot be made without sacrifice, and we do not shrink from the sacrifice involved in fighting for freedom now in order that future generations may build upon the results of our toil. But the master class of Dublin calmly and coldbloodedly calculate upon using the sufferings of the children to weaken the resistance of the parents. They wish to place us upon the horns of a dilemma. Either the parents should resist, and then the children will starve, or the parents will surrender, and the children will grow up in slavery, and live to despise the parents who bequeathed to them such an evil heritage.[28]

Eventually, the scheme had to be abandoned as it was one thing fighting the capitalists but another thing altogether to attempt to take on the Catholic Church and the media, who were quick to denounce Rand and Montefiore as 'child exporters'. The departure of these 'London Ladies' back home was heralded as a 'Splendid Victory of Catholics of Dublin'.[29] Larkin admitted later that the scheme was 'the finest tactical error ever made in the workers' fight'.

As the employers were only too willing to starve the strikers and their families into submission, assistance in the guise of food ships came from the Trade Union Congress in England. In fact, the British TUC had pledged at the outbreak of hostilities to supply food for the duration of the strike.[30] It is estimated that the British workers raised a sum just short of £100,000 for consumables. Nonetheless, these food shipments were not welcomed by the more militant strikers, who felt that their working comrades in England might have done better to come out on strike in sympathy with the Irish as some of the railwaymen in Birmingham, Manchester and Liverpool had done. The concept of one big union was not shared by the British TUC; rather, a charitable donation to their Irish counterparts seemed a more fitting gesture. Dubliners are proud people and do not always respond well to hand-outs, but perhaps one of the most enduring images from this period is the introduction of the communal kitchen to feed the hungry. Liberty Hall was used daily to distribute bread and meals. The organiser of the Irish Women Workers' Union, Delia Larkin, the sister of 'Big' Jim Larkin, and Constance Markievicz had the enormous responsibility of ensuring a steady supply of food. Markievicz not only gave her energy but also took out loans to buy food when funds were low.

Reminiscing on the reasons for the formation of the Irish Citizen Army, Frank Robbins, who joined the ICA and wrote a memoir of his time with them, maintained that it was founded to protect 'the lowly paid and despised workers' who were 'murdered, imprisoned and brutally beaten by the armed forces of the British Crown.'[31] The story of exactly *who* founded this strikers' defence force is a little more difficult to piece together, as precise dates and key figures are blurred through selective memory and politics. It seems James Connolly was initially approached by Captain Jack White with the idea of forming the workers into an army. White does not blend too well into this period. In fact, his autobiography, *Misfit*, could not have been better titled. He was the son of a unionist who was a former governor of Gibraltar and was also a decorated ex-member of the British army who had fought with distinction in the Boer War. But despite his background, White swung to the cause of socialism. Later on, he joined the Irish Volunteers, turned to anarchism in the Thirties and fought in the Spanish Civil War. In order to do his memory some justice, he deserves to be remembered as one of the key founders of the ICA.

Robbins, who became a member of the ICA, recalled that one night during October 1913 he heard Connolly speaking from a window in Liberty Hall saying 'it was intended to organise and discipline a force to protect workers' meetings.'[32] For certain, on 13 November 1913, Connolly spoke at Liberty Hall to thousands of strikers who were there for a victory parade to celebrate Larkin's release from prison that morning. 'I am going to talk sedition,' said Connolly. 'The next time we are out for a march, I want to be accompanied by four battalions of our own men … When you draw your strike pay this week I want every man who is willing to enlist as a soldier to give his name and address, and you will be informed when and where you have to attend for training. I have been promised the assistance of competent chief officers, who will lead us anywhere. I say nothing about arms at present. When we want them, we know where we will find them.' Larkin was represented at this meeting by his wife Elizabeth. Her husband was weak from his time in jail and was also preparing to go to take a fundraising tour of England the next day.

Sean O'Casey's version of the birth of the ICA is largely fictitious and the following account, although wonderfully evocative, lacks supporting evidence. Consider if you will, when reading it, that this 'meeting' would have been held on Saturday, 22 November 1913, a night that Larkin was actually in England. Nearly every account of the birth of the ICA uses O'Casey's important book as it was written in 1919 while his memory was fresh, but it contains many inconsistencies. O'Casey sets the scene outside Liberty Hall as Larkin told the assembled workers that they 'knew to their cost that a few determined men, determined because they were imbued with the force of discipline, led by men whom they looked upon as their leaders, could scatter, like spray before the wind, the largest gatherings of men, who, untaught and loosely strung together, would always be dominated by the possibility of fear and panic.'[33] Larkin announced that if 'Carson had permission to train his braves of the North to fight against the aspirations of the Irish people, then it was legitimate and fair for Labour to organise in the same militant way to preserve their rights and to ensure that if they were attacked they would be able to give a very satisfactory account of themselves.'[34] Then the figure of Jack White appeared who 'told them that work would commence immediately … He told them to attend the very next day at Croydon Park, Fairview.'[35] He asked all those who intended to second their efforts by joining the army, and training themselves for the fight for Social liberty, to hold up their hands.' O'Casey wrote that almost 'every hand was silhouetted out against the darkening sky, and a last long deafening cheer proclaimed the birth of the Irish Citizen Army.'[36] O'Casey's blanket refusal to acknowledge James Connolly's role as a co-founder of the Citizen Army can only be attributed to his personal dislike for the labour leader.

A couple of years later, Connolly, writing in the *Workers' Republic*, recalled the events surrounding the establishment of the workers' defence force:

> Three men had been killed, and one young Irish girl murdered by a scab, and nothing was done to bring the assassins to justice. So since justice did not exist for us, since the law instead of protecting the rights of the workers was an open enemy, and since the armed forces of the Crown were unreservedly at the disposal of the enemies of labour, it was resolved to create our own army to secure our rights, to protect our members, and to be a guarantee of our own free progress.[37]

Later Connolly claimed in *Forward* that the 'writer of these notes established a Citizen Army at Dublin in connection with the Irish Transport & General Workers' Union …'[38]

The army first mustered in Croydon Park, in Fairview on the northside of Dublin, on Sunday, 23 November 1913, where White did his best to organise about forty hungry, bedraggled and undisciplined men. They had no uniforms, no guns and no ammunition. All they really had at this early stage was courage and a few hurleys, but that would prove to be sufficient to keep the 'uniformed bullies of the British Government' at bay.[39]

Nora Connolly remembered one day in Croydon Park as she watched the new army at drill: 'And here were its members, marching now to the right, now to the left, at the command of Captain White. He was tireless in the work of drilling them, and the men responded as tirelessly.' She recalled that herself and Connolly watched the proceedings but 'every now and then they would glance at each other and share an understanding smile at an unspoken thought.'[40]

By early January of 1914 rumour abounded that there was little strike pay left in the union coffers and that the food shipments from the TUC in England were about to cease. This left the ITGWU in the unenviable position of having to negotiate terms with employers who knew how desperate the strikers were. On 18 January Larkin addressed an assembly in Croydon Park and told them to return to work and to negotiate the best possible terms.

There are three main reasons why the Lockout ended.

Firstly, even wealthy capitalists have a finite reserve of money. Bit by bit some employees managed to force some concessions out of their more benign bosses, who turned a blind eye to actual union membership in exchange for an assurance that they did not support the ITGWU. This also had a knock-on effect; as some businesses began to operate normally, others began to follow suit. Secondly, the hunger and depravity that existed in Dublin during that period was beyond the limits of endurance even for the most ardent supporters of the unions. No parent can stand to see their offspring go without food. The third reason behind the ending of the Lockout was the refusal of the British TUC to sanction and implement the sympathetic strike policy. The employers were not blind to the lack of assistance from the British unions and thus held out until the workers were forced to agree to deny their union.

We are left in no doubt as to where Connolly lay the blame, having 'asked for the isolation of the capitalists of Dublin, and for answer the leaders of the British labour movement proceeded calmly to isolate the working class of Dublin … And so we Irish workers must go down into Hell, bow our backs to the lash of the slave driver, let our hearts be seared by the iron of his hatred, and instead of the sacramental wafer of brotherhood and common sacrifice, eat the dust of defeat and betrayal … Dublin is isolated.'[41]

Even the *Irish Times* saw 'the miserable part which the

English trade union leaders have played in this weary dispute. We do not often enjoy the pleasure of being able to agree with Mr. Larkin, but there is considerable ground for his charge that these English leaders "betrayed" the Dublin strikers.'[42]

There were some harsh lessons to be learned. Perhaps they had underestimated the greed of the capitalists.

> As the tiger reared upon flesh can never lose his craving for that food, so the Dublin employer reared as employer upon the flesh and blood of cheap labour can never wholly relinquish, and in most cases cannot even partially relinquish, his lust after cheapness in the labour he exploits.[43]

On the other hand, it was not a clear victory for the employers. Connolly called it a draw. There were gains for the labour movement and indeed for the Irish nation as a whole. Connolly saw a new sense of strength, unity and camaraderie that had not existed in Dublin beforehand.

> Trade unionists, socialists of all kinds, anarchists, industrialists, syndicalists, all the varying and hitherto discordant elements of the labour movement found a common platform, were joined together in pursuit of a common object.[44]

The ITGWU was not defeated. It was almost financially bankrupt but was not crushed. Indeed it still exists today as Ireland's largest union, albeit under a new name, SIPTU,

**Left:** General Sir John Grenfell Maxwell GCB, KCMG, CVO, DSO, PC, sporting all his medals and honours. Maxwell instigated the court martial that resulted in the executions of the leaders of the Easter Rising.

**Below:** Wounded rebels under guard in Dublin Castle. James Connolly was held for twelve days in the temporary hospital in Dublin Castle after the Rising.

Scenes in Dublin after the Rebellion
Wounded Rebels in a Temporary Hospital in Dublin Castle, with Armed Sentries on Guard and a Priest in attendance

**Left:** Maxwell inspecting troops in the aftermath of the Rising.

**Above:** O'Donovan Rossa funeral committee, 1915.

**Below:** Members of the Dublin Metropolitan Police, waiting in reserve on a side street, Windsor Avenue, in case of a clash with strikers who were on a protest march during the 1913 Lockout.

**Above:** Volunteers and ICA in GPO during the 1916 Rising. Left to right: Desmond O'Reilly, James Mooney, Paddy Byrne, John Doyle, Tom McGrath, Hugh Thornton, John J Twamly and young Bernard Frick. Joseph Cripps took the photo. Thornton and Twamley were in the ICA.

**Below:** ICA with rifles standing in a line on Liberty Hall roof. Their uniforms were purchased wholesale in Arnotts and Captain Jack White chose to fit out the army with the 'cronje' slouch hat popularised during the Boer War. Left to right: Captain Joseph Byrne, Sergeant Christopher Poole, Philip Lacey and Patrick Fox.

**Above:** Burned-out tram used as a barricade on the corner of North Earl Street and Sackville Street.

**Below:** Ruins of the GPO; note the light pouring in through the roofless building.

**Above:** The devastation inside the GPO (with man on ladder).
**Below:** William Martin Murphy's Imperial Hotel in ruins opposite the GPO.

**Above:** Ruined buildings on Lower Sackville Street. John Gray's statue is visible.

**Below:** Liberty Hall, displaying banner with message, 'WE SERVE NEITHER KING NOR KAISER BUT IRELAND', in late 1914.

**Above:** A year after the Rising, a new banner unfurled at Liberty Hall, proclaiming 'James Connolly Murdered May 12th 1916'.

**Below:** A room in Liberty Hall, ransacked by British soldiers when the Rising was over.

Z.

O'Farrell Colonel
President of G.C.M

I do not wish to make any defence except against charges of wanton cruelty to prisoners. These trifling allegations that have been made in that direction if they record facts that really happened deal only with the almost unavoidable incidents of a hurried uprising, and overthrowing of long established authorities, and nowhere show evidence of a set purpose to wantonly injure unarmed prisoners.

We went out to break the connection between this country and the British Empire and to establish an Irish Republic. We believed that the call we thus issued to the people of Ireland was a nobler call in a holier cause than any call issued to them during this war having any connection with the war

---

Connolly's last statement at the court martial, as recorded by the British in the trial file. He smuggled a copy to his daughter, Nora, when she went to bid him farewell before his execution.

and Liberty Hall, which was for a long time Dublin's tallest building, still stands in proud memory of the struggle that began there.[45]

As the Lockout was essentially over, membership of the ICA began to dwindle, so on 22 March 1914 a meeting was held in Liberty Hall to decide the future of the army. Rather than disband it, the essential idea was to reorganise the army and make it a permanent revolutionary force. O'Casey drafted a constitution and then presented it to the committee, which included James Connolly, Countess Markievicz, PT Daly and William Partridge, the Labour councillor, ITGWU official and ICA activist. While O'Casey acted as secretary, it is interesting to note that Captain White presided over the meeting as opposed to Connolly. In fact, O'Casey noted that on the 'motion of Jim Connolly … it was unanimously decided to hold a public meeting … and to ask Jim Larkin to preside … as it was felt by all that the chief of the Labour movement should know all that was recommended.'[46]

The agreed Constitution was as follows:

Article One: The first and last principle of the Irish Citizen Army is the avowal that the ownership of Ireland, moral and material, is vested of right in the people of Ireland.

Article Two: That its principal objects should be:

(a) To arm and train all Irishmen capable of bearing arms to enforce and defend its first principle, and

(b) To sink all differences of birth, privilege and creed under the common name of the Irish people.

Article Three: The Irish Citizen Army shall stand for the absolute unity of Irish nationhood, and recognition of the rights and liberties of the democracies of all nations.

Article Four: That the Citizen Army shall be open to all who are prepared to accept the principles of equal rights and opportunities for the People of Ireland and to work in harmony with organized labour towards that end.

At Larkin's suggestion an fifth article was added, to suggest that every enrolled member must be, if possible, a member of a trade union recognised by the Irish Trades Union Congress.

Sean O'Casey remembered the reinvigorated ICA of 1914:

Two splendid companies of picked men were formed as the nucleus of the City Battalion. Captain White gave an order to Messrs. Arnott for fifty uniforms of dark green serge, and the men eagerly awaited their arrival. For the time being the rank and file wore on their left arms broad bands of Irish linen of a light blue colour, and the officers a band of crimson on their right arm.[47]

By the time they got their uniforms, the Citizen Army were a tight-knit, well trained and dapper force. Their famous slouched hats, worn in the same style as the Boers, with one side pinned up by the Red Hand union badge, marked them out as they paraded the streets.

The flag of the Irish Citizen Army, blue and gold, was known as the 'Starry Plough'. The seven gold stars on the flag represent The Plough, the seven brightest stars in the constellation Ursa Major. Of course the star is a shape that tends to represent left-wing ideology and is often found on the flags of socialist countries. The plough shape perfectly represents the dignity of physical labour. O'Casey interpreted it as follows:

> There it was – the most beautiful flag among the flags of the world's nations: a rich, deep poplin field of blue; across its whole length and breadth stretched the formalized shape of a plough, a golden-brown colour, seamed with a rusty red, while through all glittered the gorgeous group of stars enriching and ennobling the northern skies.

It seems that Billy Megahy, a Galway art teacher, 'sketched a realistic pattern, and from this the Dun Emer Guild wove' the Starry Plough.[48] 'The tallest man in the army was selected as banner-bearer, and he was always proud of his work, though the carrying of the flag, which was of large dimensions, was no easy task, particularly upon a breezy day.'[49]

The motto of the Irish Citizen Army was simple and straightforward: 'That the entire ownership of Ireland – moral and material – is vested of right in the entire people of Ireland.' On the back of the membership cards the words of John Mitchel, a leading figure in the Young Ireland insurrection of 1848, were printed:

> The Land and Sea and Air of Ireland for the People of Ireland. That is the gospel the heavens and earth are proclaiming; and that is the gospel every Irish heart is secretly burning to embrace.

For James Connolly, the 1913–14 Lockout was a personal victory, as the prize was the conversion of Dublin.

> There are times in history when we realise that it is easier to convert a multitude than it ordinarily is to convert an individual; when indeed ideas seem to seize upon the masses as contra-distinguished by ordinary times when individuals slowly seize ideas. The propagandist toils on for decades in seeming failure and ignominy, when suddenly some great event takes place in accord with the principles he has been advocating, and immediately he finds that the seed he has been sowing is springing up in plants that are covering the earth. To the idea of working class unity, to the seed of industrial solidarity, Dublin was the great event that enabled it to seize the minds of the masses, the germinating force that gave power to the seed to fructify and cover these islands.[50]

Connolly was now well known and more popular than he had been at the turn of the century. He had come to the attention of the IRB as a man of principle and strength. When Larkin decided to go to America and attempted to leave PT Daly in charge, he was compelled to give Connolly the job of acting general secretary of the ITGWU. More importantly, Connolly was left in command of the Irish Citizen Army.

## Chapter Twelve

# 1914

# The World at War

*... Ireland may yet set the torch to a European conflagration that will not burn out until the last throne and the last capitalist bond and debenture will be shrivelled on the funeral pyre of the last war lord.*[1]

**W**ynn's Hotel on Abbey Street, Dublin, was the venue chosen by a number of individuals for a historic meeting on 11 November 1913. The purpose of the conference was to discuss the possible foundation of a militia similar to the Ulster Volunteer Force, but with a nationalist outlook. Eoin MacNeill, one of the founding members of The Gaelic League, had written an encouraging article in *An Claidheamh Soluis*, entitled 'The North Began'. This article caught the attention of the Irish Republican Brotherhood leadership, conscious of the potential revolutionary possibilities of any proposed volunteer army. With this in mind, many of those present at the meeting were members of the Irish Republican Brotherhood, including Bulmer Hobson, James Deakin, Seán MacDiarmada, Piaras Beaslaí and Éamonn Ceannt.[2] Those in attendance at the meeting who were not members of the Brotherhood included Michael Joseph O'Rahilly, Col. Maurice Moore, Eoin MacNeill and Patrick Pearse (who would be sworn into the IRB later). A decision was made to hold a meeting in the Rotunda at the top of O'Connell Street on 25 November 1913. Despite the short notice, thousands of men and women packed into the Rotunda rooms. In fact, there were so many eager to join that hundreds spilled out onto the streets and into the Rotunda gardens. The net result of the evening was the recruitment of a couple of thousand men into the Irish Volunteers.

A detachment of the newly founded Irish Citizen Army was thrown out of the Rotunda. It was not for fear that the Irish Volunteers would be infiltrated by socialists; the reality of it was that these men were on strike and they objected to the presence of Laurence Kettle, as his family had locked out workers. The Citizen Army tried to shout Kettle down when he attempted to speak, which did not endear them to the majority and, despite being 'armed' with hurleys, they were sent packing. This initial distrust was fuelled by a certain section of the Volunteers and would escalate over the coming months to the extent that many halls that allowed Volunteers to train were closed to the ICA.

In March 1914 the British Prime Minister Asquith proposed that any county in Ireland which wished to opt out of Home Rule by a simple majority vote of the electors could do so. All of a sudden, majority rule no longer applied to the island as a whole; using a form of gerrymandering, democracy had been whittled down to local majorities. The Home Rule Bill, as amended, was to be a foregone conclusion; partition of Ireland was set to be the outcome. Connolly clearly stated his opinion on those advocating Home Rule in the *Irish Worker*:

> The recent proposals of Messrs. Asquith, Devlin and Redmond … reveal in a most striking and unmistakable manner the depths of betrayal to which so-called nationalist politicians are willing to sink …

In the Curragh Military Training Camp in County Kildare, where James Connolly had once been stationed as a young British soldier, a mutiny was afoot. British army officers resigned their commissions to protest their possible use against people loyal to the Crown. They were reinstated with the assurance that they would never be utilised to force Home Rule upon the Unionists. This avoided the potentially bizarre possibility that the UVF would have fought the British army in order to remain British if Home Rule were forced upon them.

Throughout the summer of 1914, Connolly found himself

again petitioning Larkin for money for the Belfast branch. In June he wrote:

Dear Jim,

In connection with our telephone conversation today I wish to remind you that our deficit on the Trade Union for the week ending 13 June was £16 1s. This included £6 12s. 3d. advanced to the Approved Society to pay claims. Of the £16 1s. – £13 is my own and £3 represents two maternity claims for which we had to borrow the money to pay them on Saturday, although I had asked for the sum over the 'phone to Dublin during the day. You will see, of course, that this state of matters is impossible.

I am entirely broke and running in debt. Of that £13 I may say that £6 represents some money I got last week as royalties on a book of mine and I had to use it to pay insurance to save the credit of the Society. I hope you will look into this matter and get this straightened out.[3]

Despite the tone of the letter, things had not improved much by the following month, when Connolly wrote to Larkin, complaining that there was no money to pay the rent on the insurance office:

We are at the end of our tether, and speaking quite quietly I am so sick of it all that I wish I was shut of it for good. The only thing that keeps me at my post is the fear that the

Orange element would say that they frightened me out of Belfast.[4]

Larkin, for many reasons, including broken health, despondency and need for rest, wanted to go to America. He told Connolly that he had been in touch with Bill Haywood, co-founder of the Industrial Workers of the World, concerning a possible tour of the USA. Connolly would clearly have expected to be in charge of the union if Larkin departed, but he was well aware of Larkin's importance for the cause of labour. Larkin tried to quit the Transport Union, but his resignation letter was ceremoniously burned and his comrades encouraged him to take a temporary rest by going to North America to recuperate. At the end of June 1914, Connolly wrote openly and sympathetically about how Larkin was 'broken down physically, run down mentally, and almost worn out. Hence he did not realise himself that what was needed was a rest ... If he were to go to America and raise funds for the new Irish Labour Party it would recuperate him, and he would be back in seven days if needed.'[5] Larkin received plenty of medical advice on his mental and physical health but, being Larkin, chose to ignore it.

Membership numbers for the Irish Volunteers were far more impressive than the few hundred that joined the ICA. By March 1914 there were 20,000 Irish Volunteers. The final reading of the Home Rule Bill was on 25 May 1914. That month saw the Volunteers membership rise to 50,000.

June saw that figure double to 100,000. On 26 July the Irish Volunteers landed a shipment of 900 rifles from a yacht at Howth, a small fishing village to the north of Dublin. The writer Erskine Childers, his wife Molly, and Mary Spring Rice had sailed *The Asgard* from Hamburg with the cargo of German Mausers. They were old as can be deduced by their full name, Mauser Model 1871 (as in made in 1871). That afternoon, angered by their failure to intercept the weapons landing, the King's Own Scottish Borderers let loose a burst of fire into a crowd of unarmed civilians on Dublin's Bachelor's Walk, killing three people. Their funerals were also a massive show of strength for the Volunteers and recruitment increased at a phenomenal rate. On 4 August 1914 war in Europe broke out. In September the Home Rule Bill received royal assent, but the Bill came with another Act suspending it for the duration of the war. By then there were 191,000 men in the Volunteers.

Redmond was in quite a fix over the Volunteers; if he was going to be the leader of Ireland under Home Rule, the last thing he needed was a private army over which he had no control. He pulled off a coup in June by demanding the right to nominate individuals of his choice to the committee. Of course, the IRB members objected to this, but in order to avoid a split in the movement Redmond's demands were acceded to.

Connolly's immediate reaction to the war was printed in

the *Irish Worker* on 8 August 1914:

Should a German army land in Ireland tomorrow we should be perfectly justified in joining it if by doing so we could rid this country once and for all from its connection with the Brigand Empire that drags us unwillingly into this war.

Should the working class of Europe, rather than slaughter each other for the benefit of kings and financiers, proceed tomorrow to erect barricades all over Europe, to break up bridges and destroy the transport service that war might be abolished, we should be perfectly justified in following such a glorious example and contributing our aid to the final dethronement of the vulture classes that rule and rob the world.

But pending either of these consummations it is our manifest duty to take all possible action to save the poor from the horrors this war has in store.

Let it be remembered that there is no natural scarcity of food in Ireland. Ireland is an agricultural country, and can normally feed all her people under any sane system of things. But prices are going up in England and hence there will be an immense demand for Irish produce. To meet that demand all nerves will be strained on this side, the food that ought to feed the people of Ireland will be sent out of Ireland in greater quantities than ever and famine prices will come in Ireland to be immediately followed by famine itself. Ireland will starve, or rather the townspeople of Ireland will starve, that the British army and navy and jingoes may be fed. Remember, the Irish farmer like all other farmers will benefit by the high prices of the war, but these high prices will mean starvation to the labourers in the towns. But without these labourers the farmers' produce cannot leave Ireland without the help of a garrison that England cannot now spare. We must consider at once whether it will not be our duty to refuse to allow agricultural produce to leave Ireland until provision is made for the Irish working class.

Let us not shrink from the consequences. This may mean more than a transport strike, it may mean armed battling in the streets to keep in this country the food for our people. But whatever it may mean it must not be shrunk from. It is the immediately feasible policy of the working-class democracy, the answer to all the weaklings who in this crisis of our country's history stand helpless and bewildered crying for guidance, when they are not hastening to betray her.[6]

William McMullen, Independent Labour Party activist and later general president of ITGWU, recalled the rampant jingoism that gathered in Belfast alongside the 'war clouds.' At one meeting, Connolly commenced without the expected chairman and was halfway through his anti-war speech when McMullen finally arrived.

The opposition was so strong that he was unable to make himself heard above the uproar. I relieved him for a spell when he took over again until the end of the meeting. He dismounted from the platform and literally bored his way through the dense hostile crowd out into Royal Avenue and proceeded on his way home to the Falls Road, followed by the angry crowd.[7]

Connolly was vehemently opposed to the war; he passionately exposed the conflict as the slaughter of the working class in Europe for the benefit of capitalists. The fight against conscription and the unmasking of the horrors of the war became his passions. His writings on the war, often considered as pro-German, were in fact a necessary and unflinching antidote to the jingoism of the media at the time, who were doing the bidding of the British army.

All these mountains of Irish dead, all these corpses mangled beyond recognition, all these arms, legs, eyes, ears, fingers, toes, hands, all these shivering putrefying bodies and portions of bodies – once warm living and tender parts of Irish men and youths – all these horrors buried in Flanders or the Gallipoli Peninsula, are all items in the price Ireland pays for being part of the British Empire. All these widows whose husbands were torn from their sides and forced to go to war, their prayers and tears for the ones who will return no more, are another part of the price of Empire. All those fatherless orphans, who for the last time have heard the cheery laugh of an affectionate father, and who must for years suffer all the bitter hardships of a childhood poorly provided for against want and hunger – all those and their misery are part of the price Ireland pays for Empire. All those shattered, maimed and diseased wrecks of humanity who for years will crowd our poorhouses and asylums, or crawl along our roads and streets affronting our health by their wounds, and our comfort by their appeals for charity – all, all are part of the price Ireland pays for the glory of being an integral part of the British Empire.[8]

Connolly predicted the real cost to the Irish homes where family members had joined the British army and headed off to fight:

Each day one of these homes, some days thousands of these homes will be stricken from the field of battle, and news will come home that this young son or that loving father has met his doom, and out there under a foreign sky the mangled remains, twisted, blown and gashed by inconceivable wounds will lie, each of them in all their ghastly horror crying out to Heaven for vengeance upon the political tricksters who lured them to their fate.[9]

His ideas are just as relevant today:

War is ever the enemy of progress ... The poor of the world

would be well advised, upon the declaration of war in any country, as their first steps to peace, to hang the Foreign Minister and Cabinet whose secret diplomacy produced such a result. If each country hanged its own Foreign Minister and Cabinet before setting out to the front, wars would not last long; and if a jingo editor were hanged each week it lasted, the most jingo being first to hang, not many angry passions would be stirred up to make the work of peaceful understanding difficult.[10]

In Woodenbridge, County Wicklow, on 20 September 1914, John Redmond made a speech encouraging Irishmen to go 'wherever the firing line extends, in defence of right, of freedom and religion in this war'. Now that Redmond had become a recruiting sergeant for the British army, the Volunteers were forced to split; over 90 per cent became the National Volunteers, or the Redmondites, and trooped off to the trenches. The remaining numbers, loyal to their chief-of-staff Eoin MacNeill, were really effectively under the control of the IRB. Those Irish Volunteers now had more in common politically with the ICA; a new sense of cordiality began to emerge. They even began to fraternise with each other. Frank Robbins, who fought in St Stephen's Green in 1916, recalled in his memoirs that, along with some of the more enthusiastic members of the ICA, he busied himself 'in perfecting a large rifle range in Croydon Park' which 'when completed, attracted a good many of the Irish

Volunteers' who practised alongside them on Saturdays and Sundays. They even constructed a miniature rifle range in a large room in Liberty Hall for use during the winter months 'by those who could afford the charge of three shots per penny'.[11]

A conference was arranged by Éamonn Ceannt to be held in the library of the Gaelic League at 25 Parnell Square on 9 September 1914. Tom Clarke, Seán MacDiarmada, Joseph Plunkett, Patrick Pearse and Thomas MacDonagh were in attendance. Also present at the meeting were Connolly, William O'Brien, Seán T O'Kelly, John MacBride and Arthur Griffith. Griffith and O'Brien were the only men at that historic meeting who would not take part in the 1916 Rising. It appears that the main topic of discussion revolved around striking a blow against the British while they were at war; England's difficulty being Ireland's opportunity. An IRB decision was made to seek assistance in the form of weapons; secret plans were made to send Roger Casement to Germany for this very purpose.

Another consequence of the meeting was the formation of the Irish Neutrality League, for which Connolly acted as President of the Provisional Committee. He was joined by a number of others, including William O'Brien, Countess Markievicz, Francis Sheehy Skeffington, Arthur Griffith, and Seán T O'Kelly. Aiming to keep Ireland neutral in what they considered an English war, they organised a number of lectures and produced a pamphlet or two, but as a pressure group it imploded very quickly. O'Brien said it was an 'organisation of leaders without members'.[12]

In early October 1914, Larkin confirmed his decision to travel to America. The union leader asked Connolly to come down from Belfast and take charge of the *Irish Worker* and the Approved Society (or insurance section) of the ITGWU. Larkin planned that PT Daly would take charge of the union. Connolly explained to O'Brien that 'such an arrangement would be unbearable and unworkable. For one thing, we could never hope to maintain an understanding with the nationalists if Daly was in command of the Transport Union. They would not trust him, have him, or co-operate with him, and the Transport Union would become a mere dues-collecting Union if a man with the character of Daly for evading difficulties was in charge.'[13] The general president of the union, Thomas Foran, supported Connolly for the role of acting general secretary; in fact, very few supported Larkin's desire to appoint Daly.

Finally, on 24 October 1914, when Larkin went to the US, Connolly left Belfast and came to Dublin on a more permanent basis. By stubbornly insisting on his position, he got his wish and became acting general secretary of the ITGWU and he would soon be commandant of the ICA. For a revolutionary such as Connolly, circumstances could not have worked out better. He began immediately to nail his colours to the mast and in of his more audacious stunts, draped a huge banner across Liberty Hall: 'We Serve Neither King nor Kaiser – but Ireland'. This was erected in October 1914 and was not removed by the 'authorities' until 19 December. This lack of action, considering the Defence of the Realm Act, under which it was an offence to print seditious material which might undermine the war effort, suggests that the British, officially at least, were hesitant to provoke trouble with the ICA and Connolly. Nonetheless, Connolly often suffered many personal attacks and physical threats from individuals in the British army. Frank Robbins remembered:

> It was not unusual for him to be subjected to vile and offensive language … There were several attempts to assault him, and on one occasion the would-be attackers were handled very roughly by members of the Irish Citizen Army. In order to overcome these annoyances it was decided to close the front door of Liberty Hall when Connolly was about to leave for home at night. He would then leave by a side gate in old Abbey Street.[14]

Countess Markievicz was presented with an illuminated address, a framed painted manuscript, in February 1915 for her 'unselfish and earnest labours … during the Great Dublin Lockout' and as a sign that the ITGWU members held her in high esteem and affection.[15] There was also a mutual affection between Markievicz and the Connolly family. Ina recalls:

> The Countess, on hearing I was out of work due to a septic hand, invited me down to Dublin. At the station I was met by one of the Fianna boys and Sir Roger Casement. Imagine the excitement and joy I felt at meeting such a wonderful man. How splendid he looked, kind, and gently he bowed and shook my hand, saying: "Is this the little northern warrior that is going to set Ulster ablaze? What is it that you want?" "An Irish Republic," I promptly replied. He looked at me seriously and in his quiet voice said: "I don't think that would satisfy your father." At once I realised I had omitted the word, "Workers."[16]

# Chapter Thirteen

• • • • • • • •

## 1915–1916

# The Re-Conquest of Ireland

*… only the Irish working class remain as the incorruptible inheritors of the fight for freedom in Ireland.*[1]

The first thing James Connolly did when he took charge of the Irish Citizen Army was to address the lack of discipline within the ranks. As a body of men, women and boys they would assemble at Liberty Hall, but could often take up to an hour to ready themselves for parade. Connolly remarked to them: 'I can always guarantee that the Irish Citizen Army will fight, but I cannot guarantee that they will be in time for such fight when it takes place.'[2] Captain Jack White had resigned his position and went over to the National Volunteers. Connolly appointed a new chief-of-staff, a man who had shown great leadership qualities during the 1913 silkweavers' strike, Michael Mallin. Having spent a total of twelve years with the British army in India, although mostly as a bandsman, Mallin was more than capable of instilling discipline within the ICA. Frank Robbins recalled in his memoirs, 'the laxity soon disappeared, as also did a number of ... the Citizen Army who, without the glamour of Larkin, had no use for the serious kind of work expected of them by Connolly and Mallin.'[3]

Mallin and his family lived in Emmet Hall, the premises of the Inchicore Branch of the ITGWU. The house was adjacent to Richmond Barracks, which provided, through judicious use of the party wall, much opportunity for the procurement of arms and ammunition. Con Colbert, who hailed from Limerick and was a dedicated Fianna scout and IRB activist, joined and helped train the Irish Volunteers, often using Emmet Hall for meetings. Colbert's section of the Volunteers would often engage in mock attacks against the Citizen Army. 'As well as being informative these exercises also proved to be very healthy and a lot of good fun. They also created firm comradeship with the Irish Volunteers.'[4]

*The Re-Conquest of Ireland* was published in 1915 to encourage the Irish to reclaim what was rightfully their own. Connolly explained in the foreword:

> The underlying idea of this work is that the Labour Movement of Ireland must set itself the Re-Conquest of Ireland as its final aim, that the re-conquest involves taking possession of the entire country, all its powers of wealth-production and

all its natural resources, and organising these on a co-operative basis for the good of all.[5]

In reality, this pamphlet was composed mainly of a collection of articles which Connolly had contributed, in the summer of 1912 to the *Irish Worker*. Now Connolly was no longer just a contributor to the *Irish Worker*; he was an editor again due to Larkin's departure in October 1914. He revamped the paper, put an end to the 'personal attack' journalistic style, and began including nationalist and revolutionary propaganda with plenty of ICA material. However, his editorship of the *Irish Worker* came to an abrupt halt after the issue of 5 December appeared with a large blank space, the printers being fearful that an editorial of Connolly's might lead to the seizure of their printing presses. Freedom of expression disappeared, as it tends to do during war, and the *Irish Worker*, *Sinn Féin* and *Irish Freedom* were all suppressed.

The blanked-out portion of the *Irish Worker* was released as a handbill under a slightly different name, *Irish Work*, and was printed in haste to avoid the censor; it was anti-recruitment propaganda designed to goad the apparently hesitant Irish Volunteers and to thwart the British:

> A resurrection! Aye, out of the grave of the first Irish man or woman murdered for protesting against Ireland's participation in this thrice-accursed war there will arise anew the Spirit of Irish Revolution ... If you strike at, imprison

or kill us, out of our prisons or graves we will still evoke a spirit that will thwart you, and, mayhap, raise a force that will destroy you. We defy you! Do your worst.[6]

Connolly was not to be beaten by the censor, and as no Irish printer would touch the contract, he made an arrangement during a visit to Glasgow to get the *Irish Worker* printed in Scotland instead. Under a slightly different name, the *Worker*, it was smuggled over to Dublin and was on the streets before the DMP could even react. But in February an entire issue was seized on a steamer – the police had discovered the origin of the newspaper and thus ended the ruse.

Matthew Nathan, the under-secretary for Ireland, prepared a list of seditious newspapers circulating in Ireland before the Rising, of which the *Workers' Republic* was one. The owner of the paper was listed as being Helena Molony of 70 Eccles Street. The editor was listed as James Connolly, 49B Leinster Road, ie Surrey House, the home of Constance Markievicz. Connolly had found an old run-down printing machine, and with a little oil and polish it was propped up on a few bricks in Liberty Hall. It spat out a reborn *Workers' Republic*, not seen on the streets of Dublin since 1903. Connolly was in the driving seat again, editing it for a full year from 29 May 1915, and even getting an issue out two days before the Easter Rising in April 1916.

The year 1915 was to be one of Connolly's busy years; he had to travel regularly to stay with his family in Belfast while he based himself in Dublin. In fact, he visited other towns as well, such as Sligo and Cork, encouraging workers to join the union. He was writing, organising and fighting a losing battle against the huge numbers that were joining the British army. At the end of May, the Phoenix Park Labour Day rally attracted a few thousand workers. Connolly avoided the usual substance of his speeches, being economic demands, and instead encouraged the workers to join the army, then he paused for effect before mentioning, 'The Citizen Army!' Another key event was held in Croydon Park in the middle of June; an Irish musical and athletic festival. The Gaelic League, the Fianna boys and all sectors of Irish nationalism engaged together in a celebration of all things Irish. There was a sense of cohesion between the various groups, also evident by the equal numbers of Citizen Army members and Irish Volunteers who formed the guard of honour at the annual Wolfe Tone pilgrimage in Bodenstown that summer.

At the beginning of April 1915, the weekly subscription to the union was increased to four pence per week. Connolly wrote 'the very large amounts payable in benefits make this necessary in order that the funds available for Trades Union purposes may be kept secure.'[7] Four pennies would have bought a pint of Guinness in 1915, so it is clear that this was a manageable amount for a worker to pay at the time. The truth was that when Larkin had left for the United States the ITGWU was close to financial ruin. The toll the

1913–14 Lockout had taken on Larkin's health had taken a similar toll on the health of the union.

Connolly, as acting general secretary, struggled with the finances. The union had called for another strike in the middle of June 1915, taking on the railway companies in a bid for better wages. The payment of strike pay was speedily depleting the resources of the ITGWU. Connolly wrote to his personal secretary, who was also the full-time secretary to the ITGWU in Belfast, Winifred Carney, and confessed that he felt 'all his boats were in danger of foundering'.[8] In fact, the financial position was so dire that the union had to relinquish the lease on that oasis of calm for the workers and the ICA, Croydon Park. Connolly managed to secure a loan of £40 from the Bricklayers' Union to cover strike pay for one week – this was the last of the funds and Connolly had to recommend a return to work, but luckily the employers caved in on the strikers' demands and increased wages by two shillings a week in August.

When the dock workers went on strike a couple of months later, Connolly enjoyed the irony that it was of great benefit to the training of the ICA.

A large section has been formed for drill, and every day the men are instructed in military exercises. We are thus rapidly becoming the best drilled body of men in Ireland. For a time it was difficult to get our men trained, as dock work keeps men employed always in the evenings, but the employers are kindly helping us to get over that difficulty. Company after company locks out its men, and then we bring them up to Liberty Hall and take advantage of the opportunity to drill and train them. When each dispute is settled that squad of men goes back to work, and some other squad gets locked out, and we get a chance to train them.

Thus the whole quay is getting drilled, and the Irish Citizen Army has a larger reserve of drilled fighting men than any force in Dublin. It is a great game! And all these men are ready to fight – in Ireland. Perhaps that is not what the employers are aiming at. Perhaps. But every musketry instructor can tell you that people often hit what they did not aim at. The great danger is that the dispute may be over before the men are thoroughly drilled. And when it is over the men will be back to work at the same rates of pay as their brothers have been conceded. And not a penny less.[9]

The legendary 'unrepentant Fenian', Jeremiah O'Donovan Rossa, exiled to America since 1871, passed away at the age of eighty-three at the end of June 1915.[10] Tom Clarke saw the potential for arousing Irish republican sentiment and immediately sent a telegram to John Devoy: 'SEND HIS BODY HOME AT ONCE.' Clarke then set about arranging the O'Donovan Rossa Committee – no one was better qualified to do so, as Tom Clarke was connected to the old Fenian movement, having spent fifteen years in English prisons. More importantly, he was also close to the younger generation and the more dedicated activists, including James Connolly. Kathleen Clarke noted that in 1914 her husband and Connolly 'became great friends, and kept friends to the end.'[11] As a mark of Clarke's respect for Labour, Connolly was included as a member of the Guards and Procession subcommittee. This ensured the ICA and the Volunteers would guard Rossa's remains and jointly form the guard of honour at his funeral. Other representatives from Labour included William O'Brien and the general secretary of the Brick and Stoneworkers' Union, Councillor Richard O'Carroll.

It is interesting to note that the Committee was mostly composed of men and women who would soon fight in the Easter Rising: Diarmuid Lynch, a member of the Supreme Council of the IRB who worked with Tom Clarke on the plans for the Easter Rising and who would act as a staff captain in the GPO in 1916; and Clarke's brother-in-law, Edward 'Ned' Daly, who would hold the Four Courts during Easter Week, joined with his sister Kathleen in organising the funeral. She accompanied Seán MacGádhra (McGarry) to Liverpool to meet Mrs O'Donovan Rossa when she arrived from America with her husband's remains. MacGádhra was to become a future president of the Supreme Council of the IRB and would later escape from Lincoln Jail in February 1919 with fellow committee member Éamon de Valera. A close comrade of theirs during the Tan War, who miraculously survived despite being shot to pieces during the Rising in the South Dublin Union, Cathal Brugha, was also a member of the Committee. Chief Marshal of the funeral was Thomas MacDonagh, who was to work very closely with Clarke on the plans for the procession to Glasnevin. The fact that Seán MacDiarmada was in prison for making a seditious anti-recruitment speech ruled him out. Three future Sinn Féin MPs, Constance Markievicz, Arthur Griffith and Joe McGuinness, sat on the Committee. Major John MacBride, who fought for the Boers in South Africa and was Tom Clarke's best man at his New York wedding in 1901, was also on board for the funeral.

Thousands of mourners gathered in Glasnevin Cemetery, on the first day of August 1915, to pay their respects to Rossa. They were also treated to the now-legendary graveside oration by Patrick Pearse, in which he clearly outlined the IRB's position:

> And while Ireland holds these graves, Ireland unfree shall never be at peace.

It should be noted that Pearse was careful to include the ICA in his oration and, in fact, it is an early indication of their unity:

> We of the Irish Volunteers, and you others who are associated with us in today's task and duty, are bound together and must stand together henceforth in brotherly union for

the achievement of the freedom of Ireland.

In a souvenir pamphlet issued for the funeral, Connolly made it clear why the Irish Citizen Army was attending the funeral:

In honouring O'Donovan Rossa the workers of Ireland are doing more than merely paying homage to an unconquerable fighter. They are signifying their adhesion to the principle of which Rossa till his latest days was a living embodiment – the principle that the freedom of a people must in the last analysis rest in the hands of that people – that there is no outside force capable of enforcing slavery upon a people really resolved to be free, and valuing freedom more than life. We in Ireland have often forgotten that truth, indeed it may be even asserted that only an insignificant minority of the nation ever learned it. And yet, that truth once properly adopted as the creed of a nation would become the salvation of the nation ... The Irish Citizen Army in its constitution pledges its members to fight for a Republican Freedom for Ireland. Its members are, therefore, of the number who believe that at the call of duty they may have to lay down their lives for Ireland, and have so trained themselves that at the worst the laying down of their lives shall constitute the starting point of another glorious tradition – a tradition that will keep alive the soul of the nation ... We are, therefore, present to honour O'Donovan Rossa by right of our faith in the separate destiny of our country, and our faith in the ability of the Irish workers to achieve that destiny.[12]

During the summer of 1915 Connolly researched and published in the *Workers' Republic* a collection of military essays under the banner 'Insurrection and Warfare'. Ranging in scope from a study of the '1905 Moscow Insurrection' to the 'Defence of the Alamo', Connolly hoped to instruct and enable discussion within the Citizen Army:

> The lessons are invaluable for all students of warfare who wish to understand the defence and attack of cities, towns, villages or houses.

He finished up the series with an article on 'Street Fighting' which included some advice on the positioning of barricades and the fortifying of strong buildings.

During this period detectives and police were fastidious in their surveillance of ICA activity. Their records make for interesting reading. One ICA tactic was to go on a route march and stay out until the early hours, just to antagonise those sent to spy on them. The following are some examples of police reports into these ICA activities:

> 6 October, 1915. Citizen Army – At 12.45 a.m. 85 members carrying rifles, in command of James Connolly and Countess Markievicz, left "Liberty Hall", Beresford Place,

and marched through portion of the city to Werburgh Street. After manoeuvring in the vicinity of Dublin Castle they returned to their Hall at 1.50 a.m.

24 October, 1915. Citizen Army – At 12.15 a.m. about 120 persons, including 12 women and 20 Sinn Fein Boy Scouts, left "Liberty Hall," Beresford Place, in command of James Connolly and Countess Markievicz, and marched to Christ Church Place. Eighty of the men carried rifles. The party divided up into small sections and manoeuvred in the neighbourhood of Francis Street and the Coombe, having been joined at the latter place by 20 other members with rifles under the command of William P. Partridge. They remained in the locality until about 3 a.m. and then left for Emmet Hall, Inchicore, where they took part in a dance which was being held there. At 5.20 a.m. 70 of the party left the Hall and marched back to College Green where they were dismissed about 6 a.m. About 35 returned to "Liberty Hall" and broke-off there, each man bringing his rifle to his home.

5 December, 1915. Citizen Army – At 12.50 a.m. 76 members (62 with rifles) assembled at "Liberty Hall", Beresford Place, in command of James Connolly, James Mallin,[13] and Countess Markievicz, and proceeded to Cross Guns Bridge, Phibsborough, where they broke up into sections – some going along Whitworth Road and others along the Canal Bank to Newcomen Bridge – and went through manoeuvres as they went

along. They returned to their Hall, at Beresford Place, at 3 a.m. and broke off there.

On 15 December 1915, Connolly wrote to Winifred Carney in Belfast, describing an anti-conscription meeting held by the Volunteers and the Citizen Army in the Mansion House and attended by two thousand people. Eoin Mac-Neill, wrote Connolly, 'was as garrulous as ever, and even declared that the "statement of Mr. Birrell that the Irish Volunteers were opposed to recruiting was a deliberate lie." The statement fell very flat, but he droned away … Pearse was beautiful, but not up to his usual high form. Mr Skeffington was well received, and I was not hissed.'[14]

The lord lieutenant or viceroy, John Campbell Hamilton-Gordon, 1st Marquess of Aberdeen and Temair, better known as 'Aberdeen' responded to the anti-recruitment demonstrations by asking the employers to 'facilitate enlistment' by dismissing young men of military age. This form of 'economic conscription', coupled with the jingoism of the war, saw recruitment continue unabated. The level of recruitment was to fall later, quite dramatically, in fact, in the summer of 1916, possibly due to the Rising and the Battle of the Somme.

That Connolly joined the IRB caused distress to some socialists, including Seán O'Casey, who said that 'Connolly had stepped from the narrow byway of Irish Socialism on to the broad and crowded highway of Irish Nationalism.' This nationalism 'became his daily rosary, while the higher creed of international humanity that had so long bubbled from his eloquent lips was silent for ever, and Irish Labour lost a Leader.'[15]

It would be wise when reading criticism of Connolly by O'Casey to bear in mind the controversy surrounding the secretary's resignation from the Irish Citizen Army. O'Casey was annoyed that Markievicz was a member of the committee of Cumann na mBan as they were clearly tied to the Irish Volunteers, an army which was 'in its methods and aims, inimical to the first interests of Labour.' O'Casey called a meeting to discuss this situation, but a vote of confidence in the countess was passed and O'Casey was told to apologise to Markievicz. He refused to do so, on a point of principle, and resigned his position and his membership of the ICA. The Citizen Army's loss was literary Ireland's gain as fate ensured O'Casey would not die by a British bullet but would go on to write such classics as *Juno and the Paycock*, *Shadow of a Gunman* and the controversial *Plough and the Stars*. Nonetheless, the incident seemed to taint O'Casey's view of Connolly.

As far back as the turn of the century, Connolly proposed a united front for all radical organisations:

> We agitate for the revolution; let those who will conspire for it; when the hour for action arrives our only rivalry need be as to which shall strike the most effective blows against the common enemy.[16]

More importantly, Connolly was always a socialist republican. He did not leave socialism and go over to republicanism; if anything he brought socialism *into* republicanism.

The details of how he was sworn into the IRB are often described as a kidnapping. Between the afternoon of Wednesday, 19 January, and the evening of Saturday, 22 January 1916, he went missing. It seems he spent most of that time in discussions with Joseph Plunkett, Patrick Pearse and Seán MacDiarmada in a secret location. Fearful that Connolly might lead the ICA out in a premature uprising, the trio informed him of their plans and let him know that the IRB Military Council had set the date of the Rising. He was told that Roger Casement was in Germany organising a shipment of arms and ammunition which would be landed in time for the Rising. Over these days and nights Connolly was co-opted on to the Military Council, thus ensuring the ICA would also be part of the army of the Irish Republic. William O'Brien recounted that he asked Connolly where he had been, to which he received the reply, 'I have been through hell these last few days, and I hope everything will be for the best. I was very tired last night when I came home. I must have walked forty miles yesterday.' Connolly told Thomas Foran, one of the five vice-chairmen of the ICA, that an urge to go walking during the spring weather came upon him and that he succumbed to the desire.

A number of points can be raised to counter the notion

that he was held against his will. Firstly, had James Connolly been held against his will, one would imagine there would have been repercussions. Secondly, it is highly likely that, once informed of the plans for the Rising, Connolly would have wanted to spend hours thrashing out the details, arguing every point, which would explain his absence. Thirdly, it is possible that Connolly did go for a 'long walk' to digest the information that the IRB had fed him. And lastly, it is highly likely that he would have been sworn to secrecy about the meeting and hence reluctant to explain his disappearance. Helena Molony asked Connolly where he had been and he was not forthcoming; he simply replied, 'Ah, that would be telling.'

Coinciding with the IRB meeting but written before it, the *Workers' Republic* issue of 22 January 1916 is decidedly defiant – he talks of 'our duty' to 'strengthen the hand of those of the leaders who are for action as against those who are playing into the hands of the enemy.' He clearly advocates revolution and cautions against delay:

> Mark well then our programme. While the war lasts and Ireland still is a subject nation we shall continue to urge her to fight for her freedom. … the time for Ireland's battle is NOW, the place for Ireland's battle is HERE. That a strong man may deal lusty blows with his fists against a host of surrounding foes, and conquer, but will succumb if a child sticks a pin in his heart.

This was the very kind of language that the IRB preferred to whisper to each other in the back rooms of secret halls. Connolly, on the other hand, proclaimed it from the rafters:

> We believe in constitutional action in normal times; we believe in revolutionary action in exceptional times. These are exceptional times.[17]

A week after he was co-opted on to the Military Council, the language in the *Workers' Republic* became more subdued, and a kind of calm sense of the inevitable is evident:

> The issue is clear, and we have done our path to clear it. Nothing we can say now can add point to the argument we have put before our readers in the past few months; nor shall we continue to labour the point ... In solemn acceptance of our duty and the great responsibilities attached thereto, we have planted the seed in the hope that ere many of us are much older, it will ripen into action. For the moment and hour of that ripening, that fruitful blessed day of days, we are ready. Will it find you ready too?[18]

The ICA internal structure was organised to ensure the force could be made ready at short notice. Connolly, or Mallin, gave orders to round up the troops; these were passed to the chief mobilisation officer, Thomas Kain; he issued the instructions to 'section mobilisers' who were responsible for getting the order to muster to a given number of men or women living near their area of the city.[19] This was put to the test with positive results. The story revolves around the union shop on Eden Quay, run as a co-operative by Jane Shanahan, Helena Molony and Rosie Hackett. They sold a 'first class worker's shirt. It had a crest of the Red Hand on it …' but they also sold some of the more radical papers, including *The Spark, Honesty, The Gael* and the *Workers' Republic*. The shop led directly into the machine room in Liberty Hall, where the print works was situated. From there, Christopher Brady, the resident union printer, witnessed a police raid on the shop a week before Good Friday, 1916:

> They rushed into the shop and proceeded to seize copies of *The Gael* … The three women were behind the counter and I was looking through a little door with two spy holes in it … I hastily went for James Connolly who was upstairs with Madame Markievicz and others. Connolly came down quickly, walked quietly to the counter with drawn gun in his hand. A few feet away Miss Molony was already covering the police with her automatic. Connolly looked sternly at the police and gave his command to them; "Drop those papers or I will drop you." At this moment Madame Markievicz who had gone out through the front door of Liberty Hall had come round the street corner and appeared at the entrance to the Co-op behind the raiding police. As she entered, a hot-headed young policeman was urging his comrades to rush Connolly, but as he spoke Madame came forward. She too

had them covered and they realised they were surrounded. At once they changed their tune … they beat a hasty retreat but it was clear that they would return with a larger force. Within an hour of this incident a large contingent of Citizen Army men were mobilised to defend Liberty Hall.[20]

The last thing Connolly needed was bunch of policemen searching the Transport Union building. He feared that they might seize the printing press. Worse still, the place was an arsenal; for three months a large number of men had been engaged in full-time munitions work in Liberty Hall. They made grenades, bullets and bombs and, just as the Volunteers in Kimmage had tried to do, a couple of men made a reasonably good attempt to engineer a machine gun. So, in essence, there were two Liberty Halls. One was upstairs, where members came and paid their dues, documents were filed, and an air of respectability reigned. Downstairs and underground, revolution was being planned and stacks of explosives were stored in preparation for the coming Rising. This storage of ammunition was of course fraught with danger. On one occasion, hundreds of live bullets were stored up a chimney. Inevitably, some genius decided to light a fire – luckily disaster was narrowly averted thanks to some speedy extinguishing. After a couple of other incidents, including a faulty detonator which exploded and injured a couple of men, the making and testing of bombs was transferred to St Enda's, Pearse's school.

The speed with which the ICA were mobilised after the police raid assured Connolly that the force was now well trained and could be trusted. It was only a few months before this that all members of the ICA were mustered at Liberty Hall to confirm their adherence to their cause. They were all asked three questions in the presence of Connolly, Mallin and Kain:

> Are you prepared to take part in the fight for Ireland's freedom?
> Are you prepared to fight alongside the Irish Volunteers?
> Are you prepared to fight without the aid of the Irish Volunteers or any other allies?

Those who answered yes to all three questions were given a secret number, which was to be embossed on a little piece of wood and worn as a dog tag; their names were recorded by Kain in case they needed to be identified if they were killed in a possible battle.[21] It was becoming increasingly clear to members that such a battle was inevitable as opposed to possible.

For the moment, not even Connolly's family knew the exact plans as secrecy was of the greatest importance. They did guess that something was afoot; although he still visited Belfast as regularly as his busy schedule allowed, his mind was on revolution. He even moved his bed into Liberty Hall and, with a number of other ICA men, slept on the premises every night. His followers also foisted a full-time bodyguard on him; they feared that the British might try to arrest, deport or even assassinate him.

# Chapter Fourteen

· · · · · · · ·

## April 1916

# Our Faith in Freedom

*For, be it well understood, an insurrection is always doubtful,*
*a thousand to one chance always exists in favour of the estab-*
*lished order and against the insurgents.*[1]

T he very first time that James Connolly appeared in the
uniform of the Irish Citizen Army was on Palm Sunday,
16 April 1916. That day, several thousand spectators had
gathered to witness the ICA hoist a republican flag over
Liberty Hall. The flag was presented to the colour bearer, a
young Citizen Army woman, Mollie O'Reilly, who ceremoniously carried it to the roof of the union building. When
the gold harp upon green background began to flutter from
the flagpole, bugles were sounded and 'tremendous cheers
from the huge crowd echoed over the Liffey, punctuated by
individual cracks from revolvers fired by enthusiastic Irish Volunteers who were amongst the spectators.'[2] In the previous

week's edition of the *Workers' Republic*, Connolly wrote that the green flag of Ireland, hoisted over Liberty Hall, was 'the symbol of our faith in freedom, and as a token to all the world that the working class of Dublin stands for the cause of Ireland, and the cause of Ireland is the cause of a separate and distinct nationality.'[3]

That night, Connolly gave a lecture to the Citizen Army and told them that a Rising was inevitable, but that 'he was going to fight the way he wanted, not the way the enemy wanted. It would be a new way and soldiers had not been trained to deal with it.' He lectured them on methods of house-fighting, of breaking through walls and on the importance of commanding rooftops. He was not overly optimistic:

> The odds are a thousand to one against us … If we win, we'll be great heroes; but if we lose, we will be the greatest scoundrels the country ever produced. In the event of victory, hold on to your rifles, as those with whom we are fighting may stop before our goal is reached. We are out for economic as well as political liberty. Hold on to your rifles![4]

Frank Henderson, a member of the Irish Volunteers who fought in the GPO in 1916, noted in his memoirs that James Connolly lectured the Irish Volunteers on street fighting 'of which it was said he had had experience in Mexico'. This notion is indeed without any foundation, but it is interesting to note Henderson's claim that Connolly 'held that the British would never use artillery against the buildings in the city [Dublin] owing to the amount of English money invested in such property.'[5] It has always been accepted that this was Connolly's firm belief, but reference to this cannot be found in his writings. In fact, there is no evidence to suggest that Connolly maintained the capitalists would not destroy private property. The story began with Desmond Ryan, Connolly's first biographer, when he wrote in 1924: 'To the end James Connolly was convinced that artillery would never be used against a Dublin in revolt; a capitalist army would never destroy capitalist property...'[6]

However, as early as January 1915 Connolly mused on capitalist bombardment in *The Worker*:

> Of like character is the outcry over the bombardment of undefended towns. One would think to read such diatribes that it was not a recognised practice of all naval warfare. ... It all depends, it appears, upon whose houses are being bombarded, whose people are being massacred, whose limbs are torn from the body, whose bodies are blown to a ghastly mass of mangled flesh and blood and bones.

Finally, Connolly also said:

> [It] is safe to assume that in the bombardment of undefended towns we have a practice authorized by the British Admiralty.[7]

A second charge often levelled at the leaders of the Rising, and directed at Connolly in particular, is that it was a 'big mistake' on the Citizen Army's part not to capture Dublin Castle. Only six weeks before Easter Week 1916, Connolly wrote a fine piece concerning previous uprisings in Ireland, from the perspective of someone who knows what is going to happen:

> March 4th is the date which by common consent is set aside for the commemoration of the heroic attempt of Robert Emmet. March 6th is the anniversary of the Fenian Rising of 1867. Does March 1916 carry in its womb anything of national importance for Ireland? Will our children be commemorating an attempt, celebrating a victory, or mourning over a lost opportunity?[8]

Emmet's 1803 uprising, he explains, might have had a greater success if the small band of United Irishmen had pushed on and taken Dublin Castle, that 'edifice of evil omen' as Connolly so eloquently described it. He then puts the castle into context in the year 1916: 'Dublin Castle is not of so much importance today in the political or military government of Ireland, but in the eighteenth and early nineteenth centuries it was the real centre of all the activities of foreign rule in this country, as it had been for centuries before.' Knowing the full plans for the coming Rising and, again, bearing in mind that he was writing six weeks before it, Connolly then muses that 'it is not probable that much blood will ever again be shed for the sake of the capture of Dublin Castle.' And as a further remonstration from the grave to those who might look back and ridicule the insurgent's plans, he says:

> Remember. It is easy for us now to be wise after the event
> … If we know where they made a mistake it is not because
> our judgment is better than was theirs, but rather because
> we are judging a crisis that is past and whose happenings are
> all therefore familiar to us.

Nonetheless, a detachment of the Irish Citizen Army was sent to City Hall, on the doorstep of Dublin Castle, their ultimate intention being to disrupt the British from coming and going within that area. One of the problems in trying to counter the notion of the so-called 'failure to take the castle' lies in the fact that the man given the command of the City Hall area, Seán Connolly, was shot dead within minutes of the Rising and his exact orders are not known.

However, the ICA bugler, eighteen-year-old William Oman, who fought in 1916 in the castle area, left a plausible witness statement; he was fifty-two when he recalled the story:

> According to the original plan, it was never intended to
> occupy Dublin Castle. The reasons given by Seán Connolly
> were that the buildings were too spread out, and also that

it contained a British military hospital. Our OC explained to us that to occupy it would be very simple, but to retain it would be very difficult with the number of men at our disposal, as we would have to hold prisoners and feed them, and also the sick and injured who were already in the hospital. We had, of course, carried out mimic attacks on Dublin Castle towards the end of 1915.[9]

Ina Connolly became aware that the Rising was due to begin over Easter. She relates:

Although the decision to rise at Easter Week was a closely guarded secret even from the main body of Volunteers, we had an inkling of it because it had been decided that my mother would break up our home in Belfast and go to Dublin.

It had been arranged for Lillie and the younger members of the family to stay in Markievicz's cottage on Three Rock Mountain.

Sadly, mother looked around the home that she cherished; here she was leaving all the convenience of modern life and the work of the last five years which it took to build up, to go to an empty cottage on the hills of Dublin, miles away from anyone she knew. But she would carry out the wishes of her husband. She left Belfast very downhearted with the feeling that once again her hopes of a happy home had been dashed to the ground.[10]

While Lillie and the younger children went down to Dublin, Nora and Ina Connolly went to Coalisland, County Tyrone, where large contingents on Volunteers had gathered to await the order to begin the Rising. But everything that could go wrong had gone wrong. The expected shipment of weapons that Roger Casement had sent from Germany had arrived on Holy Thursday. Instead of being greeted by the Irish Volunteers, the *Aud* was arrested by two British naval vessels, HMS *Zinnia* and HMS *Bluebell*, and when told to sail to Cobh, the German captain, Karl Spindler, scuttled his ship off Daunt's Rock on Saturday, 22 April, at 9.28am. In the meantime, Roger Casement landed from U19 on Good Friday to a 'lonely Banna Strand'; there were no comrades there to meet him and within a couple of hours he was in the custody of the Royal Irish Constabulary. When word reached Dublin about these two disasters, the IRB Military Council met to reassess the situation. Eoin MacNeill, as chief of staff of the Irish Volunteers, was unnerved, to say the least, and decided to do his utmost to stop the Rising. He sent emissaries all around Ireland with dispatches to cancel all Volunteer movements on Easter Sunday.

Just as in Cork, Kerry, Limerick and Galway, the Volunteers in Coalisland received an order from MacNeill to stand down. Nora, Ina and four Cumann na mBan women decided to head for the capital and arrived at Amiens Street Station, Dublin, at about 5am on Easter Sunday. They made their way towards Liberty Hall to contact Connolly.

> The building was heavily guarded. It was some time before
> we got a response to our knocking. Many questions were
> put to us before the door opened. Not until we told them
> that we were James Connolly's daughters Nora and Ina and
> that we had travelled all night to see him ... They said they
> would go and confirm our statement.
>
> The truth was that the guard did not want to disturb my
> father who had just gone to bed. There had been a military
> council meeting in Liberty Hall which lasted long into the
> early hours. I learned this from my father when I went up
> to his room. When the guard returned he opened the door
> and admitted all of us, but would only let my sister and me
> up to Room No. 7 to see father, where he lay on a bed in a
> half-sitting position, his head resting on his hand, wonder-
> ing what was the nature of our news. We rushed forward to
> hug and kiss him; we knelt on the floor beside his bed and
> told him everything that had happened since we left home.

There is no doubt that Connolly would have been scepti-
cal as at this stage, in the very early hours of Sunday morning,
he would not have heard about MacNeill's countermanding
order.

> He listened attentively, making no remark until our story
> ended. Then, lifting himself up into a sitting position, he
> said: "This is what you think happened." "Oh, no," said my

sister, "there are other members of Cumann na mBan here with us, please hear what they have to say." Our tales agreeing, father said: "This is a very serious situation and I want you to realise the importance of your message and urgency of letting the other members of the military council know. I will send you each out to relate your story to the other members. Just repeat what you have told me."[11]

The seven members of the IRB Military Council were gathered together in Liberty Hall for another long meeting. Things had become a little more urgent since the previous night, when all they were concerned with was the arrest of Casement and that the mysterious ship which had been sunk in Cork was the *Aud*. Thomas MacDonagh had informed the Military Council the night before that MacNeill had said that he was going to call off the mobilisation, but they probably had not realised how effective his countermand would be.[12] The news that the women had brought had now been confirmed by the appearance of MacNeill's countermanding order in the *Sunday Independent* newspaper:

Owing to the very critical position, all orders given to Irish Volunteers for tomorrow, Easter Sunday, are hereby rescinded, and no parades, marches, or other movements of Irish Volunteers will take place. Each individual Volunteer will obey this order strictly in every particular.

The IRB Military Council retired to room number seven,

in complete privacy, just the seven of them, for three hours, thrashing out the various options open to them. Although we can never know exactly what was said in that room, it is safe to presume that they came to a decision to comply with MacNeill's order for Sunday, despite Clarke's desire to go ahead as planned that day for 3.30pm. Instead, they decided to postpone the Rising to the following day, Easter Monday, with a start time of noon.

It was during this crucial meeting that the draft of the Proclamation was checked by the Military Council and, when it was approved, was given to the ITGWU printer, Christopher Brady, who printed two and a half thousand copies with the able assistance of compositors Liam Ó Briain and Michael Molly. The three worked under armed guard and had great difficulty in finding enough type, famously having to mix and match various fonts and even using sealing wax to make some letters.

The machine was ready for first printing at about 8.30pm on Easter Sunday night and the job was finished between 12 and 1 on Easter Monday morning … I gave the first proof to James Connolly at 9 p.m. and he checked it with the manuscript and I never saw the manuscript after that … Although I read the manuscript, I could not say in whose hand writing it was. It certainly was not Connolly's as I was familiar with his scrawl.[13]

Brady recalled seeing that Markievicz was 'in a raging temper' and he witnessed her talking to Connolly in the machine room:

> "I will shoot Eoin MacNeill," she said. Connolly replied "You are not to hurt a hair on MacNeill's head. If anything happens to MacNeill I will hold you responsible."[14]

As the ICA were not affected by MacNeill's order, they still mobilised as planned and Connolly wisely brought them on a route march around the city to divert attention away from Liberty Hall. Usually, concerts were held in the union building on Sunday nights, so an impromptu session was held that evening with Michael Mallin playing a few tunes on his flute, coupled with the singing of many Irish ballads. 'Lights Out' was called for 11pm that night and the ICA bedded down in Liberty Hall; it would be their final rest for some time to come.

## Chapter Fifteen

# 1916 Easter Week

# Our Own Red Blood

*And the best men in Ireland, the only men whom the Ireland*
*of the future will care to remember, have decided long ago that*
*if they must fight they will fight in Ireland, for Ireland, and*
*under Ireland's flag.*[1]

On Easter Monday morning, 24 April, in Liberty Hall, Patrick Pearse asked Nora and Ina Connolly and the Belfast women to study the contents of the Proclamation and bring a dispatch to the north to tell the Volunteers to rise up. Ina recalled that her father appeared at the same time:

> Clutching him tightly, I begged him to let me stay with him.
> He clasped my head with his two hands, at arm's length, and
> said: "It is not what you want or what I want, but what is
> wanted of us that counts."[2]

The efforts of the messengers proved to be in vain as the

Belfast men had dispersed home by the time the women arrived in Coalisland, County Tyrone, with the dispatch. Other messengers, who travelled at great risk to other population centres, met with a similar situation.

In the meantime, the Dublin contingent of the Irish Volunteers, Na Fianna, Cumann na mBan, the Irish Citizen Army and a few members of the Hibernian Rifles were mustering at Liberty Hall and other venues around Dublin. They were armed with the Mausers landed in Howth in 1914, described by one Volunteer as 'a very accurate and deadly weapon, although it was very heavy, it had a kick like a mule and only fired one bullet before having to be reloaded.' There was also the odd Lee Enfield; some carried shotguns; others had pikes, more symbolic than useful; and still some carried no weapon at all. Liberty Hall was not the only muster point that morning. Éamonn Ceannt and the Fourth Battalion met at Emerald Square, off Cork Street, and made their way to the South Dublin Union. The Second Battalion under Thomas MacDonagh and Michael O'Hanrahan were to take Jacob's Factory so they gathered nearby at St Stephen's Green. The majority of the Third Battalion met with their commandant, Éamon de Valera, at an old school, St Andrew's on Great Brunswick Street, from where they made their way to the South Docks area, where they intended to occupy Boland's Mills and Westland Row railway station. Edward Daly took over the Four Courts area with the First Battalion, so those Volunteers and Cumann na mBan mustered at the Gaelic League Hall on Blackhall Street. Included in Daly's area were the men and women under Con Colbert, who took over Watkin's Brewery on Ardee Street. Out in north County Dublin, Fifth Battalion commandant Thomas Ashe prepared the Fingal Volunteers for an attack on Ashbourne.

Thomas Clarke and Seán MacDiarmada made their own way to the GPO. MacDiarmada had a bad limp from polio and did not wish to hold up the rest of the Headquarters' Battalion. Clarke simply wanted to keep his close friend company. Then, sometime around 11.30am, William Oman sounded 'fall-in' on his bugle and the various armies mustered and prepared to march to their chosen positions.[3] ICA Captain Richard McCormack and his group of less than forty made their way towards Harcourt Street railway terminus. The Abbey actor, Captain Seán Connolly, and his troop of Citizen Army men and women made their way towards City Hall. Volunteer Seán Heuston led a small detachment of men and boys towards the Mendicity Institution, followed closely by ICA commandant Michael Mallin and Lieutenant Constance Markievicz, who were off to take St Stephen's Green and the College of Surgeons. The last contingent to leave from Liberty Hall formed into fours. Leading the column were Patrick Pearse, the provisional president of the Irish Republic, James Connolly, commandant-general of the Dublin Brigade of the army of the Irish Republic, and

Joseph Plunkett, fresh from a nursing home, having recently undergone an operation on his neck. He was closely followed by his aide-de-camp Michael Collins and Irish Volunteer commandant William James Brennan-Whitmore. They marched up Abbey Street, turned right on to Dublin's main thoroughfare, Sackville Street (today's O'Connell Street), and stopped outside the imposing General Post Office.

Then Connolly gave a sudden order, 'Left turn. The GPO, charge!' and when they got inside Connolly's voice rang out, in a determined tone, stating, 'Everyone outside!' There was some initial confusion amongst the GPO employees as to whether Connolly was referring to them, but as soon as they realised he did indeed mean them they cleared the building with a certain haste. Brennan-Whitmore recalled that Connolly then ordered the men to smash the windows and barricade them.[4]

While the men, and Winifred Carney, the only woman at this early stage, busied themselves securing the position, Connolly stood outside the GPO beside Pearse, who read the Proclamation to a bemused and fairly unimpressed crowd of onlookers, who may not have recognised that the seven signatories of the Proclamation were, in effect, the provisional government. When the provisional president had finished reading, Connolly grasped him by the hand and with great warmth said something like: 'Thanks be to God, Pearse, that we have lived to see this day!'[5]

Less than a couple of hours into the establishment of the republic, a number of Lancers came to the headquarters to see what was afoot. The Lancers were routed with a barrage of fire from the roof and the loop-holed windows of the GPO. This early success gave the army of the Irish Republic a great boost of confidence. Connolly was in high spirits; he laughed at one particular officer who kept showering him with messages and updates: 'If that man was standing on his right foot, he would send me a dispatch to inform me that he was shortly going to put down his left foot.'[6]

Clery's and various other department stores held the greatest sale ever that Easter Monday – everything was free. The looting was something that the revolutionaries had not anticipated. Initially, Seán MacDiarmada admonished the mob over their disrespectful attitude towards this historical declaration of independence, which their wanton destruction was sullying. His oration fell on deaf ears. Brennan-Whitmore wanted to shoot a few looters, but Connolly's orders were that no one was to harm civilians unless they were intent on attacking the insurgents.

That afternoon, Connolly dictated a communiqué to the 'Officers and Soldiers of the army of the Irish Republic' in the other districts:

> Comrades, We salute you. This day the Flag of the Irish
> Republic has been hoisted in Dublin and the armed forces
> of the Irish Republic have everywhere met the enemy and

defeated them – North, South, East and West, the Irish Army has been in action all day, and at no single point has it been driven in, nor lost a single position it has taken up. In the name of Ireland we salute you. This is the greatest day in Irish History and it is you who have made it so.

By Tuesday, the random looters had become a mob and as most of the food had already been cleared from the shops, they began to drink any available alcohol by raiding Dublin's pubs in the afternoon.

Earlier in the day, Brennan-Whitmore's position was visited first by Pearse and then by Connolly, who 'came striding briskly across the street' to them.

> The men gave [Connolly] a rousing cheer which he acknowledged with a quick wave of his hand … he strode over to the barricade and immediately found fault with it. He said it was too small and too frail, and would not stop a charge … I invited him to try and knock it down. At once he seized the leg of a table, in the centre, and gave it a vigorous pull which did not budge it. I then pointed out the way the whole structure had been wired. This seemed to please him.[7]

Later that day, Winifred Carney typed as Connolly dictated a communiqué to the officer in charge of the area diagonally across from the GPO, encompassing Reis & Co. and the Dublin Bread Company:

The main purpose of your post is to protect our wireless station. Its secondary purpose is to observe Lower Abbey street and Lower O'Connell street. Commandeer in the DBC whatever food and utensils you require. Make sure of a plentiful supply of water wherever your men are. Break all glass in the windows of the rooms occupied by you for fighting purposes. Establish a connection between your forces in the DBC and in Reis's building. Be sure that the stairways leading immediately to your rooms are well barricaded. We have a post in the house at the corner of Bachelor's Walk, in the Hotel Metropole,[8] in the Imperial Hotel,[9] in the General Post Office. The directions from which you are likely to be attacked are from the Custom House, or from the far side of the river, D'Olier street, or Westmoreland street. We believe there is a sniper in McBirney's on the far side of the river.

Winfred Carney pointed out that Joseph Plunkett looked out of place with his bangle and fine antique rings. Connolly told her that 'Joseph Plunkett can do and wear what he pleases. And as for military science, he could teach us all a thing or two. He's a clear-headed man, and he's a man of the world.'

Three flags fluttered in the wind throughout the Easter Rising. One was the tricolour of green for nationalist sentiment, white for peace, and orange for the unionists. The second flag was painted by Markievicz, with two simple words on a green background: 'Irish Republic'. Connolly gave the order that the third flag, the 'Starry Plough', should be hoisted above the Imperial Hotel opposite the GPO. That his old adversary William Martin Murphy owned this establishment, and that it was now in the hands of the ICA, no doubt amused Connolly.

By Wednesday, the British had a machine gun at the apex of Westmoreland Street and D'Olier Street, which poured a steady stream of hot lead down towards the post office. Compounding this, two 18-pounder Howitzers were brought into action, initially against Liberty Hall, 'the centre of social anarchy in Ireland, the brain of every riot and disturbance'.[10]

Later that day, a British vessel, the *Helga*, spent a good couple of hours attempting to bombard the building, in a futile attempt to dislodge the hundreds of Citizen Army members that they supposed were holed up there. However, there was only one occupant, Peter Ennis the caretaker, who escaped from the building in great haste.

Meanwhile, the 18-pounders soon trained their sights on the heart of the Rising. The bombardment was concentrated on the Metropole Hotel, right beside the GPO; it was clear that the British had decided to eliminate the protection that the hotel afforded and that they would soon have a clear shot at the headquarters. Connolly called his only son Roddy to his side and explained to him the necessity of bringing a bundle of 'important papers' to William O'Brien's house in the company of another Volunteer. Roddy was concerned that his father's eyes were welling up and tried to assure Connolly that he would be alright and that he would return as soon as possible. Then Connolly explained to him that he should stay with O'Brien to help with some important union work. Roddy had just turned fifteen and it was only much later that he realised his father was sending him away for his own safety.

Unknown to Connolly at this stage, his friend and comrade, the socialist and pacifist Francis Sheehy Skeffington, had been executed. He had been arrested on Tuesday while returning home, having unsuccessfully attempted to form a citizens' brigade to stop the looting. A British officer, Captain Bowen-Colthurst, ordered Skeffy's illegal execution in Beggars Bush Barracks the following day. On Wednesday the same officer was out with a squad on a mission seeking retribution against the Irish over the killing of British soldiers. He came across a second comrade of Connolly's, Councillor Richard O'Carroll, and shot him in cold blood; the trade unionist, who had helped to bury Rossa, died nine days later.

By Thursday the centre of Dublin was ablaze. Frank Burke, who fought in the GPO, recalled, 'the fires had now extended from Clery's right down to Hopkins' corner and from the Metropole Hotel, the next building on our right, down to O'Connell's Bridge. In fact, the whole area was one mass of flames but the GPO had not yet caught fire ... Not a soul was now to be seen, only a huge wall of flames towering to the sky and great billows of smoke. The noise of bursting shells and tumbling walls and roofs was indescribable.'[11]

The constant barrage of incendiary shells from the Howitzers ensured that the republican headquarters was in great danger of catching fire. The occupants did their best to quell the blazes, but they were fighting a losing battle. The Dublin fire brigade played a heroic role during the first three days, but the constant machine-gun fire and the bombardment made it impossible for them to beat the flames. Captain Purcell, the chief of the fire brigade, watched the Great Fire begin in the *Irish Times* reserve printing office on Abbey Street at 12.32pm. The fire crept along Abbey Street in both directions and on both sides, and down O'Connell Street, destroying the republican outpost in the DBC and taking the whole block of buildings throughout the night. He 'witnessed this terrible destruction' with 'awful pain, amounting to anguish' because he felt he could have easily stopped the fires if he 'could only have been allowed with any reasonable degree of safety to approach these premises.'[12] Under normal circumstances, streets or roads make good barriers to the spread of fires, but the huge number of barricades made of combustible material ensured that the flames were given a perfect path to leap from block to block.

During the battle in the GPO, Joseph Plunkett kept some notes in his Field Message Book. One entry reads as follows:

Thursday 4th Day of the Republic. About one o'clock Comt. General Connolly was wounded in the left arm and ten minutes later in the left leg (by a sniper). The leg wound is serious as it caused a compound fracture of the shin bone.[13]

It seems Connolly was outside on Prince's Street when he received his first wound. He was supervising the erection of a barricade and stopped a stray bullet. A young medical student, James Ryan, remembered the incident:

Then I saw James Connolly come in and walking quickly to where I was standing he asked if there was any private place where he might speak to me. I led him behind the folding screen. Here he took off his coat and showed me a flesh wound in his arm. He asked me to dress it and, when leaving, begged me not to tell anybody. He feared a garbled report of the gravity of the wound might reach his men and, perhaps, undermine their morale. He immediately returned to his duties, but before long he was carried back on a stretcher, this time suffering from a severe wound in the ankle. It was badly lacerated, probably from a rifle bullet at comparatively short range. Having no choice of anesthetic, I gave him chloroform while Dr. O'Mahony, RAMC, one of our prisoners of war, and Mr. McLoughlin put the leg in splints. Connolly suffered great pain and it was only with the help of frequent injections of morphia that got any rest ... We were kept busy on Thursday night. Connolly required a

good deal of attention. He slept very little and in the inter-
vals the pain was ever present and severe …[14]

Pearse issued a manifesto on Friday morning in which he
paid 'homage to the gallantry of the soldiers of Irish Freedom.' He singled out Connolly for praise:

> If I were to mention names of individuals, my list would be
> a long one. I will name only that of Commandant-General
> James Connolly, Commanding the Dublin Division. He lies
> wounded, but is still the guiding brain of our resistance.

The student doctor recalled that, not long after Connolly
awoke from a morphine-induced sleep, he 'asked to be put
in a bed with wheels or castors so that he could be moved to
the front hall. This was done and he resumed command of
the garrison. Nothing could conquer the will of this man …'
Connolly then dictated a message 'To Soldiers' which Winifred Carney typed up:

> This is the fifth day of the establishment of the Irish Repub-
> lic, and the flag of our country still floats from the most
> important buildings in Dublin, and is gallantly protected by
> the officers and Irish soldiers in arms throughout the coun-
> try. Not a day passes without seeing fresh postings of Irish
> soldiers eager to do battle for the old cause. Despite the
> utmost vigilance of the enemy, we have been able to get in
> information telling us how the manhood of Ireland, inspired

by our splendid action, are gathering to offer up their lives if necessary in the same holy cause. We are here hemmed in because the enemy feels that in this building is to be found the heart and inspiration of our great movement.

Let us remind you what you have done. For the first time in 700 years the flag of a free Ireland floats triumphantly in Dublin City.

The British Army, whose exploits we are for ever having dinned into our ears, which boasts of having stormed the Dardanelles and the German lines on the Marne, behind their artillery and machine-guns, are afraid to advance to the attack or storm any positions held by our forces. The slaughter they suffered in the first few days has totally unnerved them, and they dare not attempt again an infantry attack on our positions.

Our Commandants around us are holding their own.

Commandant Daly's splendid exploit in capturing Linen Hall Barracks we all know. You must know also that the whole population, both clergy and laity of this district are united in his praises. Commandant MacDonagh is established in an impregnable position reaching from the walls of Dublin Castle to Redmond's Hill, and from Bishop street to Stephen's Green.

In Stephen's Green, Commandant — [15] holds the College of Surgeons, one side of the square, a portion of the other side, and dominates the whole Green and all its entrances and exits.

Commandant De Valera stretches in a position from the Gas Works to Westland row, holding Boland's Bakery, Boland's Mills, Dublin South-Eastern Railway Works, and dominating Merrion square.

Commandant Kent holds the South Dublin Union and Guinness's Buildings to Marrowbone lane, and controls James's street and district.

On two occasions the enemy effected a lodgement and were driven out with great loss.

The men of North County Dublin are in the field, have occupied all the Police Barracks in the district, destroyed all the telegram system on the Great Northern Railway up to Dundalk, and are operating against the trains of the Midland and Great Western.

Dundalk has sent 200 men to march upon Dublin, and in other parts of the North our forces are active and growing.

In Galway Captain —[16], fresh after his escape from an Irish prison, is in the field with his men. Wexford and Wicklow are strong, and Cork and Kerry are equally acquitting themselves creditably. (We have every confidence that our Allies in Germany and kinsmen in America are straining every nerve to hasten matters on our behalf.)

As you know I was wounded twice yesterday and am unable to move about, but have got my bed moved into the firing line, and, with the assistance of your officers, will be just as useful to you as ever.

> Courage, boys, we are winning, and in the hour of our victory
> let us not forget the splendid women who have everywhere
> stood by us and cheered us on. Never had man or woman a
> grander cause, never was a cause more grandly served.[17]

Connolly was now a living metaphor for the Rising. As a wounded leader, he did his best to encourage morale, but it took a sudden drop when it became apparent that the GPO was hopelessly surrounded and that parts of the roof were caving in on top of them. The fires were so intense that the great fear was that they would be roasted alive in the post office. Flames were also licking around the headquarters; the basement of the GPO contained an arsenal of homemade explosive devices which, if they caught fire, would have blown the place asunder.

That evening an evacuation of the GPO was inevitable. The O'Rahilly, who had done his absolute best to stop the Rising but joined in when he saw it was going ahead, led a charge of Volunteers down Moore Street to get to Great Britain Street. Their destination was Williams and Woods, manufacturers of soap and sweets, a large factory which they hoped could become their new headquarters. As it transpired, this area was already in British hands. The O'Rahilly, handgun blazing, followed by about a dozen others, ran against a British barricade at the bottom of Moore Street and bore the full brunt of a machine gun. He slumped into a doorway and wrote a note to his wife, to explain the circumstances of his death, in which he also stated, 'It was a good fight anyhow.' The remainder of the GPO garrison made their way out on to Henry Street and down a back alley called Henry Place which, being L-shaped, led into Moore Street. Cogan's, a modest grocer's shop, at 10 Moore Street, was quickly occupied and Connolly was carried there by stretcher to spend the night in acute pain. The Red Cross nurse Elizabeth O'Farrell knelt beside him at one stage and asked him how he was feeling. Connolly replied: 'Bad – the soldier who wounded me did a good day's work for the British government.'

Connolly's position as commandant-general was passed to young Seán McLoughlin for the remainder of the Rising. McLoughlin had fought in the Mendicity Institution, but after that position fell to the British he ended up in the GPO. He had shown some leadership qualities during the evacuation, barking orders to the men and bringing some sense of discipline to what had been a very haphazard affair. McLoughlin's rank was never discovered, thanks to the kind action of a British captain who removed his commandant tabs immediately after the surrender. If not for this gesture, he could have been court-martialled and executed.[18]

Connolly spent a sleepless night in 10 Moore Street. The medic James Ryan spent a lot of time looking after him. He recalled what happened early the next day:

On Saturday morning we moved from house to house through bored walls. The openings were small and Connolly's

stretcher would not pass through. We had to put him in a
sheet and so carry him northwards. He must have suffered
torture during that journey but he never complained.[19]

The five members of the provisional Irish government
made their new headquarters in 16 Moore Street. The
majority of those who had escaped with their lives were in
all the houses which stretched along this row. Others were
haphazardly scattered all around the area, some crouching in
doors, others smashed their way into yards, shops or homes.
The machine guns of the British army were in overdrive, the
fires were raging, and innocent local people were wounded
and dead. A conference was held in number sixteen. Clarke
was keen to fight on; fifteen years in an English prison was
not something he wished to repeat. Gangrene had set in
on Connolly's wound and Plunkett was white with tiredness
and pain. Pearse and MacDiarmada were convinced that a plan
of young Seán McLoughlin's to link up with the Four Courts
would result in too great a loss of their men and, indeed, civilians. A decision was made, and a little after noon the nurse,
Elizabeth O'Farrell, with tremendous bravery, stepped out
into the street under a white flag to seek terms of surrender.
When she returned a little later, she made the journey again,
this time with Pearse, to meet General Lowe and formally
surrender. The 'surrender document' had to be typed up and
brought to the other commandants around Dublin, some of
whom thought it was all a British ploy:

In order to prevent further slaughter of unarmed people and in the hope of saving the lives of our followers, now surrounded and hopelessly outnumbered, members of the Provisional Government at present at headquarters have agreed to unconditional surrender, and the commanders of all units of the republican forces will order their followers to lay down their arms.

(Signed) PH Pearse

29th day of April, 1916.

I agree to these conditions for the men only under my own command in the Moore street district, and for the men in the Stephen's Green Command.

April 29th, 1916. James Connolly.

On consultation with Commandant Ceannt and other officers, I have decided to agree on unconditional surrender also.

Thomas MacDonagh

Pearse typed one copy for the Volunteers who were 'out' in Enniscorthy, County Wexford, as they refused to believe that Dublin had surrendered.

# Chapter Sixteen

## • • • • • • • •

# May 1916

# Field General Court Martial

*The readiness of the ruling class to order killing, the small value the ruling class has ever set upon human life, is in marked contrast to the reluctance of all revolutionists to shed blood.*[1]

One of the nurses working in the temporary Red Cross hospital in Dublin Castle, during and after the Rising, left an interesting account of Connolly's time in their care:

> The arrival of James Connolly caused an unusual stir. From the window I could see him lying on the stretcher, his hands crossed, his head hidden from view by the archway. The stretcher was on the ground and at either side stood three of his officers, dressed in the Volunteer uniform; a guard of about thirty soldiers stood around. The scene did not change for ten minutes or more; they were arranging where he should be brought, and a small ward in the Officers'

Quarters, where he could be carefully guarded, was decided upon. The nurses in charge of him acknowledged, without exception, that no one could have been more considerate, or have given less trouble.[2]

From the archway entrance, topped by the statue of Justice, he was carried directly across Upper Castle Yard and brought up the stairs to the first floor.

A Capuchin friar, Father Aloysius, noted on 1 May that he went to visit Connolly in Dublin Castle, where he was under armed guard. 'The soldiers left and I was alone with Connolly. I told him I had given my word I would act only as a priest and not in any political capacity. "I know that, Father," he said. "You would not get this privilege otherwise, and it is as a priest I want to see you. I have seen and heard of the brave conduct of the priests and nuns during the week and I believe they are the best friends of the workers." I then heard Connolly's confession.'

The following morning, Tuesday 2 May, he gave Holy Communion to Connolly. Although Connolly had not practised his faith for many years, he often insisted that religious and socialist beliefs were not mutually exclusive. However, we must be guarded against any claims by a Church hostile to socialism that Connolly found religion at the last minute.

Later, the same priest went to see Pearse in Kilmainham: 'You will be glad to know that I gave Holy Communion to James Connolly this morning,' he said to Pearse. 'Thank God,' replied Pearse, 'it is the only thing I was anxious about.'[3] Pearse, it appears, had very little to be anxious about, despite the fact that he was due to be executed the following day.

Nora, who visited Connolly in the castle, recorded that her father was clearly a dying man.

> Gangrene had set in, and he had little chance of living. He could not even sit up, and was unable to lift more than his head from the pillow, and his shoulders a little bit. The gangrene began affecting his whole body.[4]

Most of the leaders of the Easter Rising were tried in Richmond Barracks, but Connolly had the dubious pleasure of having his court martial held around his bed in the hospital in Dublin Castle. The irony of being tended by British doctors and nurses so that he might get well enough to be shot was not lost on Connolly. Nor was it necessarily a new low within the British army to shoot a wounded man. In fact, Connolly mentioned to Nora the case of Gideon Scheepers, a sick Boer Commandant who was strapped to a chair and executed.[5] Connolly was not given the benefit of a proper trial by jury with a defence council. In fact, the trials were held *in camera* and were, in reality, a foregone conclusion. Connolly pleaded not guilty, not in an attempt to save his life, but because he simply was not guilty of the charges that were brought against him. The following details are taken from the James Connolly trial file held in the British Public Records Office, Kew; it was released to the public only in 1999.[6]

The British had a typed 'Form for Assembly and Proceedings of Field General Court Martial on Active Service'. This was signed the day before Connolly's trial and was a requirement if 'Ordinary General Court Martial' was 'not practicable' or if the offence was of a major character. General Maxwell, who had arrived in Ireland towards the end of the Rising, was the commander of the forces in Ireland. He convened the Field General Court Martial of Connolly and appointed a president in the guise of Colonel D Sapte, who was joined by two members, Lieutenant Colonel AM Bent and Major FW Woodward.

James Connolly was prisoner number ninety and the court martial was convened around his bed on 9 May 1916 in the Red Cross Hospital, Dublin Castle. He was charged with two offences.

The first:

Did an act to wit did take part in an armed rebellion and in the waging of war against His Majesty the King, such an act being of such a nature as to be calculated to be prejudicial to the Defence of the Realm and being done with the intention and for the purpose of assisting the enemy.

The second:

Did attempt to cause disaffection among the civilian population of His Majesty.

Connolly entered a plea of 'Not Guilty' on both charges and the members of the court and witnesses were duly sworn in.

The 'Summary of Evidence' details the evidence of the first witness for the prosecution. Second Lieutenant SL King of the Royal Inniskilling Fusiliers:

> In Sackville Street Dublin about 11a.m. on the 25 April 1916, I was taken prisoner by the rebels upstairs in the General Post Office. There were two other officers confined in the same room. There were many armed rebels in the building. I saw firing from the Hotel Metropole. I saw the accused, in uniform and equipped with a revolver etc., going across to the Hotel Metropole. I saw him pointing out as if to order a window to be broken in the Hotel which was done, and fire opened from the window. I saw the accused on 3 or 4 occasions near the General Post Office.

King was cross-examined by Connolly, who was in no fit state to be defending himself, but was determined to have his say. Of course, his words were unrecorded, but we can get an idea of what he said from the replies to his questions.

Lieutenant King then stated:

> I was in the Post Office from 25 to 28 April when I was

marched out of it by one of the rebels. We were very well treated generally by the rebels. The window broken gave a good field of fire across Sackville Street. The uniform the accused wore was the green Volunteer uniform with rings on his arm, and a wideawake hat. I cannot remember any feathers in it.

The witness was clearly unable to identify Connolly's darker green uniform as that of the Irish Citizen Army, but Connolly was more concerned with recording the fact that British soldiers fired on the POWs during the evacuation of the GPO.

King replied to this re-examination:

When we were put out of the Post Office we were told to run for our lives and we were fired on by the rebels, and two of us were hit. I cannot state whether the British troops were firing at the time.

The fact is that British prisoners were released and given the choice to either make a break for their own 'lines' or stick with their captors who were making a break for Moore Street. The POWs were taken to the Henry Street exit where The O'Rahilly bid farewell to them.

Connaught Ranger Private Peter Richardson told a newspaper reporter:

We were placed near the door where we could rush for our

liberty. Then shaking hands with each one of us in turn, The O'Rahilly said, "Good-bye … I may never see you again. Good bye and good luck to you." Then the door was pulled open. Lieutenant Chalmers led the party, with a Dublin Fusilier following close behind … He was running west towards Moore Street when a machine gun opened up and caught him in the thigh. Beside him the Dublin Fusilier fell dead with a bullet in his head.[7]

As it was only the British who had machine guns during the Rising, this was an unfortunate case of 'friendly fire', but Connolly wanted to make sure that it was recorded that the POWs were not abused, beaten or shot by the army of the Irish Republic, hence his reason for cross-examining the witnesses.

The second witness for the prosecution was Captain HE de Courcy Wheeler, who stated:

I saw the accused, James Connolly, in bed at the Dublin Castle Hospital on the 29 April 1916 between 3 and 4 p.m. I had previously seen the rebel leader P.H. Pearse surrender at the top of Moore Street off Great Britain Street. I produce a document which I brought to the accused from Pearse, which he signed in my presence.

This was the 'Surrender Document' which was 'Marked X, signed and attached', but is missing from the file in Kew. There is a note attached to the file which says: 'Received from the Judge Advocate General a document signed P. H. Pearse, James Connolly and Thomas MacDonagh, which was attached as exhibit X to the proceedings of the FGCM held at Dublin on James Connolly on 9 May 1916.' The note is dated 2 July 1918 and is signed by 'J.G. Maxwell'.

The third witness for the prosecution called was Second Lieutenant SH Jackson of the Third Royal Irish Regiment who stated:

> On the 1 May 1916 I searched the rebel John MacBride and found on him the document I produce to the court. It purports to be signed by James Connolly and I consider the signature the same as that shown to me by the Court.

This document, marked 'Y', is still on the Kew file; it was the communiqué issued by Connolly on Easter Monday afternoon – not that this was a crucial piece of evidence against Connolly, but the question remains as to why Mac-Bride, a man of great intelligence and military experience, would retain an incriminating document.

The fourth and final witness for the prosecution was Second Lieutenant AD Chalmers of the Fourteenth Royal Fusiliers. Chalmers stated:

> About 12.10 p.m. on 24 April 1916 I was in the General Post Office Dublin when about 300 armed rebels entered and seized the Post Office and made me prisoner. I saw the accused present among them. The accused ordered me to

be tied up in the telephone box. This was done. I was kept
there about 3 hours. One of the rebels came and asked me
how I was getting on.[8] I replied I was about suffocated.

Apparently the man went to the accused. I then heard
the accused say "I don't care a damn what you do with
him." The words were obviously concerned with me. I was
kept in the General Post Office until 28 April 1916. On the
25 and 26 April from the window of the room I was in, I
saw the accused giving orders about firing from the Hotel
Metropole. I heard him give orders for firing on more than
one occasion.

Lieutenant Chalmers had been the author of his own misfortune. Desmond Ryan, who had fought in the GPO and
wrote about his experiences during the revolutionary period,
recalled that Chalmers, instead of making himself scarce, had
'bandied indignant words with Plunkett, Brennan-Whitmore and Michael Collins outside on the very steps.' He was
brought into the GPO by a group of Volunteers and tied up
by the future leader of the IRA, Michael Collins.

Connolly cross-examined him on the treatment of prisoners and seems to have enquired whether he had heard the
accused 'order the witness to be tied up'. Chalmers replied:

I think I last saw the accused on the 26 April. Up to that,
I had frequently seen him. The rebels did their best for us
whilst we were in the Post Office. The accused was in dark

green uniform with a distinctive hat with cock's feathers in it. The distinctive uniform was very noticeable from the other Volunteer uniforms. I saw the accused close while he was in the Post office. I did not actually hear the accused order me to be tied up in the box. One of the rebels went up to the accused and on his return I was tied up.

Connolly had prepared a written defence; the document is marked 'Z' and is in Connolly's handwriting. He cleverly made another copy, which differs only slightly from this one, and is known as 'Connolly's Last Statement', which he slipped to Nora on 11 May. Before Connolly read the document, he asked 'that a copy of these proceedings shall be given to his wife.' The president of the court martial directed him to make a formal application to Headquarters Irish Command – not an easy task for a prisoner lying in bed with a shattered ankle. He read out his defence:

> I do not wish to make any defence except against charges of wanton cruelty to prisoners. These trifling allegations that have been made in that direction if they record facts that really happened deal only with the almost unavoidable incidents of a hurried uprising, and overthrowing of long established authorities, and no where show evidence of a set purpose to wantonly injure unarmed prisoners.
>
> We went out to break the connection between this country and the British Empire and to establish an Irish Republic.

We believe that the call we thus issued to the people of Ireland was a nobler call in a holier cause than any call issued to them during this war having any connection with the war.

We succeeded in proving that Irishmen are ready to die endeavouring to win for Ireland their national rights which the British Government has been asking them to die to win for Belgium. As long as that remains the case, the cause of Irish freedom is safe. Believing that the British Government has no right in Ireland, never had any right in Ireland, and never can have any right in Ireland, the presence in any one generation of even a respectable minority of Irishmen ready to die to affirm that truth makes that Government for ever a usurpation and a crime against human progress. I personally thank God that I have lived to see the day when thousands of Irishmen and boys, and hundreds of Irish women and girls, were equally ready to affirm that truth and seal it with their lives if necessary.[9]

Connolly was found 'Not Guilty' of the second charge, the less serious charge of causing disaffection among the civilian population. He was, however, found guilty of the first charge 'in the waging of war against His Majesty', being 'for the purpose of assisting the enemy.'

The nurse that tended him was clearly quite taken with her patient.

About a week after his arrival he had an operation on his leg. All through, his behaviour was that of an idealist. He was calm and composed during the court-martial, and he is reported to have said: "You can shoot me if you like, but I am dying for my country." He showed no sign of weakness till his wife was brought to say goodbye to him, the night he was to be shot.[10]

On Thursday, 11 May, at midnight, Nora Connolly and her mother, Lillie, were brought by ambulance to Dublin Castle to see James Connolly. Nora had a good idea why they were being brought there, but it seems Lillie was ever hopeful that some leniency might yet be shown to her wounded husband. Nora recalled that Connolly turned to them when they entered his room:

> 'Well, Lillie. I suppose you know what this means?'
>
> 'James, James. It's not that – it's not that,' mama wailed.
>
> 'Yes, Lillie,' he said, patting her hand. 'I fell asleep to-night for the first time. I was awakened at eleven and told I was to be shot at dawn.'
>
> Mama was kneeling, her head on the bed, sobbing heart-breakingly.
>
> Daddy laid his hand on her head.
>
> 'Don't cry, Lillie,' he pleaded. 'You'll unman me.'
>
> 'But your beautiful life, James,' mama sobbed. 'Your beautiful life.'

'Hasn't it been a full life, Lillie,' he said. 'And isn't this a good end?'

Connolly slipped a piece of paper into Nora's hand, the copy of his last statement that he read at his trial. An officer announced that they had five more minutes, which over-whelmed Lillie and she briefly collapsed. Connolly tried to clasp her in his arms but he was immobilised by his wounds. His daughter laid her head on his chest and he whispered, 'Goodbye, Nora.'

The officer called out that the time was up. Nora went to Lillie but could not move her. 'She stood as if turned to stone, and with white face looked at daddy.' A nurse put her arm around Lillie and guided them towards the door. Nora and Lillie 'stood on the threshold, taking a last look at him.' They 'would never see him again.'[11]

Sometime after 1am that morning, on Friday, 12 May, Father Aloysius arrived and heard Connolly's confession and administered Holy Communion. Connolly was then given a final meal in his bed. As he was lifted into a stretcher, some of the nurses were in tears and one nurse in particular, Lucinda McDermott, held his hand as the guards carried him down the stairs to Upper Castle Yard.[12] He was lifted into a waiting ambulance in a stretcher, which he lay on for the journey to Kilmainham Gaol. Father Aloysius and another Capuchin friar, Father Sebastian, accompanied him in the rear of the ambulance.[13] When they reached Kilmainham a blindfold was placed around his head whilst he was still in the ambulance, but his hands were not tied.

The side entrance into the stone-breakers' yard in the jail was opened wide enough to allow the ambulance to drive right in. Connolly was removed from the stretcher and, as he was unable to stand unaided, was placed in a chair, wearing only his pyjamas. His head was lolling backwards; the injection of morphine, which had been administered in Dublin Castle by the military doctor, affected his senses.

The firing squads used in Dublin in 1916 consisted of twelve men and one sergeant, under the direction of an officer who loaded the rifles for the men. Of the thirteen bullets used, one was a blank or 'conscience' round; therefore each man was left not knowing whether he had personally shot the victim or not.[14]

Ready. Present. Fire. These were the last words that Connolly heard.

Two shots hit his head and one shot entered his abdomen. The rest of the firing squad aimed for the piece of white paper pinned to Connolly's chest. The intensity of their firing was such that a large chunk of the back of the chair was blown away.

Father Eugene McCarthy, who had attended Seán Mac-Diarmada, executed a half an hour earlier, anointed Connolly immediately after the shooting.

Although it would have provided some small comfort to

his family, they were denied the right to bury Connolly after he was executed. He was buried in the cemetery attached to a British military prison at Arbour Hill.

Nora recalled that they would not even return any part of his uniform except for his blood-stained under-shirt. When Lillie spoke to the chief-of-intelligence, she was informed that they were keeping his clothes as evidence. She wryly enquired as to what evidence they required now that they had shot him.[15]

# Conclusion

*Apostles of Freedom are ever idolised when dead, but crucified when living.*[1]

*Our real geniuses and inspired apostles we never recognised, nor did we honour them. We killed them by neglect, or stoned them whilst they lived, and then went in reverent procession to their graves when they were dead.*[2]

**C**onnolly was not the only leading socialist to die as a result of the Easter Rising. Francis Sheehy Skeffington, pacifist, suffrage campaigner and socialist, was executed by British soldiers despite having nothing to do with the Rising. Councillor Richard O'Carroll, general secretary of the Brick and Stoneworkers' Union, died a little over a week after he was shot by British troops, despite the fact that he had surrendered. ICA Captain Se`n Connolly was one of the first casualties of the Rising, having been shot dead at City Hall, where he was in command of the garrison. Michael Mallin was executed by firing squad. William Partridge was sentenced to twenty-five years' penal servitude for his part in the Rising, but was released from Dartmoor in April 1917. He died three months later. Peadar Macken, once vice-president of the Dublin Trades Council, was killed by one of his own men in Boland's Mills.[3]

Lillie Connolly had suffered lengthy periods of separation from her husband. In the last sixteen years of their time together Connolly was away lecturing, touring, and organising for a total of four years. After the Rising she was to be separated from him forever and she was to struggle even more than before. Roddy and Fiona were still children and, although little money was around while Connolly was alive, there was to be be even less now he was dead. Immediately after her husband's execution, Lillie resolved to return to New York with the family and try to rebuild their life there. Permission to do so was denied. She lived in Dublin until she passed away in 1938.

Nora Connolly carried on the work of her father: she went on lecture tours of the US, was active with the IRA, maintained her republican beliefs throughout her life, and became a member of Seanad Éireann. She passed away just before her book *We Shall Rise Again* was published in 1981.

Roddy Connolly became the first president of the Communist Party of Ireland and later assisted in the setting up of the Workers' Party of Ireland. He fought with the Anti-Treaty IRA during the Civil War and much later was elected to the Dáil as a Labour candidate. Like his sister, he was also a member of Seanad Éireann. Roddy was 79 years of age when he died just before Christmas 1980.

Ina Connolly was active during the Civil War and ran a first aid station with Nora in Talbot Street during the fighting in Dublin. She married Archie Heron, a trade unionist and organiser for the Labour Party who was elected to Dáil Éireann in 1937.

Moira Connolly studied medicine and became a doctor; she married Richard Beech and lived in Harrow, London.

Aideen Connolly married Hugh Ward from Monaghan and lived first in Kildare and later in Manchester.

Fiona Connolly completed her education in France and studied to become an English teacher. She carried out a large amount of research for Dorothy McArdle's *The Irish Republic*. She married Leonard Wilson and was an active member of the British labour party. Fiona Connolly passed away in 1976.

The legacy James Connolly left when he was executed is unquantifiable. There are those who might argue that the Rising was premature, needless bloodletting, and was unnecessary. There are others who believe that Connolly's passionate words, words that he transformed into deeds, gave hope to the aspirations of more than one generation and will continue to stimulate and encourage until his vision of an equitable world is achieved.

John Leslie, Connolly's old comrade from Edinburgh, the man responsible for Connolly moving to Dublin in 1896, in a letter to William O'Brien, ISRP comrade and faithful collector of Connolly's correspondence, stated quite profoundly in late 1916:

Personally, my day of active work in the movement is done, but to the last I will treasure as one of the most consoling remembrances of that work, that it brought me into friendship with James Connolly.[4]

It seems only fair to allow Connolly have the last word. On 8 April 1916, only a couple of weeks before the Easter Rising, he penned these words in the *Workers' Republic*:

We are out for Ireland for the Irish. But who are the Irish? Not the rack-renting, slum-owning landlord; not the sweating, profit-grinding capitalist; not the sleek and oily lawyer; not the prostitute pressman – the hired liars of the enemy … Not these, but the Irish working class, the only secure foundation upon which a free nation can be reared.

# Appendix 1

## Wages, Marriage and The Church

• • • • • • • • • • • • • • •

Connolly's letter on 'Wages, Marriage and The Church' was
published in *The People*, 9 April, 1904. This is the letter that
caused a long-term battle of words between Connolly and
Daniel De Leon.

> There is a tale told of an inmate of a lunatic asylum who was
> asked by a visitor to the institution how he came to be there.
> "Well," he replied, "I thought the people outside were mad, and
> they thought I was mad. They were in the majority, and, here I
> am." This tale often occurs to my mind when I run up against
> things in our movement contrary to my own views of Social-
> ism and the essentials of Socialist propaganda. I find myself in
> complete accord with the S.L.P. (of which I am proud to be
> a member) on all questions of policy and of discipline and of
> revolutionary procedure. When it comes down to holding our
> position as against an opponent, no matter how well equipped,
> I am not aware of any case in any country in which the com-
> rades found fault with my defence or attack, or my exposition
> of our principles. And yet I have found in the party speakers

and writers, and comrades who professed to be neither, who held and gave expression to views on policy, and conceptions of Socialism with which I would not for a moment agree. And the thought occurs to me: Which of us is mad? To settle this question, I am here setting down some of the points on which I find myself in disagreement with numbers of the comrades, and hope to see in the Weekly People – the only one of our organs available for me – an earnest discussion thereon.

Lately when reading the report of the meetings held by one of our organizers in the West, I discovered that in the course of a discussion with a spokesman of the Kangaroos, this comrade held that the workers could not even temporarily benefit by a rise in wages "as every rise in wages was offset by a rise in prices."[1] When the Kangaroo quoted from Marx's "Value, Price and Profit," to prove the contrary, our S.L.P. man airily disposed of Marx by saying that Marx wrote in advance of, and without anticipation of, the present day combinations of capital.[2] I am afraid that that S.L.P. speaker knew little of Marx except his name, or he could not have made such a remark. The theory that a rise in prices always destroys the value of a rise in wages sounds very revolutionary, of course, but it is not true. And, further-more, it is no part of our doctrine. If it were it knocks the feet from under the S.T. & L.A. and renders that body little else than a mere ward-heeling club for the S.L.P.[3] I am prepared to defend this point if any one considers me wrong upon it. It was one of the points in dispute between my opponents at the Schenectady meeting and myself. Until the party is a unit upon such points, our propaganda in one place will nullify our propaganda in another.

Again, when touring this country in 1902, I met in Indianapolis an esteemed comrade who almost lost his temper with me because I expressed my belief in mono-gamic marriage, and because I said, as I still hold, that the tendency of civilization is towards its perfection and completion, instead of towards its destruction. My com-rade's views, especially since the publication in The People of Bebel's "Woman," are held by a very large number of members, but I hold, nevertheless, that they are wrong, and, furthermore, that such works and such publications are an excrescence upon the movement.[4] The abolition of the capitalist system will, undoubtedly, solve the economic side of the Woman Question, but it will solve that alone. The question of marriage, of divorce, of paternity, of the equality of woman with man are physical and sexual ques-tions, or questions of temperamental affiliation as in mar-riage, and were we living in a Socialist Republic would still be hotly contested as they are today. One great element of disagreement would be removed – the economic – but men and women would still be unfaithful to their vows, and questions of the intellectual equality of the sexes would still be as much in dispute as they are today, even although economic equality would be assured. To take a case in point: Suppose a man and woman married. The man after a few years ceases to love the woman, his wife, and loves another. But his wife's love for him has only increased with the passage of years, and she has borne him children. He wishes to leave her and consort with his new love. Will the fact that her economic future is secured be any solace to the deserted mother or to her children? Decidedly not! It is a human and sexual problem, not an economic problem at all. Unjust economic conditions aggravate the evil, but do not create it. Comrade De Leon says in his preface, which I have just seen, that Bebel's "Woman" raises up for the proletaire friends in the camp of the enemy. I consider that it is, on the contrary, an attempt to seduce the proletariat from the firm ground of political and economic science on to the questionable ground of physiology and sex. Instead of raising up friends in the camp of the enemy, it engenders the fatal habit of looking outside our own class for help to the members of a class – the "enemy" referred to – whose whole material interests are opposed to ours. In the days of battle will the claims of sex or the claims of their class weigh most with the ladies of the capitalist class? Bebel's "Woman" is popular because of its quasi-prurient revelations of the past and present degradation of womanhood, but I question if you can find in the whole world one woman who was led to Socialism by it, but you can find hundreds who were repelled from studying Socialism by judicious extracts from its pages. I believe it is destined to be in the future a potent weapon against us in this country. And it is a weapon put into the enemy's hands without obtaining any corresponding advantage for our side. The valuable propaganda material in the book is absolutely nullified by its identification with a debatable physiological question on which the party as a whole has never been consulted, and could not be.

The attitude of the party toward religion is another one on which I believe there is a tendency at present to stray from the correct path. Theoretically every S.L.P. man agrees that Socialism is a political and economic question, and has nothing to do with religion. But how many adhere to that position? Very few, indeed. It is scarcely possible to take up a copy of the Weekly People of late without realizing from its contents that it and the party are becoming distinctly anti-religious. If a clergyman anywhere attacks Socialism the tendency is to hit back, not at his economic absurdities, but at his theology, with which we have nothing to do. In other words, we occupy a strongly entrenched position based upon demonstrable facts. When a clergyman attacks this position our wisest course is to remain in our entrenchments and to allow him to waste his energy and demonstrate his ignorance by futile attacks upon our position. Instead of which, our comrades descend from their entrenchments and engage the enemy in combat over a question of the next world – a question that were we to argue for another century could not be proven or disproved on one side or the other. That is to say, we attack the enemy where he is strongest, and instead of relying upon appeals to the class interests of the workers we tangle their minds up in questions which even the trained intellect of scientists cannot solve. All of which must be very satisfactory to our enemies. The prominence given to the absurd article of M. Vandervelde illustrates this clearly.[5] Mr. Vandervelde is a middle class doctrinaire, who, on every question of tactics, has proven himself unsafe as a guide. His performances as an upholder of Millerand ought to be well known to readers of The People, his botchy handling of the late Universal Strike in Belgium, when he and his party sacrificed the interests of hundreds of poor workingmen and their families in order to "teach a lesson" to the amused capitalist government, is also well known.[6] His general Kangarooism is recognized by every thinking student of the European Socialist movement, but, lo! he speaks against the Catholic Church, and presto, he is become an oracle. But I refuse to worship at this Delphic shrine, and I laugh at the words of the oracle. Indeed, those words contain their own refutation. They are not a reasoned appeal to the working class, but an appeal to the free-thinkers to look to the Socialists to fight their battles for them. That is the tenor of the whole article. See how tenderly he speaks of the English Liberals. "Justice forbids, however, to reproach English Liberalism as a body with the reactionary complaisance of the right wing." We read how he approves of the sleek bourgeois governmental dodge to disorganize Socialist forces by the corruption of Millerand and Jaures. For the extract in The People omits a word, which I will put in brackets, and which, whether in the "Independent" or not, obviously from the context ought to have been there: "The Republican middle class and the radical Democracy do (not) hesitate to accept the help of the Social Democracy in the fight against the Catholic Church by enrolling Millerand in the Ministry and elect-ing Jaures Vice President of the Chamber of Deputies." To this doctrinaire the great struggle of the working class for freedom is but a kind of side show, or, perhaps, an auxiliary, to the free-thinking movement. The betrayal of the work-ers by his kind in France is justifiable in the exigencies of the free-thought campaign. His statement that he does "not know and cannot conceive of a free-thinking workingman who is not at the same time a Socialist," only goes to show how little he knows about the working class. I am sure few readers of The People could echo his words. His whole soul is perturbed with the fear that when Socialism crushes out the free-thinking middle class, there will be nobody left to fight the Church unless Socialism kindly consents to become a catspaw for the propagandists of free-thought. How the capitalist editor of the English "Freethinker," or the staunch Republican soul of Bob Ingersoll would rejoice to see us linking the propaganda of our *knowledge* with that of their *speculations*. We have seen how the free-thinking capitalist governments of France knew how to utilize an anti-clerical Dreyfus agitation to corrupt our movement, we see to-day how a similar free-thinking administration in the same country initiates against religious orders a campaign which the Parti Ouvrier has seen fit to denounce as a mere bourgeois dodge to divert public attention from the social question, and if we but pause to think we will see in the anti-religious tone of our papers and speakers how the ground here is being unwittingly prepared for the same confusion and emasculation. I shall certainly do my share toward repelling every such tendency as strongly as I would fight to prevent the movement being identified even by implication with the tenets of the Catholic Church, or the Protestant, or the Shinto, or the Jew.

The S.L.P. is a political and economic party, seeking the conquest of public power in order to clear the way for the Social Revolution. Let it keep to that. It is a big enough proposition.

But I have said enough to arouse discussion, and will reserve further criticism to another time. I hold that mine is the correct S.L.P. doctrine. Now, will some one please tread on the tail of my coat?

JAMES CONNOLLY, Troy, N.Y., 23 March [1904].

# Appendix 2

## Ballads and Poems of James Connolly

• • • • • • • • • • • • • • •

In the introduction to *Songs of Freedom*, which was published in New York in 1907, James Connolly wrote:

> No revolutionary movement is complete without its poetical expression. If such a movement has caught hold of the imagination of the masses, they will seek a vent in song for the aspirations, the fears and hopes, the loves and hatreds engendered by the struggle. Until the movement is marked by the joyous, defiant, singing of revolutionary songs, it lacks one of the distinctive marks of a popular revolutionary movement—it is a dogma of a few, and not the faith of the multitude ...

Connolly published a little over twenty songs during his life. 'Be Moderate' was published in *Songs of Freedom* and 'The Watchword' or 'The Watchword of Labour' was written during his time in the US and printed in the *Irish Worker* in December 1913. 'The Legacy' is a poem written for his son, Roderick Connolly, when James Connolly was suffering a severe illness. It was published in *The Harp* in February 1908 and in the *Irish Worker*, on 23 May 1914.

# Be Moderate

## Air – A Nation Once Again

*Some men, faint-hearted, ever seek*
*Our programme to retouch,*
*And will insist, when'er they speak*
*That we demand too much.*
*'Tis passing strange, yet I declare*
*Such statements give me mirth,*
*For our demands most moderate are,*
*We only want THE EARTH.*

*'Be moderate,' the timorous cry,*
*Who dread the tyrants' thunder,*
*'You ask too much, and people fly*
*From you aghast, in wonder.'*
*'Tis passing strange, and I declare*
*Such statements cause me mirth,*
*For our demands most moderate are,*
*We only want THE EARTH.*

*Our masters all – a godly crew,*
*Whose hearts throb for the poor –,*
*Their sympathies assure us, too,*
*If our demands were fewer.*
*Most generous souls, But please observe,*
*What they enjoy from birth,*
*Is all we ever had the nerve*
*To ask, that is, THE EARTH.*

*The 'Labour Fakir,' full of guile,*
*Base doctrine ever preaches,*
*And, whilst he bleeds the rank and file,*
*Tame moderation teaches.*
*Yet, in his despite, we'll see the day*
*When, with sword in its girth,*
*Labour shall march in war array,*
*To seize its own, THE EARTH.*

*For Labour long with groans and tears*
*To its oppressors knelt,*
*But, never yet to aught save fears*
*Did the heart of tyrant melt.*
*We need not kneel; our cause is high,*
*Of true men there's no dearth,*
*And our victorious rallying cry*
*Shall be, WE WANT THE EARTH.*

## The Watchword

*O, hear ye the watchword of Labour!*
*The slogan of they who'd be free,*
*That no more to any enslaver,*
*Must Labour bend suppliant knee;*
*That we on whose shoulders are borne*
*The pomp and pride of the great,*
*Whose toil they repaid with their scorn,*
*Shall meet it at last with our hate.*

**Chorus**

*Then send it aloft on the breeze, boys,*
*That watchword, the grandest we've known,*
*That Labour must rise from its knees, boys,*
*And claim the broad earth as its own.*

*Aye, we who oft won by our valour*
*Empire for our rulers and lords,*
*Yet knelt in abasement and squalor*
*To that we had made by our swords,*
*Now valour with worth will be blending*
*When, answering Labour's command,*
*We rise from the dust, and, ascending*
*To manhood, for freedom take stand.*

*Then out from the field and the city,*
*From workshop, from mill and from mine,*
*Despising their wrath and their pity,*
*We workers are moving in line,*
*To answer the watchword and token*
*That Labour gives forth as its own,*
*Nor pause till our chains we have broken*
*And conquered the spoiler and drone.*

# The Legacy: The Dying Socialist to his Son

Come here my son, and for a time put up your childish play,
Draw nearer to your father's bed, and lay your games away,
No sick man's 'plaint is this of mine, ill-tempered at your noise,
Nor carping at your eagerness to romp with childish toys.
Thou'rt but a boy, and I, a man outworn with care and strife,
Would not deprive you of one joy thou canst extract from life;
But o'er my soul comes creeping on death's shadow, and my lips
Must give to you a message now ere life meets that eclipse.
Slow runs my blood, my nether limbs I feel not, and my eyes
Can scarce discern, here in this room that childish form I prize.

Aye, death's grim hand is on my frame, and helpless it lies here,
But to my mental vision comes the power of the seer,
And time and space are now as nought as with majestic sweep,
I feel my mind traverse the land and encompass the deep;
Search backward over history's course, or with prophetic view,
And sounding lines of hope and fear, gauge man's great destiny too,
The chasm deep 'twixt life and death, I bridge at last tonight,
And with a foot on either side absorb their truths and light.
And thus, though 'reft of strength, my limbs slow turn to clay,
Fired by this light I call you here to hear my Legacy.

'My legacy!' Ah, son of mine! Wert thou a rich man's pride,
He'd crown thee with his property, possessions far and wide,
And golden store to purchase slaves, whose aching brain and limb
Would toil to bring you luxury as such had toiled for him.
But thy father is a poor man, and glancing round you here,
Thou canst see all his property — our humble household gear,

*No need we will by lawyers drawn, no witnesses attest,*
*To guard for you your legacy, your father's last bequest.*


*'Thy father is a poor man,' mark well what that may mean,*
*On the tablets of thy memory that truth write bright and clean,*
*Thy father's lot it was to toil from earliest boyhood on,*
*And know his latent energies for a master's profit drawn;*
*Or else, ill-starred, to wander round and huckster-like to vend*
*His precious store of brain and brawn to all whom fate may send,*
*Across his path with gold enough to purchase Labour's power*
*To turn it into gold again, and fructify the hour.*
*With sweat and blood of toiling slaves, like unto us, my son,*
*Aye, through our veins since earliest days, 'tis poor man's blood has*
*run.*
*Yes, son of mine, since History's dawn two classes stand revealed,*
*The Rich and Poor, in bitterest war, by deadliest hatred steeled,*
*The one, incarnate greed and crime, disdaining honest toil,*
*Had grasped man's common birthright and treasure house, the soil.*
*And standing 'twixt their fellow man and all that earth could give,*
*Had bade them render tribute if they would hope to live.*
*And, building crime on top of crime, had pushed their conquests on,*
*Till, arbiters of life and death, they stood with weapons drawn,*
*And blades athirst to drink the blood, on land and over sea,*
*Of him who dared for human rights to stem their tyranny,*
*They held our lands, our bodies ruled, and strove to rule the mind,*
*And Hell itself could not surpass their evil to mankind,*
*And all who strove for human rights to break their cursed yoke –*
*The noblest of our race, my child – went down beneath their stroke,*
*And over all earth's sweetest spots, in nature's loveliest haunt,*

*Each built his fort or castle grim the poor of earth to daunt.*

*And issuing forth from walls of stone, high over cliff and pass,*
*With sword in hand, would gather in the tribute for his class,*
*And grimmest emblems of their rule, flaunting to human ken,*
*The pit to drown our women, the gibbet for our men,*
*Stood, aye, beside their fortresses; and underneath the moat*
*Tier upon tier of noisome cells for those the tyrant smote.*
*Thumbscrews and rack and branding rod, and each device of Hell*
*Perverted genius could devise to torture men to sell*
*(For brief respite from anguish dire to end their wretched lives)*
*The secret of their comradeship, the honour of their wives.*

*As the fabled upas tree of old, by ancient poets sung,*
*Consumed with blight each living thing then 'neath its branches*
*sprung,*
*The rich man's power o'er all the earth had spread its baleful blight,*
*Respecting neither age nor sex to sate its lust and might.*
*It stole the harvest from the field, the product of the loom,*
*Struck down the old man in his age, the young man in his bloom,*
*It robbed the carrier on the road, the sailor on the tide,*
*And from the bridegroom of the hour it took the new-made bride,*
*Such crimes it wrought not Hell itself and its satanic school*
*Could fashion crimes to equal those wrought by the rich man's rule.*

*'The past?' Aye, boy, the method's past, the deed is still the same,*
*And robbery is robbery, yet cloaked in gentler name.*
*Our means of life are still usurped, the rich man still is lord,*
*And prayers and cries for justice still meet one reply – the sword!*

*Though hypocrites for rich men's gold may tell us we are free,*
*And oft extol in speech and print our vaunted liberty,*
*But freedom lies not in a name, and he who lacks for bread*
*Must have that bread tho' he should give his soul for it instead,*
*And we, who live by Labour, know that while they rule we must*
*Sell Freedom, brain and limb to win for us and ours a crust.*

*The robbers made our fathers slaves, then chained them to the soil,*
*For a little longer chain – a wage – we must exchange our toil.*
*But open force gave way to fraud, and force again behind*
*Prepares to strike if fraud should fail to keep men deaf and blind.*
*Our mothers see their children's limbs they fondled as they grew,*
*And doted on, caught up to make for rich men profits new.*
*Whilst strong men die for lack of work, and cries of misery swell*
*And women's souls in cities' streets creep shuddering to Hell.*
*These things belong not to the past, but to the present day,*
*And they shall last till in our wrath we sweep them all away.*

*'We sweep them!' Ah, too well I know my work on earth is done,*
*Even as I speak my chilling blood tells me my race is run.*
*But you, my last-born child, take the legacy I give,*
*And do as did your father whilst he yet was spared to live.*
*Treasure ye in your inmost heart this legacy of hate,*
*For those who on the poor man's back have climbed to high estate.*
*The lords of land and capital – the slave lords of our age,*
*Who of this smiling earth of ours have made for us a cage,*
*Where golden bars fetter men's souls, and noble thoughts do flame*
*To burn us with their vain desires, and virtue yields to shame.*
*Each is your foe, foe to your class, of human rights, the foe,*

*Be it your thought by day and night to work their overthrow;*
*And howsoe'er you earn your wage, and whereso'er you go,*
*Be it beneath the tropic heat or 'mid the northern snow,*
*Or closely penn'd in factory walls or burrowing in the mine*
*Or scorching in the furnace hell of steamers 'cross the brine,*
*Or on the railroad's shining track you guide the flying wheel,*
*Or clambering up on buildings high to weld their frames of steel,*
*Or use the needle or the type, the hammer or the pen,*
*Have you one thought, one speech alone, to all your fellow-men.*
*The men and women of your class, tell them their wrongs and yours,*
*Plant in their hearts that hatred deep that suffers and endures,*
*And treasure up each deed of wrong, each scornful word and look,*
*Inscribe it in the memory, as others in a book,*
*And wait and watch through toiling years the ripening of time,*
*Yet deem to strike before that hour were worse than folly – crime!*

*This be your task, oh, son of mine, the rich man's hate to brave,*
*And consecrate your noblest part to rouse each fellow-slave.*
*To speed the day the world awaits when Labour long opprest,*
*Shall rise and strike for Freedom true, and from the tyrant wrest,*
*The power they have abused so long. Oh ever glorious deed!*
*The crowning point of history, yet child, of bitterest need.*

*Ah, woe is me, thy father's eyes shall not behold the day.*
*I faint and die; child, hold my hand –*
*Keep–thou–my–leg–a–cy!*

# Notes

## Introduction

[1] *Shan Van Vocht,* January 1897.

[2] *Workers' Republic,* 3 September 1898.


## Chapter One

[1] *Workers' Republic,* 8 April 1916.

[2] Connolly, James, *Labour in Irish History,* Dublin, Maunsel, 1910.

[3] *Sinn Féin Rebellion Handbook,* Dublin, *The Irish Times,* 1916, p272.

[4] Desmond Ryan also asserts that Connolly was born in 1870, which goes in some way to explain why his official death certificate indicates that he was 46 when he was executed, whereas he was really 47, just three weeks short of his 48th birthday.

[5] Greaves, C Desmond, *The Life and Times of James Connolly,* London, Lawrence & Wishart, 1961, p17.

[6] *Irish Felon,* 24 June 1848.

[7] Connolly, *Labour in Irish History.*

[8] Connolly O'Brien, Nora, *Portrait of a Rebel Father,* Dublin, Talbot Press, 1935, p86.

[9] Samuel Levenson suggested that Connolly may have joined the Second Battalion, Royal Scots, but the evidence is insufficient.

[10] Connolly, *Labour in Irish History.*


## Chapter Two

[1] *Irish Worker,* 29 August 1914.

[2] National Library of Ireland, NLI Ms. 13,911. This letter, although undated, was penned around April 1889.

[3] Ibid. This undated letter was written in April 1890.

[4] Greaves says it was 13 April, Levenson says 20 April, Cronin says 30 April. An examination of the marriage certificate clearly shows it was the thirtieth.

[5] NLI Ms. 13,942.

[6] Ryan, Desmond, *James Connolly, His Life, Work and Writings*, Dublin, Talbot Press, 1924, p16.

[7] NLI Ms. 13,933.

[8] Greaves, *The Life and Times of James Connolly*, p60.


## Chapter Three

[1] Connolly, *Labour in Irish History*.

[2] Greaves says 76 Charlemont Street, but a letter from Connolly in the NLI clearly states number 75.

[3] Ryan, *James Connolly, His Life, Work and Writings*, p22.

[4] Connolly O'Brien, Nora, *Portrait of a Rebel Father*, p24.

[5] *Shan Van Vocht*, January 1897.

[6] NLI Ms. 16,292.

[7] Levenson, Samuel, *James Connolly*, London, Martin, Brian & O'Keefe, 1973, p51.

[8] NLI Ms. 13,939.

[9] Greaves, *The Life and Times of James Connolly*, p99.

[10] Ibid. p86.

[11] Ryan, *James Connolly, His Life, Work and Writings*, p3.

[12] Ibid. p122.

[13] Bell, Thomas, *Pioneering Days*, London, Lawrence & Wishart, 1941, p47.


## Chapter Four

[1] *Workers' Republic*, 19 August 1899.

[2] Connolly O'Brien, *Portrait of a Rebel Father*, p9.

[3] *Irish Press*, 24 January 1938.

[4] Bureau of Military Archives (BMH), Ina Connolly Heron, Witness Statement (WS) 919.

[5] Ibid.

[6] Nevin, Donal, *James Connolly, A Full Life*, Dublin, Gill & Macmillan, 2005, p97.

[7] Connolly, *Labour in Irish History*.

[8] *Workers' Republic*, 2 October 1915.

[9] Connolly O'Brien, *Portrait of a Rebel Father*, p49.

[10] *On Doctrine* by Samuel Butler (1835–1902).

[11] Translated, The Sword of Light.

[12] NLI Ms. 13,932.

[13] *Workers' Republic*, 20 August 1898.

[14] Ibid. 19 August 1899.


## Chapter Five

[1] *Irish Worker*, 19 September 1914.

[2] *Workers' Republic*, 10 February 1900.

[3] Greaves, *The Life and Times of James Connolly*, p122.

[4] McCarthy, Michael JF, *Five Years in Ireland, 1895–1900*, p504.

[5] *Inghinidhe na hÉireann* translates directly as 'Daughters of Ireland'.

[6] *Workers' Republic*, 24 November 1900.

[7] Connolly O'Brien, *Portrait of a Rebel Father*, p62.

[8] Ina Connolly Heron, WS 919.

[9] Greaves, *The Life and Times of James Connolly*, p133.

[10] NLI Ms. 13,912.

[11] Valentine McEntee (1871–1953) Dublin born ISRP and later SDF activist, later Labour MP in England.

[12] AP Hazell, SDF comrade and author of a pamphlet *A Summary of Marx's 'Capital'*.

[13] NLI Ms. 13,912.

[14] Later known as Con Lehane, he co-founded the Cork ISRP with Tom Lyng, he would be forced to leave Cork after socialism was condemned from the pulpit.

[15] NLI Ms. 13,939.

[16] *Workers' Republic*, March 1902.

[17] NLI Ms. 13,932.

[18] Ibid.

[19] NLI Ms. 13,908.

[20] Greaves maintained they moved here in 1897, but he missed the fact that the family lived on Queen Street for a couple of years.


## Chapter Six

[1] Connolly, James, *The Re-Conquest of Ireland*, Dublin, 1915.

[2] Ryan, *James Connolly, His Life, Work and Writings*, p30.

[3] Levenson, *James Connolly*, p92.

[4] Reeve, Carl and Ann, *James Connolly and the United States*, New Jersey, Humanities Press, 1978, p27.

[5] NLI Ms. 13,932.

[6] Ibid.

[7] Connolly O'Brien, Nora, *We Shall Rise Again*, London, Mosquito Press, 1981, p42.

[8] NLI Ms. 13,932.

[9] ibid.

[10] Reeve, *James Connolly and the United States*, p34.

[11] Nevin, *James Connolly, A Full Life*, p199.

[12] Connolly O'Brien, *Portrait of a Rebel Father*, p63.

[13] Reeve, *James Connolly and the United States*, p38.

[14] Greaves, Reeve and Nevin record they were called Helen and Thomas Humes. See text further on in chapter on research that shows they were Margaret and Thomas Humes.

[15] Nevin, *James Connolly, A Full Life*, p202. Reeve gives the same date. Greaves gives the date as 2 January 1903.

[16] Reeve, *James Connolly and the United States*, p41.

[17] Ibid.

[18] Fox, RM, *James Connolly, The Forerunner*, Tralee, Kerryman, 1946, p47.

[19] Connolly, James, *Wood Quay Ward Election Address*, Dublin, January 1903.

[20] NLI Ms. 13,915.

[21] NLI Ms. 13,906.

[22] Bell, *Pioneering Days*, pp 47–48.

[23] Ibid p49.

[24] NLI Ms. 13,932.

[25] NLI Ms. 13,939.

[26] NLI Ms. 13,906.

[27] For detailed analysis of this controversy see; Greaves, pp171–181; Reeve, pp51–63; Allen, pp 60–64.

[28] Reeve, *James Connolly and the United States*, p51.

[29] Greaves, *The Life and Times of James Connolly*, p170.

[30] NLI Ms. 13,906.

## Chapter Seven

[1] *Forward*, 1 November 1913.

[2] NLI Ms. 13,906.

[3] Ibid.

[4] Ina Connolly Heron, WS 919.

[5] Ibid.

[6] Plot number JL 174 Glasnevin Cemetery.

[7] First Name, *Mona*. Last Name, *Connolly*. Ethnicity, *Ireland, Irish*. Last Place of Residence, *Dublin*. Date of Arrival, *Aug 14, 1904*. Age at Arrival, *13yr*. Gender, *F*. Marital Status, *S*. Ship of Travel, *Cedric*. Port of Departure, *Queenstown*. Manifest Line Number, *0014*.

[8] NLI Ms. 13,909.

[9] Not 76 Ingalls Ave. as Greaves maintained. The Troy directory for 1905 lists Connolly at 96 Ingalls Ave. Also letters from Connolly bear the address 96 but sometimes Connolly's nines look like sevens.

[10] Ina Connolly Heron, WS 919.

[11] NLI Ms. 13,909

[12] Greaves, *The Life and Times of James Connolly*, p185.

[13] Ina Connolly Heron, WS 919.

[14] NLI Ms. 13,909.

[15] Ibid.

[16] Ina Connolly Heron, WS 919.

[17] NLI Ms. 13,940.

[18] NLI Ms. 13,906.

[19] Ina Connolly Heron, WS 919.

[20] NLI Ms. 13,906.

[21] Connolly O'Brien, *Portrait of a Rebel Father*, p90.

[22] Ina Connolly Heron, WS 919.

## Chapter Eight

[1] *Workers' Republic*, 9 October 1915.

[2] Dutton Savage, Marion, *Industrial Unionism in America*, New York, The Ronald Press Co., 1922, p150.

[3] Levenson, *James Connolly*, p125.

[4] Connolly O'Brien, *We Shall Rise Again*, pp8–9.

[5] *Tír gan teanga, tír gan anam,* PH Pearse.

[6] Gurley Flynn, Elizabeth, *I Speak My Own Piece*, New York, Masses & Mainstream, 1955, p64.

[7] Connolly O'Brien, Nora, *Portrait of a Rebel Father*, p96.

[8] NLI Ms. 13,906.

[9] Gurley Flynn, *I Speak My Own Piece*, p75.

[10] NLI Ms. 13,906.

[11] Ibid.

[12] Reeve, *James Connolly and the United States*, p121.

[13] NLI Ms. 13,906.

[14] Ibid.

[15] Ibid.

[16] NLI Ms. 13,908.

[17] *The Harp*, May 1908.

[18] Flynn, Elizabeth Gurley, *I Speak My Own Piece*, p 76.

[19] NLI Ms. 13,906.

[20] Reeve, *James Connolly and the United States*, p108.

[21] *Liberty Magazine*, Recollections of Ina Connolly-Heron, Dublin, ITGWU, April 1966, p19.

[22] NLI Ms. 13,906.

[23] NLI Ms. 13,939.

## Chapter Nine

[1] Connolly, *Labour in Irish History.*

[2] NLI Ms. 13,945. The play was performed in Liberty Hall in March 1916 and again a week before the Rising. The protagonist was played by Seán Connolly. who was killed in action on Easter Monday at City Hall.

[3] NLI Ms. 13,928.

[4] Reeve, *James Connolly and the United States*, p144.

[5] Ibid. p159.

[6] NLI Ms. 13,908.

[7] Ibid.

[8] Ibid.

[9] NLI Ms. 13,911.

[10] NLI Ms. 13,908.

[11] Ibid.

[12] Ibid.

[13] Ibid.

[14] Ibid.

[15] Ibid.

[16] Nevin, Donal (ed.) *Between Comrades, Letters and Correspondence*, Dublin, Gill & Macmillan, 2007, pp421–422.

[17] *The Harp*, August 1909.


## Chapter Ten

[1] *Forward*, 2 August 1913.

[2] *Fifty Years of Liberty Hall*, Dublin, Sign of the Three Candles, 1959, p28.

[3] Ibid. p33.

[4] Connolly, James, *Labour, Nationality and Religion*, 1910.

[5] NLI Ms. 13,906.

[6] NLI Ms. 13,908.

[7] Ibid.

[8] Ina Connolly Heron, WS 919.

[9] Connolly O'Brien, *Portrait of a Rebel Father*, p110.

[10] Ryan, *James Connolly, His Life, Work and Writings*, p27.

[11] Ina Connolly Heron, WS 919.

[12] Ibid.

[13] NLI Ms. 13,908.

[14] Nevin, *Between Comrades, Letters and Correspondence*, p457.

[15] Ina Connolly Heron, WS 919.

[16] NLI Ms. 13,908.

[17] The two main unions being the Textile Operatives' Society and the Amalgamated Union of Labour.

[18] Dudley Edwards, Ruth, *James Connolly*, Dublin, Gill & Macmillan, 1981, p83.

[19] Ina Connolly Heron, WS 919.

[20] NLI Ms. 13,908.

[21] Ina Connolly Heron, WS 919.

[22] NLI Ms. 13,908.

[23] Ryan, Desmond (ed.), *The Workers' Republic, A Selection from the Writings of James Connolly, With Introduction by William McMullen*, Dublin, Sign of the Three Candles, 1951, p24.

[24] NLI Ms. 13,908. The letter to O'Brien is dated 3 January 1913.

[25] Election Address, Dock Ward, Belfast, January 1913.

[26] NLI Ms. 13,908.

[27] *Forward*, 23 August 1913.

[28] Nevin, *Between Comrades, Letters and Correspondence*, p493.

[29] NLI Ms. 13,908.

## Chapter Eleven

[1] *Irish Worker*, 4 April 1914.

[2] Murphy founded the DEF in June 1911.

[3] Chesterton, GK, *Irish Impressions*, London, Collins, 1916, p75.

[4] Ryan, *James Connolly, His Life, Work and Writings*, p62.

[5] Lionel Cranfield Sackville, 1st Duke of Dorset and Lord Lieutenant of Ireland from 1731–37 and from 1751–55. Many Dubliners referred to the street as O'Connell Street following an attempt by Dublin Corporation to rename it so in 1884. The residents of the street took legal action against the Corporation and were successful in blocking the renaming, but the name O'Connell Street was popularised. It was officially renamed O'Connell Street when the Free State was established in 1922.

[6] Nevin, Donal (ed.), *1913, Jim Larkin and the Dublin Lockout*, Dublin, Workers' Union of Ireland, 1964, p30.

[7] Fox, RM, *The History of the Irish Citizen Army*, Dublin, James Duffy & Co, 1943, p25.

[8] Great Brunswick Street was renamed Pearse Street in 1922 to honour Patrick and Willie Pearse who were born in number 27. The building has been restored by the Ireland Institute.

[9] Nearly every DMP station had a barrel and a tap.

[10] Yeates, Padraig, *Lockout, Dublin 1913*, Dublin, Gill & Macmillan, 2000, p51.

[11] Once known as World's End Lane, Montgomery Street provided the nickname for the immediate area, Monto, Dublin's notorious red light district. Montgomery Street was renamed Foley Street in 1930.

[12] Corporation Buildings contained over 450 flats housing over 2000 residents. Corporation Street was renamed Store Street in 1925.

[13] Helena Molony (1884–1967), Abbey actress and future secretary of the Irish Women Workers' Union and member of the ICA. She fought in City Hall in 1916.

[14] Helen Ruth 'Nellie' Gifford (1880–1971), founding member of Irish Citizen Army. Took part in 1916 Rising as a member of St Stephen's Green garrison. Sister of Grace Plunkett and Muriel MacDonagh.

[15] Larkin, Jim, *In The Footsteps of Big Jim*, Dublin, Blackwater Press, 1995, p43.

[16] Amiens Street Station was renamed Connolly Station in 1966.

[17] There were other 'Bloody Sundays' to follow over the course of the twentieth century in Ireland; Sunday, 26 July 1914, Bachelor's Walk, Dublin; Sunday, 21 November 1920, Croke Park, Dublin; Sunday, 30 January 1972, The Bogside, Derry.

[18] *Irish Worker*, 27 September 1913.

[19] *Workers' Republic*, 29 May 1914.

[20] Ina Connolly Heron, WS 919.

[21] *Forward*, 4 October 1913.

[22] *Irish Worker*, 13 December 1913.

[23] Irish Women Workers' Union (IWWU) – founded in 1911. First General Secretary was Delia Larkin, Big Jim's younger sister.

[24] Yeates, *Lockout, Dublin 1913*, p498.

[25] *Evening Herald*, 21 October 1913.

[26] Yeates, *Lockout, Dublin 1913*, p249.

[27] Joyce, James, 'Gas From A Burner', 1912.

[28] *Forward*, 1 November 1913.

[29] *Evening Herald*, 29 October 1913.

[30] Ryan, *James Connolly, His Life, Work and Writings*, p68.

[31] Robbins, Frank, *Under The Starry Plough*, Dublin, Academy Press, 1977, p58.

[32] Ibid. p16.

[33] O'Cathasaigh, PS (Sean O'Casey), *The Story of The Irish Citizen Army*, Dublin, 1919, p4.

[34] Ibid. p5.

[35] Croydon Park, Fairview was rented by the ITGWU. O'Casey noted that it was 'situated well within the boundaries of the city' and was 'singularly pastoral and peaceful'.

[36] O'Cathasaigh, *The Story of The Irish Citizen Army*, p6.

[37] *Workers' Republic*, 30 October 1915.

[38] *Forward*, 30 May 1914.

[39] *Workers' Republic*, 30 October 1915.

[40] Connolly O'Brien, *Portrait of a Rebel Father*, pp154–155.

[41] *Forward*, 9 February 1914.

[42] *Irish Times*, 3 February 1914.

[43] *Irish Worker*, 28 February 1914.

[44] *Forward*, 9 February 1914.

[45] Services Industrial Professional Technical Union was formed in 1990 when the Federated Workers' Union of Ireland united with the ITGWU.

[46] O'Cathasaigh, *The Story of The Irish Citizen Army*, p12.

[47] Ibid. p17.

[48] O'Casey, Sean, *Drums under the Windows, Autobiography, Book 3, 1906–1916*, London, 1945, p230.

[49] O'Cathasaigh, *The Story of The Irish Citizen Army*, p42.

[50] *Forward*, 9 February 1914.

## Chapter Twelve

[1] *Irish Worker*, 8 August 1914.

[2] Martin, FX, *The Irish Volunteers 1913–15*, Dublin, James Duffy, 1963, p25.

[3] Nevin, *Between Comrades, Letters and Correspondence*, p516.

[4] Ibid. p517.

[5] *Forward*, 27 June 1914.

[6] *Irish Worker*, 8 August 1914.

[7] Ryan, Desmond (ed.), *The Workers' Republic, A Selection from the Writings of James*

*Connolly, With Introduction by William McMullen*, p28.

[8] *Workers' Republic*, 20 November 1915.

[9] *Irish Worker*, 29 August 1914.

[10] *Irish Worker*, 14 November 1914.

[11] Robbins, *Under The Starry Plough*, p17.

[12] Nevin, *James Connolly, A Full Life*, p604.

[13] NLI Ms. 13,908.

[14] Robbins, *Under The Starry Plough*, pp31–32.

[15] Marreco, Anne, *The Rebel Countess*, London, Weidenfeld & Nicolson, 1967, p187.

[16] Ina Connolly, WS 919.


## Chapter Thirteen

[1] Connolly, *Labour in Irish History*.

[2] Robbins, *Under The Starry Plough*, p27.

[3] Ibid.

[4] Ibid. p45.

[5] Connolly, James, *The Re-Conquest of Ireland*, 1915.

[6] *Irish Work*, 19 December, 1914.

[7] NLI Ms. 13,910.

[8] Nevin, *Between Comrades, Letters and Correspondence*, p529.

[9] *Workers' Republic*, 6 November 1915.

[10] Born Rosscarbery, County Cork, 11 September 1831, died Staten Island, New York, 29 June 1915.

[11] Clarke, Kathleen, *Revolutionary Woman, My Fight for Ireland's Freedom*, Dublin, O'Brien Press, 1991, p43.

[12] Souvenir of the Public Funeral of O'Donovan Rossa to Glasnevin Cemetery, Dublin on 1 August 1915.

[13] The police seem to have had the incorrect name for Michael Mallin.

[14] Nevin, *Between Comrades, Letters and Correspondence*, pp536–537.

[15] O'Cathasaigh, *The Story of The Irish Citizen Army*, p52.

[16] *Workers' Republic*, 23 June 1900.

[17] Ibid. 4 December 1915.

[18] Ibid. 29 January 1916.

[19] Robbins, *Under The Starry Plough*, p48.

[20] Christopher Brady, WS 705.

[21] Robbins, *Under The Starry Plough*, p55.


## Chapter Fourteen

[1] *Workers' Republic*, 13 November 1915.

[2] Robbins, *Under The Starry Plough*, p69.

[3] *Workers' Republic*, 8 April 1916.

[4] Fox, *The History of the Irish Citizen Army*, p189.

[5] Henderson, Frank, *Easter Rising, Recollections of a Dublin Volunteer*, Cork University Press, 1998, p32.

[6] Ryan, *James Connolly, His Life, Work & Writings*, p126.

[7] *The Worker*, 30 January 1915.

[8] *Workers' Republic*, 11 March 1916.

[9] William Oman, WS 1574.

[10] Ina Connolly Heron, WS 919.

[11] Ibid.

[12] Macardle, Dorothy, *The Irish Republic*, London, Victor Gollancz, 1937, p163.

[13] Christopher Brady, WS 705.

[14] Ibid.


## Chapter Fifteen

[1] *Workers' Republic*, 11 March 1916.

[2] Ina Connolly Heron WS 919.

[3] William Oman, WS 1574.

[4] Brennan-Whitmore, WJ, *Dublin Burning*, Dublin, Gill and Macmillan, 1996, p39.

[5] Ryan, *The Rising*, Dublin, Golden Eagle Books, 1949, p127.

[6] Ibid. p134.

[7] Brennan-Whitmore, *Dublin Burning*, p67.

[8] Corner of Princes Street and O'Connell Street, right beside the GPO.

[9] Opposite the GPO, currently Clery's department store.

[10] *Sinn Féin Rebellion Handbook*, p19.

[11] Fergus (Frank) Burke WS 694.

[12] *Sinn Féin Rebellion Handbook*, pp30–31.

[13] NLI Ms. 4,700.

[14] *Capuchin Annual*, Dublin, 1966, pp173–174.

[15] It's possible that Michael Mallin's name does not appear here to avoid implicating him.

[16] As per note above. The captain in question was Liam Mellows who led a huge contingent in Galway, consisting of over 1,000 Volunteers. Mellows had been smuggled back from banishment in Britain, in time for Rising, with the assistance of Nora Connolly. There is no doubt James Connolly knew of this. Mellows escaped to America after the Rising. He returned in 1921 as director of purchases for the IRA. Mellows was executed by Free State forces on 8 December 1922.

[17] *Sinn Féin Rebellion Handbook*, pp46–47.

[18] McGuire, Charlie, *Sean McLoughlin, Ireland's Forgotten Revolutionary*, London, Merlin Press, 2011, pp30–32.

[19] *Capuchin Annual*, 1966, p177.


## Chapter Sixteen

[1] *Workers' Republic*, 27 November 1915.

[2] *1916 Rebellion Handbook*, p13.

[3] *The Capuchin Annual*, 1966, p288.

[4] Connolly O'Brien, *We Shall Rise Again*, p27.

[5] Jooste, Graham & Webster, Roger, *Innocent Blood*, Capetown, Spearhead, 2002, pp149–164. Gideon Scheepers was executed in Graff-Reniet on 18 January 1902.

[6] Public Records Office, Kew, England, PRO WO71/354.

[7] Caufield, L Max, *The Easter Rebellion*, Dublin, Gill & Macmillan, 1963, p257.

[8] It was The O'Rahilly who was concerned for the lieutenant's well-being.

[9] PRO WO71/354.

[10] *1916 Rebellion Handbook*, p13.

[11] Connolly O'Brien, *Portrait of a Rebel Father*, pp320–323.

[12] Nevin, *James Connolly, A Full Life*, pp667–668.

[13] *The Capuchin Annual*, 1966, p290.

[14] War diary of Capt. A.A. Dickson, Sherwood Foresters Archives, England.

[15] Connolly O'Brien, *We Shall Rise Again*, p34.

## Conclusion

[1] *Workers' Republic*, 13 August 1898.

[2] *Workers' Republic*, 4 December 1915.

[3] The man who shot Macken had lost his reason and ran amok, firing wildly at his comrades. He, in turn, was shot dead. It serves to illustrate the tension in Boland's due to the lack of action within de Valera's position.

[4] NLI Ms. 13,942.

## Appendix 1

[1] In 1901 the Social Democratic Party and a section of the SLP which had split, merged into a new organisation called the Socialist Party of America. The old SLP called them Kangaroos because they 'jumped'.

[2] 'Value, Price & Profit' is a pamphlet dealing with Karl Marx's theory of Surplus Value.

[3] S. T. & L. A. refers to the Socialist Trade and Labour Alliance, the Industrial Union aligned to the SLP.

[4] August Bebel (1840–1913) was a founding member of the Social Democratic Party of Germany and a member of the First International. His book *Woman and Socialism* was translated into English with a preface by Daniel De Leon and was serialised in *The People* as *Woman Under Socialism*.

[5] Emile Vandervelde (1866–1938) was a member of the Parti Ouvrier Belge (Belgian Labour Party).

[6] Alexandre Millerand (1859–1943) was a member of the French Socialist Party who entered government alongside a French General, Gaston Alexandre Auguste, who had taken part in the suppression of the Paris Commune of 1871 and was known as the 'Commune's Executioner'.

# Bibliography

Allen, Kieran, *The Politics of James Connolly*, London, Pluto Press, 1990.

Anderson, WK, *James Connolly and the Irish Left*, Dublin, Irish Academic Press, 1994.

Bateson, Ray, *They Died by Pearse's Side*, Dublin, Irish Graves Publications, 2010.

Bell, Thomas, *Pioneering Days*, London, Lawrence & Wishart, 1941.

Berresford Ellis, Peter, *A History of the Irish Working Class*, London, Victor Gollancz, 1972.

Berresford Ellis, Peter (ed.), *James Connolly, Selected Writings*, London, Pelican, 1973.

Brennan-Whitmore, WJ, *Dublin Burning*, Dublin, Gill and Macmillan, 1996.

*Capuchin Annual*, Dublin, 1966.

Caulfield, Max, *The Easter Rebellion*, Dublin, Gill & Macmillan, 1963.

Clarke, Helen, *Sing a Rebel Song, The Story of James Connolly*, Edinburgh District Council, 1989.

Clarke, Kathleen, *Revolutionary Woman, My Fight for Ireland's Freedom*, Dublin, O'Brien Press, 1991.

Coates, Tim (ed.), *The Irish Uprising 1914–21, Papers from the British Parliamentary Archive*, London, The Stationery Office, 2000.

Connolly, James, *Erin's Hope, The End and the Means* (1897) & *The New Evangel, Preached to Irish Toilers* (1901), Dublin, New Books, 1972.

Connolly, James, *Socialism Made Easy*, Chicago, Charles H Kerr, 1909.

Connolly, James, *Labour, Nationality and Religion,* (1910), Dublin, New Books Publications, 1969.

Connolly, James, *Labour in Irish History,* Dublin, Maunsel, 1910.

Connolly, James, *The Re-Conquest of Ireland* (1915), Dublin, New Books Publications, 1983.

Connolly, James, *Collected Works Volume One and Volume Two*, Dublin, New Books Publications, 1987.

Connolly O'Brien, Nora, *Portrait of a Rebel Father,* Dublin, Talbot Press, 1935.

Connolly O'Brien, Nora, *We Shall Rise Again*, London, Mosquito Press, 1981.

deCourcy Ireland, John, *The Sea and the Easter Rising*, Dublin, Maritime Museum, 1996.

Cronin, Seán, *Young Connolly*, Dublin, Repsol, 1978.

Davis, Richard P, *Arthur Griffith and Non-Violent Sinn Féin*, Dublin, Anvil Books, 1974.

Deasy, Joseph, *Fiery Cross, The Story of Jim Larkin*, Dublin, New Books, 1963.

Devine, Francis, *Organising History, A Centenary of SIPTU, 1909–2009*, Dublin, Gill and Macmillan, 2009.

*Dublin's Fighting Story, 1916–21*, Tralee, The Kerryman, 1949.

Dudley Edwards, Owen, *The Mind of an Activist, James Connolly*, Dublin, Gill and Macmillan, 1971.

Dudley Edwards, Ruth, *James Connolly*, Dublin, Gill and Macmillan, 1981.

Dutton Savage, Marion, *Industrial Unionism in America*, New York, The Ronald Press Co., 1922.

Ebenezer, Lyn, *Fron-goch and the Birth of the IRA*, Wales, Gwasg Carreg Gwalch, 2006.

Feeney, Brian, *Sinn Féin, A Hundred Turbulent Years*, Dublin, O'Brien Press, 2002.

Fintan Lalor, James, *Collected Writings*, Dublin, Talbot Press, 1947.

Fox, RM, *The History of the Irish Citizen Army*, Dublin, James Duffy & Co, 1943.

Fox, RM, *James Connolly, The Forerunner*, Tralee, Kerryman, 1946.

Foy, Michael and Barton, Brian, *The Easter Rising*, Gloucestershire, Sutton Publishing, 1999.

Gonne MacBride, Maud, *A Servant of the Queen*, Dublin, Irish Academic Press, 2004.

Greaves, C Desmond, *The Life and Times of James Connolly*, London, Lawrence & Wishart, 1961.

Greaves, C Desmond, *1916 As History, The Myth of the Blood Sacrifice*, Dublin, Fulcrum Press, 1991.

Gurley Flynn, Elizabeth, *I Speak My Own Piece*, New York, Masses & Mainstream, 1955.

Hegarty, Shane & O'Toole, Fintan, *The Irish Times Book of the 1916 Rising*, Dublin, Gill & Macmillan, 2006.

Henderson, Frank, *Easter Rising, Recollections of a Dublin Volunteer*, Cork University Press, 1998.

Holt, Edgar, *Protest in Arms*, London, Putnam, 1960.

Jooste, Graham & Webster, Roger, *Innocent Blood*, Capetown, Spearhead, 2002.

Kostick, Conor, *Revolution in Ireland, Popular Militancy 1917 to 1923*, London,

Pluto Press, 1996.

Kostick, Conor & Collins, Lorcan, *The Easter Rising*, Dublin, O'Brien Press, 2000.

Larkin, Jim, *In The Footsteps of Big Jim*, Dublin, Blackwater Press, 1995.

Levenson, Samuel, *James Connolly, A Biography*, London, Martin, Brian & O'Keefe, 1973.

Lynch, David, *Radical Politics in Modern Ireland, The Irish Socialist Republican Party 1896–1904*, Dublin, Irish Academic Press, 2005.

Macardle, Dorothy, *The Irish Republic*, London, Victor Gollancz, 1937.

MacAonghusa, Prionsias, *What Connolly Said*, Dublin, New Island Books, 1995.

Marx, Karl and Engels Frederick, *Ireland and the Irish Question*, New York, International Publishers, 1971.

McGarry, Fearghal, *The Rising, Ireland, Easter 1916*, Oxford University Press, 2010.

McGuire, Charlie, *Sean McLoughlin, Ireland's Forgotten Revolutionary*, London, Merlin Press, 2011.

McHugh, Roger (ed.), *Dublin 1916*, New York, Hawthorn Books, 1966.

McKenna, Rev. Lambert, SJ, *The Social Teachings of James Connolly*, Dublin, Veritas, 1991.

MacLochlainn, Piaras F, *Last Words*, Dublin, Stationery Office, 1990.

McCarthy, Michael JF, *Five Years in Ireland, 1895–1900*, London, Simpkin, Marshall, Hamilton, Kent, 1901.

McCoole, Sinéad, *No Ordinary Women*, Dublin, O'Brien Press, 2003.

Marreco, Anne, *The Rebel Countess*, London, Weidenfeld & Nicolson, 1967.

Martin, FX (ed.), *The Irish Volunteers 1913–15,* Dublin, James Duffy, 1963.

Martin, FX (ed.), *The Leaders and Men of The Easter Rising, Dublin 1916*, London, Methuen, 1967.

Metscher, Priscilla, *James Connolly and the Reconquest of Ireland*, Minneapolis, MEP Publications, 2002.

Mitchel, John, *Jail Journal*, Dublin, MH Gill & Sons, 1914.

Nevin, Donal (ed.), *1913, Jim Larkin and the Dublin Lockout*, Dublin, Workers' Union of Ireland, 1964.

Nevin, Donal (ed.), *James Larkin, Lion of the Fold*, Dublin, Gill & Macmillan, 1998.

Nevin, Donal, *James Connolly, A Full Life*, Dublin, Gill & Macmillan, 2005.

Nevin, Donal (ed.), *Between Comrades, Letters and Correspondence*, Dublin,

Gill & Macmillan, 2007.

Nevin, Donal (ed.), *James Connolly, Political Writings 1893–1916*, Dublin, SIPTU, 2011.

Nevin, Donal (ed.), *Writings of James Connolly, Collected Works*, Dublin, SIPTU, 2011.

O'Broin, León, *Dublin Castle and the 1916 Rising*, Dublin, Helicon, 1966.

O'Casey, Sean, *Drums under the Windows, Autobiography, Book 3, 1906–1916,* London, Macmillan, 1945.

O'Cathasaigh, Aindrias (ed.), *The Lost Writings, James Connolly*, London, Pluto Press, 1997.

O'Cathasaigh, PS (Sean O'Casey), *The Story of The Irish Citizen Army*, Dublin, 1919.

O'Connell, Joseph EA, *Dublin in Rebellion, A Directory 1913–1923*, Dublin, Liliput, 2009.

O'Donnell, EE, SJ, *The Annals of Dublin*, Dublin, Wolfhound Press, 1988.

O'Donnell, Ruán (ed.), *The Impact of the 1916 Rising*, Dublin, Irish Academic Press, 2008.

O'Farrell, Padraic, *Who's Who in the Irish War of Independence and Civil War 1916–1923*, Dublin, Liliput Press, 1997.

O'Mahony, Sean, *Frongoch, University of Revolution*, Dublin, FDR Teoranta, 1987.

O'Neill, Brian, *Easter Week*, New York, International Publishers, 1939.

O'Rahilly, Aodogán, *Winding the Clock, O'Rahilly and the 1916 Rising*, Dublin, Lilliput Press, 1991.

O'Shannon, Cathal (ed.), *Fifty Years of Liberty Hall*, Dublin, Sign of the Three Candles, 1959.

Reeve, Carl and Ann, *James Connolly and the United States*, New Jersey, Humanities Press, 1978.

Robbins, Frank, *Under The Starry Plough*, Dublin, Academy Press, 1977.

Ryan, Desmond, *James Connolly, His Life, Work and Writings*, Dublin, Talbot Press, 1924.

Ryan, Desmond (ed.), *Socialism and Nationalism, A Selection from the Writings of James Connolly*, Dublin, Sign of the Three Candles, 1948.

Ryan, Desmond (ed.), *Labour and Easter Week, A Selection from the Writings of James Connolly, With Introduction by William O'Brien*, Dublin, Sign of the

Three Candles, 1949.

Ryan, Desmond, *The Rising, The Complete Story of Easter Week*, Dublin, Golden Eagle Books, 1949.

Ryan, Desmond (ed.), *The Workers' Republic, A Selection from the Writings of James Connolly, With Introduction by William McMullen*, Dublin, Sign of the Three Candles, 1951.

Ryan, WP, *The Irish Labour Movement*, Dublin, Talbot Press, 1919.

*Sinn Féin Rebellion Handbook*, Dublin, *The Irish Times*, 1916.

Stephens, James, *The Insurrection in Dublin*, Dublin, Maunsel, 1916.

*The James Connolly Songbook*, Cork, Cork Workers' Club, 1972.

White, JR, *Misfit, An Autobiography*, London, Jonathon Cape, 1930.

Yeates, Padraig, *Lockout, Dublin 1913*, Dublin, Gill & Macmillan, 2000.

Yeates, Padraig, *A City in Wartime, Dublin 1914–18*, Dublin, Gill and Macmillan, 2011.

The Military Archives in Cathal Brugha Barracks have a collection of 1,773 Witness Statements (WS) covering the period 1913–1921, collected and recorded between 1947 and 1957, sealed and stored by the government and only opened in 2003. They are also available for viewing in the National Archives on Bishop Street. Any Witness Statements used for this book have been referenced by their name and number, eg Ina Connolly Heron, WS 919.

The National Library of Ireland hold an extensive collection of material on James Connolly collected by William O'Brien and donated to the Irish State. The collection is available for viewing in the Manuscript Room but is also available on microfilm in the main library. Any material quoted from this source has been reference to the National Library of Ireland O'Brien Papers, eg NLI Ms. 13,906.

The British National Archives in Kew, Surrey released the Courts Martial files of the executed leaders and men from the Rising. They are available to the public for viewing and James Connolly's file has been referenced in this work as: Public Records Office, Kew, England, PRO WO71/354.

# Index